FEARON'S

# United States History

SECOND EDITION

Joanne Suter

Globe Fearon Educational Publisher
Paramus, New Jersey

Paramount Publishing

**Pacemaker Curriculum Advisor: Stephen C. Larsen**

Stephen C. Larsen holds a B.S. and an M.S. in Speech Pathology from the University of Nebraska at Omaha, and an Ed.D. in Learning Disabilities from the University of Kansas. In the course of his career, Dr. Larsen has worked in the Teacher Corps on a Nebraska Indian Reservation, as a Fulbright senior lecturer in Portugal and Spain, and as a speech pathologist in the public schools. A full professor at the University of Texas at Austin, he has nearly twenty years' experience as a teacher trainer on the university level. He is the author of sixty journal articles, three textbooks and six widely used standardized tests including the Test of Written Learning (TOWL) and the Test of Adolescent Language (TOAL).

**Subject Area Consultant: Jan Grodeon**

Jan Grodeon, M.A., San Jose State University, has been teaching U.S. and World History for twenty years. She was Santa Clara County Teacher of the Year in 1989 and has been a District Mentor Teacher for several years in the Campbell (California) Union School District.

**Editor:** Joseph T. Curran
**Contributing Editors:** Tony Napoli, Lisa Kass Roth, Stephen Feinstein
**Contributing Writers:** Stephen Lewin, Ted Silveira
**Production Editor:** Teresa A. Holden
**Cover Design:** Mark Ong, Side by Side Studios
**Text Design:** Dianne Platner
**Graphics Coordinator:** Joe C. Shines
**Cartographers:** Jean Ann Carroll, Sharon Johnson, Colleen Forbes, Carolyn Buck Reynolds
**Photo and Illustration Credits:** The BETTMANN ARCHIVE, with the following exceptions: Culver Pictures, 246; AP/Wide World Photos, 360, 456, 472; Stanford News Service, 465

**About the Cover Photograph:** *Henryk Kaiser/Leo de Wys, Inc.* Mount Rushmore National Monument, which was carved in the Black Hills of South Dakota during the years 1927 to 1941, shows the faces of George Washington, Thomas Jefferson, Theodore Roosevelt, and Abraham Lincoln. Sculpted in granite using drills and dynamite, each head is taller than a five-story building.

**Acknowledgments:** page 161: from *Eyewitness: The Negro in American History*, William Loren Katz, copyright © 1974 by Fearon Education, 500 Harbor Boulevard, Belmont, CA 94002

ISBN 0–8224–6894–8

Printed in the United States of America

3. 10 9 8 7 6 5 4 3
Cover Printer/NEBC
DO

# Contents

# A Note to the Student

Just a little more than 200 years ago, our great nation wasn't a nation at all. Mostly it was a vast wilderness. How did the United States get to be one of the world's largest, richest, and most powerful countries in such a short time? (On the clock of history, 200 years is just a brief moment. Countries like Egypt and Greece and China are thousands of years old.)

This book tells the amazing story of our country and its people. The story begins with the Native Americans who lived here long before white settlers arrived. And it goes on to tell about the men and women from all around the world who came to America over the years. Chapter by chapter, you will learn how these people and their descendants worked together to build the United States.

By the time you finish this book, you will be able to name the most important events in American history. You will know when they happened and why they happened. The photographs and maps will show you many people who influenced history and some of the places where historic events took place. You will learn about the key ideas that guided our country's growth and that still shape our lives today. In short, you will have a new and better understanding of your precious American heritage.

Further study of history can help prepare you for an interesting career. Perhaps you would like to work in a government office, a library, or at a newspaper. Perhaps you are interested in writing or politics or teaching. These are just a few of the job opportunities that require a solid knowledge of history.

Look for the notes in the margins of the pages. These friendly notes are there to make you stop and think. Sometimes they comment on the material you are learning. Sometimes they give examples. Sometimes they remind you of something you already know.

You will also find several study aids in the book. At the beginning of every chapter, you'll find **Learning Objectives**. Take a moment to study these goals. They will help you focus on the important points covered in the chapter. **Words to Know** will give you a preview of some key vocabulary you'll find in your reading. And at the end of each chapter, a **Summary** will give you a quick review of what you've just learned.

We hope you enjoy reading about the history of our country and its people. Everyone who put this book together worked hard to make it interesting as well as useful. The rest is up to you. We wish you well in your studies. Our success is in your accomplishment.

# The New World

**Chapter 1**

# This Land Is Our Land

**1200 B.C.**
Earliest Civilization in the Americas

**A.D. 1492**
Columbus Discovers America

**Columbus**

## Chapter Learning Objectives

- Explain the effect of land and climate on the settlement of America.
- Identify the first people to settle America.
- Tell how Europeans happened to find America.

# Words to Know

**civilization**   the way of life of a people who have developed their own government, arts, and sciences

**climate**   the typical weather of a place over a period of years

**colonies**   lands settled and ruled by people from other countries

**natives**   people who live in the place where they were born

**plains**   large stretches of almost flat, nearly treeless land

The picture on the left shows Columbus landing in the West Indies in 1492. Of course you know that Columbus became famous for his discovery of America. But in this chapter you will learn about people who reached America long before Columbus. You will learn that the history of America really began thousands of years ago.

## The Americans and Their Story

People came from all around the world to live in America. That fact makes America different from other places. The story of American history is the story of all these people. As you read America's history, think about what life is like today. Then try to imagine what America would be like if people of long ago had made different decisions.

## The American Land

The land and climate help people decide where and how they will live. Look at the map of America on page 5. There are very large **plains** in the middle of the country. One set of plains is called the Central Plains. To the west of the Central Plains is the Great Plains. The Central Plains receive plenty of rain.

The land is rich and good for farming. Less rain falls in the Great Plains. Much of this area is used for raising sheep and cattle.

There are mountain ranges in America's East and West. The Appalachian Mountains of the East made westward expansion difficult for the colonists. Frontiersmen had to find gaps in the mountains to cross to the West. The Cumberland Gap in Kentucky was one such passage.

Find the Rocky Mountains on the map of the United States. The Rocky Mountains are the largest mountain range in North America. They extend 3,000 miles through the United States and Canada. The Rocky Mountains were once seen as a barrier between the eastern two-thirds of the United States and the West Coast. Pioneers during the 1800s faced great hardships crossing the Rockies.

The crest of the Rocky Mountains forms the Continental Divide. The Continental Divide separates rivers that flow eastward into the Mississippi River and the Gulf of Mexico from rivers that flow west into the Pacific Ocean. Find the Rio Grande and Platte Rivers on your map. They flow east from the Continental Divide. Notice the Columbia and Colorado Rivers which flow westward to the Pacific. America's river valleys make rich farmlands.

The different parts of the United States have very different climates. Much of the country has cold snowy winters. But in some places it is warm all year long. There are a few deserts in the West that get hardly any rain. However, most of the country gets enough rain for growing crops. The American land and climate have offered people a good place to live, to farm, and to build their homes.

**How would people's lives and work be different if America were mostly desert land? How is your life affected by climate?**

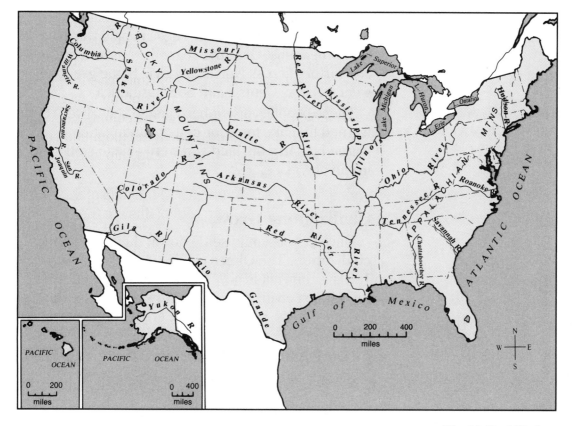

**The United States**

**Map Study**

Study the map. Then answer the questions on a separate sheet of paper.

1. What large mountain range is found in eastern America?
2. Name two rivers that flow into the Mississippi River?
3. Which rivers shown on the map lie east of the Appalachian Mountains?

# They Came by Land

How did the first people come to America? Scientists think that long ago there may have been a bridge of land. They say it stretched 56 miles between Asia and what is now Alaska. The land bridge was later covered by the sea when great fields of ice melted.

Groups of people may have crossed that bridge looking for better hunting. These people were the first Americans. Over the years they moved further and further across North America. Some groups went as far as Central and South America.

These people worked hard just to stay alive. They learned to make tools for better hunting. Some learned to farm the land and were able to settle and live in one place.

Before people learned to farm, they were often on the move. Why do you think this was so?

## Civilizations Grow

Once people could settle down, they could build a **civilization**. The Olmec civilization began around 1200 B.C. in what is now Mexico. It is thought to be the earliest civilization in the Americas. Later the Mayas, Aztecs, and Incas built great kingdoms in Mexico and Central and South America.

Native Americans of different regions had different life styles and different needs. Coastal dwellers had to learn to make canoes. People living in the Southwest had to learn to build channels to bring water to their crops. The process of bringing water to fields is called *irrigation*.

"B.C." means "Before Christ." So something that happened in the year 1200 B.C. happened 1200 years before Christ was born.

In North America people settled along river valleys where the soil was rich. The Hopewell tribes settled in the Ohio River Valley around 100 B.C. They are known to have built great burial mounds. The Mississippians lived along the Mississippi River. In the West, the Pueblo people built villages in the sides of cliffs. And in the North, the Eskimos learned to survive in one of the coldest places in the world.

## The First Visitors from Europe

A hardy group of seafaring people once lived in Northern Europe. They were called Norsemen, or Vikings. Many Europeans feared Viking raiders, who were after new lands and new riches.

About 1,000 years ago, Vikings sailed across the Atlantic Ocean from Norway. They set up **colonies** in Iceland and in Greenland. Then a Viking named Leif Ericson reached eastern North America. He spent a winter camped there with his crew. The

**A Viking Ship**

People learn what happened in the past in many ways. Sometimes they learn from old stories, such as the Viking "sagas."

Vikings returned to Greenland with tales of a rich and wonderful land. "Green forests grow down to the water's edge," Leif Ericson reported. He called the new land Vinland, because of the grapes that grew there. Today we call Leif Ericson's new land "Newfoundland."

The Vikings never returned to the new land that Leif Ericson had discovered. Historians believe that the climate became colder around that time. In fact, the Vikings even had to give up their colonies in Greenland. For the next 400 years or so, Europeans showed little interest in exploring the Atlantic again.

## A Route to Riches

The Atlantic Ocean was once the "Great Unknown." What areas today are considered "unknown territories" waiting to be explored?

In 1477 an Italian trader named Marco Polo wrote a book about his travels to the East. He spoke of visits to China and to islands called the Indies. Marco Polo told of "fabulous wealth."

European merchants who read Marco Polo's stories wished for a quick route to the East. They thought that perhaps there was a way to reach the East by sea. The problem was that most sailors at that time were afraid to sail very far from shore. They knew nothing of the earlier voyages of the Vikings. Most people believed the Earth was as flat as the top of a table. If a ship were to sail too far in one direction, it would fall off the edge of the Earth!

## Christopher Columbus Reaches the New World

A young man named Christopher Columbus lived in Italy during the late 1400s. Columbus was fascinated with the sea. He read all he could about trade and travel. Columbus believed that the world was round. So he decided that he could reach the Indies by sailing west across the Atlantic Ocean.

At first, no one would listen to Columbus's plans. He tried to get money and ships from the kings of Portugal and England. But they turned him away. At last King Ferdinand and Queen Isabella of Spain agreed to help Columbus. They gave him three ships: the *Niña*, the *Pinta*, and the *Santa Maria*. In return, Columbus promised to claim for Spain any lands that he discovered.

On October 12, 1492, Columbus and his crews landed on an island. Columbus thought that he was somewhere close to China and Japan. He claimed the island in the name of King Ferdinand and Queen Isabella and named it San Salvador. Believing he had landed in the East Indies, Columbus called the **natives** of the land "Indians." The natives were, in fact, Arawaks. Arawaks lived on the chain of islands that stretch from the tip of Florida to South America.

The Arawaks were curious about the strangers. They brought Columbus and his men gifts of parrots, cotton thread, and tobacco. The Arawaks introduced Columbus and his crews to tobacco, corn, and potatoes.

"They ought to make good, skilled servants," Columbus wrote. "They repeat very quickly whatever we say to them." Like most Europeans of his day, Columbus saw the natives as a people to be conquered and forcibly "taught" a European way of life. During their time on San Salvador and the other islands they visited, Columbus and his men enslaved and mistreated many of the natives.

When Columbus returned to Spain, he brought back several captured Arawaks and a few pieces of gold to show to the King and Queen. He was greeted with a hero's welcome and was named Admiral of the Ocean Sea.

During the following years, Columbus made three more voyages to the New World. Although he was

The king and queen of Spain were the only ones who would listen to Columbus's ideas. How much would history have changed if Columbus had given up when the first person turned him away?

disappointed that he never found the riches of the Indies, he did find a new land and a new culture. That land that he discovered would someday be called America.

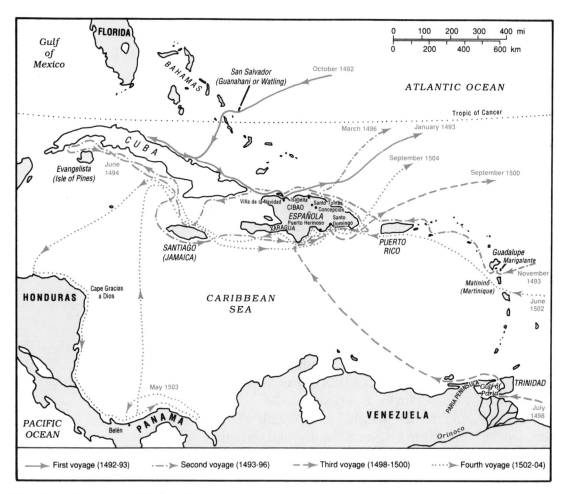

The Four Voyages of Columbus

## Words from the Past

Columbus wrote these words in his diary just two days before he discovered America!

"The people could stand it no longer and complained of the long voyage. I cheered them as best I could, and added that it was useless to complain. I had come to go to the Indies, and had to continue until I found them...."

## History Practice

Answer these questions on a separate sheet of paper.

1. Why is climate important to the development of a country?

2. What areas make good farmlands?

3. What were four of the earliest civilizations in the Americas?

4. Why do you think European merchants were interested in finding a sea route to the East?

5. Where did Christopher Columbus think he had landed when he reached America?

# Chapter Review

## Summary

| CHRONOLOGY OF MAJOR EVENTS | |
| --- | --- |
| 1200 B.C. | Olmec civilization begins |
| A.D. 250 | Mayan civilization begins |
| A.D. 1000 | Leif Ericson and Vikings reach the New World |
| A.D. 1200 | Inca civilization begins |
| A.D. 1300 | Aztec civilization begins |
| A.D. 1492 | Christopher Columbus reaches the New World |

- What happened in the past shapes our lives today.
- America's plains and river valleys make rich farmland.
- Most lands and climates in America offer good places for people to live.
- Scientists think people first came to America across a land bridge from Asia.
- Native American civilizations grew up across North, Central, and South America.
- Viking sagas named Leif Ericson as the first European visitor to America, in a.d. 1000.
- In the 1400s Europeans began looking for a sea route to the East.
- Christopher Columbus, under the flag of Spain, sailed west across the Atlantic Ocean. He hoped to reach the Indies but landed in the New World.

## Chapter Quiz

Answer these questions on a separate sheet of paper.

1. Why did people cross the land bridge from Asia to America?

2. What did people have to do before they could build a civilization in the Americas?

3. Why do you think Indians living in different regions developed different life styles?

4. Why did the Vikings have to give up their colonies in Greenland?

5. Who was Marco Polo, and what was he known for?

## Thinking and Writing

1. Describe the climate and land where you live. How do the climate and the land help determine the kind of industry in your region? The type of recreation available? The kinds of food you eat and the type of house you live in? What other things are affected by weather and land?

2. Why were most sailors in the 1400s afraid to sail very far out to sea?

3. Why did Columbus think he could reach the East Indies by sailing west across the Atlantic Ocean?

4. Imagine you are a native watching Columbus and his crews sail toward your island. Describe how you feel about the approaching strangers.

# Chapter 2

# The Newcomers:
# Explorers, Conquerors, and Settlers

| 1519 | 1636 |
|------|------|
| Spanish conquistadors come to the New World | Roger Williams founds Rhode Island |

**The Pilgrims**

## Chapter Learning Objectives

- Identify the European nations that sent the earliest settlers to America.
- Describe three differences among European colonies.
- Name three reasons settlers came to the New World.
- Explain what the Mayflower Compact was.

# Words to Know

**charter**   an official government paper granting people certain rights
**conquistador**   Spanish conqueror
**empire**   a group of countries or territories ruled by the same government
**galleon**   a Spanish ship
**legislature**   a group that makes laws

On the left is a drawing of the Pilgrims arriving on the shores of America. Many different kinds of people came to the New World. In this chapter you will learn about them, and why they came. You will also learn how the earliest settlers helped to make America what it is today.

## America Gets a Name

Europeans soon heard about Columbus's discovery. There was a wave of excitement. Nations dreamed of riches and glory and of **empires** to be built. Other explorers set out across the Atlantic.

One of the first to sail was an Italian named Amerigo Vespucci. He sailed in 1497, under the flag of Portugal. Amerigo Vespucci was interested in the study of the stars. He served as a pilot on the voyages. Vespucci realized that the lands Columbus had found were neither China nor the Indies. So he called the place a "new land." Soon this land would be named America, after Amerigo Vespucci.

## Words from the Past

This passage comes from a speech by U.S. President John F. Kennedy. It points out the many races and nationalities involved in the early exploration of America. From the time of its discovery, America has long been a land of different peoples.

"The name 'America' was given by a German mapmaker to honor an Italian explorer. The three ships which discovered America sailed under a Spanish flag and were commanded by an Italian sea captain. They included in their crews an Englishman, an Irishman, a Jew, and a Negro."

## Spanish Explorers and Conquerors

The Spanish heard tales of wealth in the New World. They heard about cities filled with gold, silver, and jewels. Many Spanish adventurers came to America after Columbus. They made discoveries and claimed new lands in the name of Spain.

An age of discovery and exploration had begun. But it was also an age of conquerors. In fact, the Spanish called their adventurers **conquistadors**.

Hernando Cortes was a Spanish explorer who went to Mexico in search of treasures. There he found the great empire of the Aztecs. The Aztec chief, Montezuma, greeted Cortes as a white god. But Cortes was really a greedy conquistador. He and his soldiers destroyed the Aztec cities and stole the Aztec treasures. In 1521, Cortes became the ruler of the land.

Another conquistador, Francisco Pizarro, conquered the Incas of Peru. The South American Incas, like the Aztecs, had a mighty empire. They had fine cities and a giant network of roads. But the

Incas were no match for the gold-hungry Spaniards. Before long, Pizarro ruled Peru.

By gaining the treasures of the New World, Spain was becoming a wealthy nation.

## Spanish Explorers Head North

Then Spanish explorers in South America and Mexico heard of rich lands to the north. Soon expeditions set out to explore what is now the United States.

Juan Ponce de Leon was the first of these explorers. In 1513, Ponce de Leon set out from a West Indies settlement with a band of men. He wanted to find gold. He also wanted to find a very special fountain. He had heard stories of a "Fountain of Youth" whose waters could make a person stay young forever. Ponce de Leon searched and searched, but he never did find gold or his special fountain. However, he did reach a beautiful land filled with trees and flowers. So he called that land Florida, from *flores*, the Spanish word for flowers.

Some explorers thought America was an enchanted place indeed. Ponce de Leon looked for the Fountain of Youth. An African explorer named Estevanco led a Spanish expedition to find "the seven cities of gold." And Francisco de Coronado also searched for a city of gold.

Coronado brought many men on his expedition. They explored what is now New Mexico, Arizona, Texas, and Kansas. Coronado met Pueblo people. These Native Americans lived in houses of sun-dried brick called adobe. Coronado never found a city of gold. But his travels gave Spain claim to large sections of the United States.

From 1539 to 1542, Hernando de Soto explored the southeastern section of what is now the United States. He too was searching for gold.

Horses and cattle weren't always in the old West. In the mid-1500s, Coronado brought the first horses and cattle onto the plains of the United States.

After marching through Florida, de Soto and his men went all the way to the Mississippi River. The Muskogee tribes they met soon realized that the Spanish explorers were enemies. De Soto and his men took the Muskogees' food and forced them to carry supplies and serve as guides.

DeSoto, the first European to see the mighty Mississippi, died on his expedition. He never found the gold he was looking for.

## The Spanish Settlers

Spaniards built cities in the New World. The first city was founded in 1565 when Spanish soldiers came to Florida. There the soldiers built a wooden fort and some huts. They named this town St. Augustine. It was the first permanent European settlement in the United States.

The city of St. Augustine still stands today. As the oldest city in the United States, it has many buildings that have stood for hundreds of years.

In 1609, the Spanish settled Santa Fe on land that is now New Mexico. Santa Fe is considered the second oldest city in the United States.

## Spanish Rule

The Spaniards tried to make life in the New World just like life in Spain. The king of Spain chose men who would strictly govern the new colonies.

The Native Americans suffered under Spanish rule. They lived in poverty. Their gold and silver were sent back to Europe on Spanish ships called **galleons**.

When the Spanish needed more workers, they brought slaves from Africa. The Native Americans and the Africans did the work. The Spanish ruled the land.

In the Spanish colonies, the people who did the hardest work were usually the poorest. Is that often the case in other places?

## History Practice

Answer these questions on a separate sheet of paper.

1. What was the major reason the Spanish came to the New World?

2. What is the oldest city in the United States?

3. How did the Spanish treat the Indians in the New World?

4. Who did most of the work in the Spanish colonies?

# French Explorers

The Spanish were not the only explorers. The French were interested in new lands, too. In 1534, around the time Pizarro conquered the Incas, France sent explorer Jacques Cartier to North America. Cartier was to search for an east-west water passage to the Pacific Ocean. When he discovered the St. Lawrence River, he thought he had found that passage. But after three trips on the river, he found he was wrong. The St. Lawrence flowed through land we now call Canada. Cartier claimed that land for France.

After Cartier's voyage, the king of France lost interest in the New World. After about 70 years, another Frenchman, named Samuel de Champlain, came to settle Canada. Champlain set up forts at Quebec and Montreal. He began a fur trade with the Indians.

French settlers arrived slowly. Some hoped to grow rich from the fur trade. Others wanted to teach the Native Americans about Christianity.

Frenchmen traveled on the St. Lawrence River and across the Great Lakes. They discovered the Ohio River and the Mississippi River. The explorer La Salle claimed the lands of the Mississippi Valley for France.

## French Colonies

The French settlers called their lands New France. The king of France chose a governor to rule his colonies.

The French got along well with the Native Americans. They did not force them to accept French ways. They made fair trades of guns, knives, and beads for furs. The fur trade helped make France a rich and powerful country.

The French made friends with the Native Americans and began to trade fairly for their furs. How was this different from the Spanish settlers?

---

Great Names in History:
Joliet and Marquette

Frenchmen Louis Joliet and Father Jacques Marquette began a long journey in 1673. They were searching for a great river they had heard of in stories. They hoped this river would flow to the Pacific Ocean.

The river the two Frenchmen found did not flow west to the Pacific Ocean. Instead it flowed southward. Joliet and Marquette paddled down the river in canoes. Their travels were hard, and at last they were forced to turn back. They did not know they had traveled on the great Mississippi.

The journeys of these two French explorers, and of others that followed them, gave France claim to much land. However, there were never enough French settlers in the United States to really develop the claims.

---

**Father Jacques Marquette**

## History Practice

Answer these questions on a separate sheet of paper.

1. Why did the French come to the New World? Give three reasons.

2. How did the French treat the Native Americans?

3. What did Marquette and Joliet hope to find? What did they find?

Why did Europeans feel that American lands were open to claim? Didn't the Native Americans who lived there already have a claim to the land?

## The English Build Colonies in America

A few years after Columbus discovered America, England began to show interest in the New World. In 1497, an explorer named John Cabot explored the east coast of North America. He claimed land there for England.

Many years passed. Then England and Spain began fighting for control of the seas. In 1588, the Spanish navy attacked England. A sea captain named Sir Francis Drake led the English navy to defeat the Spanish navy. Drake's victory left England ruler of the seas. The way was now open for English ships to sail to the New World.

## The First English Colony: A Mystery for All Time

What could have happened to the settlers at Roanoke? Think of something that may have happened to force them to leave their colony.

In 1587 a settlement called Roanoke was set up on an island off the coast of North Carolina. An Englishman named Sir Walter Raleigh founded the Roanoke colony. Roanoke became one of history's mysteries. No one knows how, but the colony simply disappeared. Two years after its settlement, the colony and the settlers had vanished. Roanoke became known as the Lost Colony.

## The Colony of Jamestown

The first permanent English settlement in America was Jamestown. It was in what is now the state of Virginia. In 1607, three shiploads of English settlers arrived on the east coast. They had a **charter** from King James I. The charter gave them the right to settle and trade. The settlers had been sent by an English trade company, called the London Company. They had come to trade and to find gold and silver. They would send their riches back to the London Company.

The Jamestown colony had problems right from the start. The land the settlers chose was swampy and poor. Most of the men were not anxious to farm. They would rather look for gold. Captain John Smith, the leader of the colony, told them they must farm the land or starve!

As time went by, the Jamestown colony lost settlers to hunger and to diseases. Native Americans were afraid of the newcomers and attacked them. But in spite of its problems, Jamestown became a strong colony.

The London Company sent supplies and granted the colonists their own land. This encouraged settlers to work hard. They produced enough tobacco to trade with England.

Soon the London Company realized that Jamestown could not grow and prosper without family life. In 1620 the first women were sent to the colony. America no longer was a place just for adventurers. It was to be a home for families.

## Government in Jamestown

The London Company controlled Jamestown, but colonists were allowed to have a say in their government. The Company chose a governor, and the settlers chose men to speak for them in the **legislature**. Now the settlers could help make their own laws. They had found a new kind of freedom in the land called America.

## Pilgrims in America Sign the Mayflower Compact

Roanoke and Jamestown were only the first of many English colonies in America. In 1620, about a hundred Pilgrims set sail from England on the Mayflower.

In late November, the ship arrived far north of Jamestown at Plymouth Rock on Cape Cod Bay. The Pilgrims had arrived at what is now Massachusetts.

Many people on board the Mayflower were Separatists. They were called Separatists because they wanted to separate from the Church of England and start their own religion. They came to America to worship God as they chose.

The rest of the settlers made the trip for their own reasons. Pilgrims from every walk of life wanted to get a new start in a new land. All of the Pilgrims wanted to be free to govern themselves.

Leaders from both groups gathered together before leaving the Mayflower. They wrote an agreement. It said the new colony would have its own laws. Those laws would be "just and equal." All men on board the Mayflower promised to obey the laws of the new government. This written agreement was called the Mayflower Compact. This document is important to America. In it, the Pilgrims gave us our first form of self-government.

## Pilgrims Face Hardships

If you went to live in the woods, what would you bring? What skills would you want to have?

The future of the Pilgrim colony in Massachusetts didn't look good. The Pilgrims had come to America with little more than guns and gunpowder. And they had landed in late November. There was no time to plant crops before the winter snows came.

But the Pilgrims were determined to make it. They made a peace treaty with Massasoit, Chief of the Massachusetts people. These Native Americans helped the Pilgrims survive that first winter.

They showed the Pilgrims how to trap deer and how to tap maple trees for syrup. Still, by the end of the winter, about half the Pilgrims had died.

In the spring, the Native Americans taught the Pilgrims how to plant corn, beans, and pumpkins. The Pilgrims harvested these crops in the summer of 1621.

In the face of hardship, the Pilgrims showed courage. They did not give in to fear and danger. Many English settlers would follow the Pilgrims to America's Atlantic coast. They, too, would show bravery and strength.

**Have you ever had to show courage in your life? What was the hardship or danger you had to face?**

## The Puritans in Massachusetts

Like the Pilgrims, the Puritans had suffered in England because of their religion. In 1630, they founded Boston and other settlements on Massachusetts Bay. The Puritans did well. They traded furs and other goods with England. Soon their settlements fanned out around Massachusetts Bay.

But the Puritans tried to force everyone in their colony to follow their religion. Only members of the Puritan church were allowed to vote. Anyone who broke church or state laws was punished.

## Roger Williams and Anne Hutchinson

Those who did not agree with Puritan leaders were often treated badly. Roger Williams was a minister who did not agree with the leaders. Williams believed that the Indians should be paid for the land the settlers took. He also believed that all people should have the right to worship as they pleased.

Puritan leaders arrested Williams. He went to trial and was found guilty of "spreading new and dangerous ideas." In 1635 he was ordered to leave Massachusetts. The next year Williams started a new colony in Rhode Island. Settlers there could elect their own governor and worship as they wished.

Other people who angered Puritan leaders were also forced to leave. A woman named Anne Hutchinson claimed it was more important to lead a holy life than to obey church leaders. Disagreeing with the ministers was against the law in Puritan New England. Hutchinson was arrested, tried, and sentenced. She was ordered to stay away from Massachusetts forever.

After five years, word reached Boston that Anne Hutchinson was dead. Native Americans, afraid of losing their land, had killed Anne and many of her 14 children. The people who opposed Anne thought their deaths were God's will. Many in Boston, though, shed tears for the woman who was brave enough to speak out.

**Anne Hutchinson**

| COMPARING PILGRIMS AND PURITANS | | |
| --- | --- | --- |
| | **Pilgrims** | **Puritans** |
| Where When/how | Plymouth, Mass. Arrived in 1620; *Mayflower* | Boston, Mass. Arrived in 1630 15 ships |
| Charter/ government | Chartered by London Company; Governed themselves with permission of English Governor | Chartered by Charles I to form Massachusetts Bay Company |
| Economy | Small farmers and fishermen; poor colony | Colonists were successful traders in fur, fish, and grain; well-to-do colony |
| Growth | 300 people in 1630; stayed small | 2,000 people in 1631; 20,000 in 1640; rapid growth |

## History Practice

Answer these questions on a separate sheet of paper.

1. What was the first permanent English settlement in America? What problems did its settlers face?

2. The Mayflower Compact was an agreement among the Pilgrims to obey the laws they made. Why was this important?

3. Which colony, Pilgrim or Puritan, grew faster? Which colony was more successful?

4. Why were Roger Williams and Anne Hutchinson forced to leave Massachusetts?

# Chapter Review

## Summary

| CHRONOLOGY OF MAJOR EVENTS | |
|---|---|
| 1519 | Cortes conquers Aztecs |
| 1532 | Pizarro conquers Incas |
| 1565 | Spanish found St. Augustine |
| 1587 | English found Roanoke Colony |
| 1603 | French settle Quebec |
| 1607 | English found Jamestown |
| 1620 | Pilgrims sign Mayflower Compact |
| 1630 | Puritans arrive in Massachusetts |
| 1636 | Roger Williams founds Rhode Island |

- Spanish explorers and conquerors sailed to Mexico and South America. They took over lands of the Aztecs and Incas.

- Early Spanish settlements in North America included St. Augustine and Santa Fe.

- The Spaniards treated the natives badly and brought slaves from Africa to work on plantations.

- The French explored Canada and the Mississippi River Valley. They traded for furs with the Indians.

- The English built colonies along the east coast of North America.

- Jamestown became the first permanent English settlement.

- The Pilgrims came from England on the Mayflower seeking self-government. They agreed to make their own laws and to obey them.

- The Puritans in the Massachusetts Bay Colony didn't accept other religions or different ideas.

## Chapter Quiz

Answer these questions on a separate sheet of paper.

1. How did Spain become a wealthy nation in the early 1500s?

2. What was Ponce de Leon looking for? What did he find?

3. Name three rivers that were discovered by French explorers.

4. What was different about the government of Jamestown?

5. Why did the Pilgrims and the Puritans come to America?

6. Name three differences between the Pilgrims and Puritans.

## Thinking and Writing

1. Imagine you are a Native American living around 1600. Would you rather live in lands colonized by the Spanish, French, or English? Explain your choice.

2. The Jamestown government and the Mayflower Compact were important steps toward democracy in America. Why?

3. Today the government does not punish people for breaking church laws. We keep church and state separate. Why is that important?

**Chapter 3**

# The Growth of the Thirteen Colonies

| 1624 | 1760 |
|---|---|
| Dutch settle New Amsterdam | King George III becomes King of England |

**Colonial plantation**

## Chapter Learning Objectives

- Tell who settled the New England Colonies, the Middle Colonies, and the Southern Colonies.
- Name three ways life was different in the three regions.
- Describe the "New American" spirit.

# Words to Know

**debt**  money that is owed

**indentured servants**  people bound to work without pay for a certain number of years. After that time, the person is set free.

**independent**  not controlled by others

**frontier**  the edge of settled country that lies next to wild, unsettled land

**jury**  a group of people who decide if a person on trial is guilty or not guilty

**plantation**  a large farm that usually produces one main product. The workers live on the grounds.

**refuge**  a place a person can go for safety

**smallpox**  a deadly disease that Europeans brought to the New World. It spreads rapidly.

**tolerate**  to let others have their own beliefs; to accept ways that may not be to one's liking

**wilderness**  a wild place that people have not changed and that has no settlers

---

In colonial times, most southerners lived on large **plantations.** But that was just one way of life in the colonies. In this chapter, you will learn how people lived in the New England, Middle, and Southern colonies. And you will learn what they had in common. You will learn what made all of them "Americans."

## Colonies Grow and Develop Differently

The thirteen colonies that grew up along the Atlantic coast were divided into three regions: New England, the Middle Colonies, and the Southern Colonies. Look at the map on the next page to see how the colonies were divided.

Ways of life were different in the three different regions. For one thing, the land and climate differed.

Also, the colonies varied in how they governed themselves and in the kinds of crops they grew. And the colonists often had different religions and different outlooks on life.

## The New England Colonies

The Pilgrims and the Puritans came to America searching for religious freedom. Yet the Puritans would not **tolerate** other religions in their colonies. And they controlled both the church and the government of most of New England.

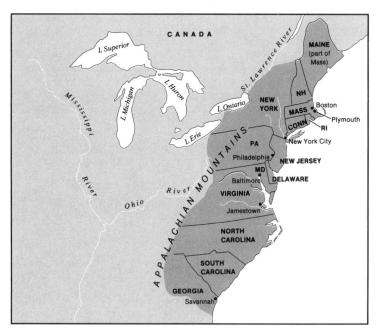

**The 13 original colonies**

In 1691, the Pilgrims and Puritans united and formed the colony of Massachusetts. The colonies of New Hampshire and Maine were founded as settlers spread out and moved north.

The colony of Connecticut was founded in 1636 by Thomas Hooker. Hooker was a Puritan minister who believed the leaders in Massachusetts had become too powerful.

You'll remember from the last chapter that Rhode Island was founded by Roger Williams.

## Life in Colonial New England

Most New Englanders worked on farms or at trades. Some made their livings from the sea. Ships called schooners sailed out to fish for cod. Whaling ships set out from New England ports. They returned with valuable whale oil to burn in lamps. New England harbors were busy places where ships from around the world came and went.

Towns were the center of life in New England. Most colonists lived in the towns or on small nearby farms. Some towns grew into cities. Boston was the largest city in the New England colonies.

Most children in New England towns went to school. New Englanders believed that children should learn to read so that they could study the Bible. In 1647, the Massachusetts government passed a law about public education. The law said that every town with 50 families or more must have a school.

The New England colonists were serious, hard-working people, and their settlements grew.

Laws often reflect the beliefs or values of society. The Massachusetts school law shows how important education was to the colonists who lived there.

## The Middle Colonies

The Middle Colonies were a home for many different kinds of people. Most New England Colonies were settled by the English. But the Middle Colonies were settled by people from all over Europe. Settlers came from Holland, Sweden, England, Germany, and other countries.

The Dutch were the first to settle the Middle Colonies. In 1609, Henry Hudson sailed from Holland to the New World. He explored the waterway that is called the Hudson River. He claimed lands along the river. Dutch settlers arrived there 15 years later. The Dutch built a settlement called New Amsterdam. It was on the island of Manhattan.

New Amsterdam was attacked by English ships in 1664. The English were strong, and New Amsterdam soon fell under English control. The English renamed the settlement of New Amsterdam. They called it New York.

The land just to the south of New York was given to two Englishmen by the Duke of York. That land was named New Jersey.

**Swedish colonists built the first log cabins in America.**

A small group of colonists from Sweden founded New Sweden at the mouth of the Delaware River in 1638. The English captured New Sweden in 1682 and renamed it Delaware.

## The Middle Colony of Pennsylvania

**Pennsylvania means "Penn's Woods."**

William Penn was an English Quaker. During Penn's time, the Quakers in England had few rights. They did not belong to the Church of England. They were peace-loving people who would not fight in England's wars. Because of this, they were beaten, jailed, and even hanged.

**William Penn and Native Americans**

William Penn was a rich English lord. But he was won over to the Quaker view of helping the poor and sick. He wanted to find a safe place for the Quakers to live.

England's King Charles II owed Penn money. The king paid Penn with land in America. Penn said he would use that land for a "free colony to help all mankind." In 1682, he founded the colony of Pennsylvania.

The Quakers in England were jailed because they would not fight in England's wars. What would you do if the United States became involved in a war that you believed was wrong?

Pennsylvania became a special place of freedom. All the people who lived there enjoyed freedom of religion. If they were charged with a crime, they had a right to a trial by **jury**. Penn also insisted that the Native Americans be treated fairly.

People came to live in Pennsylvania from England, Scotland, Ireland, Sweden, France, and other lands. They were Protestants, Catholics, and Jews. No matter what their differences were, all people had the same rights in Pennsylvania.

## Life in the Middle Colonies

People from many lands learned to live together in the Middle Colonies. After a while, they all thought of themselves as "Americans." That was the beginning of what we call the "melting pot."

Most people in the Middle Colonies lived on large farms that were far apart from each other. There were fewer towns there than in the New England colonies. Schools were too far away for most children to attend. Families taught their children at home.

The colonists' farms were successful. They produced grains such as wheat and corn. The Middle Colonies became known as the "Breadbasket of America."

Not all of the Middle Colonists were farmers. Some made their living through fur trading. Beaver hats were popular then in Europe, and loads of beaver furs were shipped across the Atlantic.

## The Southern Colonies

People came to the Southern Colonies for several reasons. Some people, like their neighbors in the Middle Colonies, came looking for religious freedom.

The Catholics, like the Puritans and Quakers, wanted to worship as they pleased. An English Catholic named Lord Baltimore founded the colony of Maryland in 1634. In 1649, Maryland was the first colony to pass a law granting freedom of religion. It was called the Act of Toleration.

The colony of Georgia was not founded for religious freedom. Rather, it was founded as a **refuge** for English prisoners. Most of these prisoners were not really criminals. They were poor people. They had been jailed because they didn't have enough money to pay their **debts**.

An Englishman named James Oglethorpe thought this was unfair. He wanted to find a place where poor English prisoners could settle. Oglethorpe founded Georgia, where people could work hard and get a new start.

The Carolinas were founded in a different way. In 1663, King Charles II gave a large area of southern land to eight English noblemen. Many people came to the beautiful Carolinas. They came for religious freedom and the chance to prosper. By 1712, so many people had settled there that the colony was divided into two new colonies. They were called North Carolina and South Carolina.

## Farms and Plantations in the Southern Colonies

Most of the Southern colonists lived on large farms or even larger plantations. Many of the farms and plantations produced rice and tobacco. There were few large cities or towns in the Southern Colonies. Most children did not go to school.

The big plantations were started along the rivers and near the coast. Each plantation was too big to be worked by one family. Owners used slaves to do the work on the plantations.

Is it unfair to put a man in jail because he can't pay his debts? Oglethorpe thought so. How could someone in jail earn money to get out of debt?

| COMPARING THE NEW ENGLAND, MIDDLE, AND SOUTHERN COLONIES (AROUND 1700) | | | |
|---|---|---|---|
| | **New England** | **Middle Colonies** | **Southern Colonies** |
| Homeland | England | Germany, England, Holland, Sweden and other lands | Mostly England |
| Religion | Mostly Puritan | Quaker, Catholic, and others | Mostly Church of England |
| Lifestyle and Schools | Lived on farms or in towns; public schools | Fewer towns and schools than in New England | Lived on large farms and plantations; they kept slaves; children were taught at home |

**Chart Study**

Answer these questions on a separate sheet of paper.

1. Which colonies had settlers from many countries?
2. Which colonists used slaves as workers?
3. If you were a young colonist in New England, would you probably go to school? Why or why not?

## Slavery in the Southern Colonies

Unlike most people, black Africans did not find freedom in America. The first Africans who came to America arrived as **indentured servants**. In exchange for their free trip to America, indentured servants worked without pay. After three to seven years, an indentured servant would be set free.

**A slave auction**

But during the 1600s, that freedom was taken away. South Carolina passed laws making African servants slaves. Soon plantation owners began to buy slaves from people called slave traders. The slaves were brought from Africa on large slave ships.

Slaves had no rights. To their owners, they were property. And like property, they were bought and sold. Many of the owners worked their slaves like animals.

As early as 1688, some white people in Pennsylvania had spoken out against slavery. Even so, by 1750, slaves made up one-fifth of the population of the colonies. Some lived and worked

Slavery was kept going because some people believed black people weren't as good as white people. Do some people still feel that one race is better than another?

in the Middle Colonies and in New England. But most lived in the Southern Colonies.

## Learn More About It:
## Life on a Slave Ship

Slaves were brought to America on large ships. The cruel way they were treated began the moment they boarded the ships in Africa.

Slaves were crammed in below deck. They were so close together they could hardly breathe. Usually slaves were chained to each other. Diseases spread, and many died on board ship.

If the slaves tried to rebel, they would be beaten and sometimes even thrown overboard. But at times, through great effort, the slaves won out. There were more than one hundred successful slave revolts at sea.

### History Practice

Answer these questions on a separate sheet of paper.

1. Which colonies made up the New England Colonies? The Middle Colonies? The Southern Colonies?

2. Give two reasons why people came to live in the American colonies.

3. Why did William Penn found Pennsylvania?

4. Where did most slaves live? Why?

**The frontier**

## The Colonial Frontier Moves West

In the early 1600s, all settlements, including the main towns of Boston, Plymouth, and Jamestown, were near rivers. These towns also were on the Atlantic coast. They served as ports.

Land that was not yet settled was called the **wilderness** or the **frontier**. As more people came, they spread westward. They founded new towns on what had been wilderness. First settlers moved up the rivers. Then they reached the east side of the Appalachian Mountains.

People did not only move west. They also moved north, into Maine, Vermont, and New Hampshire.

Today, people sometimes call space "the new frontier."

# Life on the Frontier

Life on the frontier was often difficult and dangerous. Like New England farmers, frontier farmers raised crops for themselves. They also hunted deer, bear, and other wild game. Frontiersmen and women had to be skillful. They cleared their own land. They built their own homes. They made and repaired their own tools, furniture, and household goods.

Alone in the wilderness, the frontier farmer was **independent**. Frontier families had to protect themselves against wild animals and unfriendly Indians. There were no schools or even nearby towns. Frontier people relied on their own skills, courage, and religious beliefs.

Early settlers stayed east of the Appalachian Mountains. Find the Appalachians on the map on page 4.

# Native Americans Driven West

The colonists usually treated the Native Americans badly. Often, settlers just took their land, or paid very little for it. The settlers moved onto more and more of the natives' hunting grounds. So the Native Americans had to move farther and farther west.

The settlers brought diseases such as measles and **smallpox** to the Indians. The Native Americans had never known these European diseases. There were times when whole native villages died.

Sometimes the settlers had good relations with the natives. A powerful tribe called the Iroquois lived in New York. The settlers let the Iroquois alone. They traded with them for furs and other goods.

# The New American

From 1620 to 1760, the 13 colonies spread from New Hampshire in the North to Georgia in the

South. By the 1700s, there were many different types of Americans. Most worked on farms. But there were tradespeople and merchants in the cities and towns. Fishermen hunted and trapped in the wilderness to the west. And, there were large plantations owned in the South.

But in spite of the different ways of life in the 13 colonies, the people were alike in many ways.

First, Americans had come to see themselves not as Englishmen or Germans. They saw themselves simply as Americans.

Second, they had come to believe in certain rights. They insisted on the right to govern themselves and on the right to a trial by jury.

Third, colonists had come to believe in freedom of religion. Each person should be able to practice any religion in peace.

These three beliefs made up the "New American" spirit.

In 1760, King George III became king of England. The colonists were under his rule. But they had learned to take care of themselves. They began to think about what true independence might mean.

The idea of a jury trial came from an English document called the Magna Carta. The Magna Carta set down the rights of Englishmen. It was written in 1215.

## History Practice

Answer these questions on a separate sheet of paper.

1. What kinds of skills did a frontiersman need?

2. How did the settlers treat the Native Americans? Give examples.

3. Name an important belief of the "New American."

# Chapter Review

## Summary

| CHRONOLOGY OF MAJOR EVENTS | |
|---|---|
| 1624 | Dutch settle New Amsterdam |
| 1633 | English settle Georgia |
| 1634 | English settle Maryland |
| 1636 | English settle Rhode Island and Connecticut |
| 1638 | Swedes settle Delaware |
| 1663 | English settle the Carolinas |
| 1664 | English claim New York, settle New Jersey |
| 1682 | Penn founds Pennsylvania |
| 1760 | George III becomes king of England |

- New England settlers came seeking religious freedom. They lived on small farms or in towns.

- Settlers in the Middle Colonies came from different lands and had many religions.

- William Penn founded Pennsylvania, where all kinds of people had the same rights.

- Lord Baltimore and other Catholics settled Maryland. Maryland passed a law granting freedom of religion.

- Many southern colonists lived on large plantations and brought African slaves to do their work.

- The colonial frontier kept moving west.

- Settlers treated Native Americans badly and pushed them farther west.

- The "New American" believed in the rights of self-government, trial by jury, and freedom of religion.

## Chapter Quiz

Answer these questions on a separate sheet of paper.

1. Name the three regions the colonies were divided into.

2. Which region had the most towns and cities?

3. What did most people in the Middle Colonies do for a living?

4. Why was Georgia founded?

5. In which direction did the frontier mainly move? Why did it keep moving?

6. What rights did the "New American" believe in?

## Thinking and Writing

1. Philadelphia was the largest city in Pennsylvania. The name "Philadelphia" is a Greek word meaning "brotherly love." Why do you think it was called the city of brotherly love?

2. Imagine that you live during the 1600s. Choose one of the 13 colonies and tell what your life there might be like.

3. What qualities would a person need to become a frontiersman?

# Unit One Review

Use the information you have learned in Chapters 1 through 3 to complete this page. Write your answers on a separate sheet of paper.

**A. Who did it?**

1. He gave Native Americans the name "Indians."
2. He went to Mexico in search of treasure and conquered the Aztecs.
3. He signed a peace treaty with the Pilgrims promising his tribe's friendship.
4. She angered Boston Puritans and was forced to leave Massachusetts.
5. He founded the colony of Georgia.

**B. Give one reason...**

1. ...why Europeans were interested in exploring the Atlantic Ocean.
2. ...why Native Americans liked the French settlers better than the Spanish.
3. ...why Roger Williams and Anne Hutchinson were forced to leave their homes.
4. ...why Africans were brought to the colonies as slaves.

**C. Think about what you have learned.**

1. Give three reasons why settlers came to the New World.
2. Compare and contrast the French settlement of Canada with the Spanish settlement of South America. Describe one thing that was the same and one thing that was different.
3. Tell how the Mayflower Compact served as a beginning of democracy in the New World.
4. Compare and contrast the Pilgrims and the Puritans. What did the two groups have in common? What were their differences?

# Unit Two

# Winning Liberty

# Chapter 4

# The Road to Independence

| 1754 | 1774 |
|---|---|
| French and Indian War | First Continental Congress |

**Samuel Adams**

## Chapter Learning Objectives

- Tell how the French and Indian War gave England control of the New World.
- Describe the laws that angered the colonists.
- Describe how the colonists showed their anger toward British control.
- Describe the First Continental Congress.

# Words to Know

**act**  a law

**committee**  a group of people chosen to do certain work

**correspond**  to write letters to someone and receive letters back

**declaration**  a public statement

**delegate**  chosen spokesperson

**duty**  a tax on goods brought in from a foreign country

**hostile**  hateful, angry

**loyal**  faithful to someone or something

**protest**  speak out or act against

**repeal**  cancel, put an end to

**statesman**  a person who is good at handling government business

**tax**  money people must pay to support a government

**united**  joined together

---

Today, Americans like the British royalty. We hold parades and parties when England's queen, princes, and princesses visit the United States. But that was not the case back in the mid–1700s. At that time, King George III ruled England. In this chapter, you'll learn what the king did to make the colonists furious. And you'll find out what happened as the colonists became angrier and angrier.

## Colonists Look for New Lands

The English colonies grew quickly. The colonists wanted to spread out, and they began to push west.

There were rich lands on the other side of the Appalachian Mountains. English colonists wanted to cross the Appalachians and settle in the Ohio River Valley.

But France had already claimed the Ohio Valley. They had explored the land, made friends with the Native Americans there, and started a fur trade.

## The French and Indian War Breaks Out

Which nation, France or England, should control the Ohio Valley? That question led to war.

This war between England and France began in 1754. The two nations fought battles in Europe and in the American colonies. In America, the French received a lot of help from the Native Americans. That's why the fighting was called the French and Indian War.

British soldiers marched to war to the beat of battle drums. They dressed in bright red uniforms. The French and Native Americans fought in a quieter style. They used surprise attacks to confuse their enemy. The French had learned this way of fighting from their Native American friends.

At first, France seemed to be winning the war. But then England sent more soldiers and supplies to the colonies. England began to win the battles.

In 1763, England won the French and Indian War. The English claimed not only the Ohio Valley, but all of North America east of the Mississippi River. England also took control of Canada.

**The end of the French and Indian War put England in control of the New World. What might have happened to America if France had won? What language might we be speaking today?**

## Victory for England Brings New Problems

The colonists had helped England in the French and Indian War. But after England's victory, the British government took actions that seemed very unfair to the colonists.

During the war, the colonists had fought hard for the right to settle the Ohio Valley. But King George III of England now passed a law saying no colonists could settle there. The law was called the Proclamation of 1763. The American settlers were angry.

# Land Claims After 1763

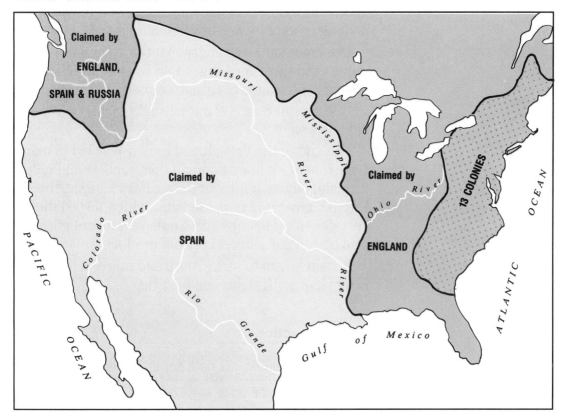

## Map Study

Study the map. Then answer the questions on a separate sheet of paper.

1. Which country claimed the 13 colonies?
2. What was the boundary between the English and Spanish land claims?

Why couldn't colonists settle in the Ohio Valley? The British government explained that it could not protect its people against the hostile Native Americans. But there were other reasons. England did not want the colonists spreading out and moving beyond its control. Also, the colonists had always bought goods from England. Britain worried that if the colonists moved west, they would buy their goods from other colonies instead. Then they would no longer send money to England.

The colonists were angry that they could not move. And they were angry that King George III was keeping thousands of British soldiers in America.

"We can take care of ourselves!" the angry colonists said.

The end of the French and Indian War led to many British **acts**, or laws. Some of these acts would help England pay its huge war debts. For example, the English government passed acts which forced the colonies to trade only with England. The colonists also had to pay a **tax** on certain products.

Britain began to make more and more demands. King George III tightened his grip.

## History Practice

Answer these questions on a separate sheet of paper.

1. What area did France and England fight over?

2. Who joined the French in their battle against the English?

3. Name the areas England claimed after the French and Indian War.

4. Give two reasons the colonists were unhappy with England after the war.

# New Acts Seem Unfair

In the years following the French and Indian War, England passed one act after another. Each act made the colonists more angry. They liked the new freedoms they had found in America. They did not want to give them up.

Look at the chart on this page to learn about some of the acts passed by the English government.

| BRITISH ACTS | | |
|---|---|---|
| **Act** | **Year** | **What the Act Did** |
| Sugar Act | 1764 | Taxed items like sugar and molasses that were bought in countries other than England. |
| Quartering Act | 1765 | Forced colonists to provide "quarters" for British soldiers. Quarters are places to eat and sleep. |
| Stamp Act | 1765 | Taxed newspapers, playing cards, and official documents. The colonists had to buy special stamps to place on such items. |
| Townshend Acts | 1767 | The colonists had to pay **duty** on tea, paper, lead, and paint. These acts were named after the English Minister of Finance. |

**Chart Study**

Study the chart to answer the following questions. Write your answers on a separate sheet of paper.

1. Which act forced colonists to give British soldiers a place to sleep?
2. Name two items taxed under the Stamp Act.
3. Name two items taxed under the Townshend Acts.

## "No Taxation Without Representation"

Most of the money collected from British taxes went back to England. It was not used to improve life in the colonies.

The colonists **protested** the British acts in different ways. Some Americans stopped buying goods from England. Others refused to pay taxes. They went to jail. Protest groups called the "Sons of Liberty" were formed in towns all over the colonies.

"No taxation without representation!" These words became the cry of colonial leaders like James Otis, Patrick Henry, and Samuel Adams. This phrase meant that the colonists thought that representatives of the people should make tax laws. They wanted a voice in decisions affecting the colonies.

Do Americans have the right to vote on new taxes today?

Learn More About It:
A Woman's Place in the 1700s

Until about the middle of the 1700s, women did many kinds of jobs. In fact, back then, women had more freedom than at almost any other time in history. Colonial women were blacksmiths, butchers, lawyers, innkeepers, hunters, and much more. Before 1776, ten American women were newspaper publishers.

## British Acts Bring Bloodshed

The colonists grew angrier. But they tried to reason with King George III. "We want to be **loyal**. We are British subjects," they wrote in letters to the king. "Just give us back our rights!"

But tensions were building between the colonists and the red-coated English soldiers. Something was bound to happen.

On March 5, 1770, trouble was in the air in Boston, Massachusetts. Some angry colonists began to yell insults at a group of British soldiers. Soon they were throwing snowballs at the redcoats.

The Boston Massacre was the result of an excited mob and some frightened soldiers. Can you think of a more recent time when an excited group caused a riot that ended in tragedy?

More colonists gathered on that snowy winter night. The British soldiers became frightened by what was turning into an angry mob. When a soldier was hit with a rock, the British opened fire. For the first time, blood was shed in a conflict between the British and the Americans.

**The Boston Massacre**

Five colonial men died as a result of what was called the Boston Massacre. The first to fall was a tall black man. He was a former slave named Crispus Attucks.

After the Boston Massacre, England realized the problems caused by the Townshend Acts. Many of the acts were **repealed**.

But King George III insisted that at least one tax be kept. So England kept the tax on tea. Its purpose was to remind the colonists that they were still under British rule.

### History Practice

Answer these questions on a separate sheet of paper.

1. What was meant by the colonial cry, "No taxation without representation"?

2. Name three acts passed by the British government between 1764 and 1767.

3. Explain what touched off the Boston Massacre.

## The Committees of Correspondence Unite the Colonies

Colonial **statesman** Samuel Adams was not happy with the continued British control of the colonies. So in 1772 he persuaded Boston colonists to set up a **Committee** of Correspondence. This committee would **correspond,** or write, to people in other towns and colonies. The letters would explain the rights of the colonists.

Soon many colonies had committees. This allowed the colonists to share ideas and learn about problems as they happened. It was a step toward banding together to face conflict with England.

## The Boston Tea Party

More conflicts came. The colonists were tired of the tax on tea. Also, England had passed a new Tea Act. This act said that only a British company could supply the tea. This would put colonial tea merchants out of business. How long would it be before other acts would close other businesses?

In protest, colonists refused to drink tea. They also tried to stop tea ships from entering harbors.

One December night in 1773, a group of colonists dressed themselves in Native American costumes. Then they boarded the British ships that were loaded with tea. They threw all the tea into Boston Harbor. This protest became known as the Boston Tea Party.

The British were furious. As punishment to Boston, they passed new, stricter laws. They were called the Intolerable Acts. These laws closed Boston

It is believed that Samuel Adams gave the signal to dump the tea.

Britain answered the Boston Tea Party by becoming stricter than ever. How do you think that pushed the colonists closer to war?

**Boston Tea Party**

Harbor for a while and put even more soldiers in Massachusetts. And the colonists were no longer allowed to hold meetings.

## Learn More About It: How the Committees of Correspondence Came to the Rescue

As you've read, one of the Intolerable Acts closed Boston Harbor. Word about that act spread quickly through the Committees of Correspondence. The response of other colonies was quick and helpful. South Carolina sent rice to Massachusetts, and Pennsylvania sent flour.

**Some colonies wanted to remain under British control. They liked the protection of the stronger country. Others wanted to separate from Britain. They wanted to make their own laws.**

## The First Continental Congress

In 1774, representatives from all the colonies except Georgia met to discuss England's laws. Men of many different backgrounds and opinions came together in Philadelphia, Pennsylvania. The meeting was called the First Continental Congress.

The First Continental Congress brought together strong leaders from the different colonies. Among the **delegates** were George Washington, Samuel Adams, John Adams, and Patrick Henry.

At this meeting, many of the colonists insisted they were still loyal to England. They argued that the problems could be worked out. "All we want," the colonists said, "are the same rights granted other Englishmen."

The idea of breaking away from England was not discussed at the First Continental Congress. But a new spirit came out of the meeting. It was the spirit of a **united** America. As Patrick Henry of Virginia said, "The differences between Virginians,

Pennsylvanians, New Yorkers, and New Englanders are no more. I am not a Virginian, but an American."

The delegates sent a **Declaration** of American Rights to England. In it, they listed the unfair ways England had treated colonists. And they asked that the hated Intolerable Acts be repealed. The delegates agreed to meet again if the king didn't act on their declaration. They would do this in May of 1775.

But British government did not change. And the colonists prepared for war.

---

### Great Names in History: Phyllis Wheatly

In 1773, around the time of the Boston Tea Party, a black woman named Phyllis Wheatly published a book. It was her first book of poems. And it was the second book of poetry ever published by a woman in America. Wheatly was a slave. She had been kidnapped in Africa at age nine and sent to a family in Boston.

---

## History Practice

Answer these questions on a separate sheet of paper.

1. What was the purpose of the Committees of Correspondence?

2. How did England react to the Boston Tea Party?

3. Name three of the famous statesmen present at the First Continental Congress.

4. What did delegates to the First Continental Congress ask Britain to do? How did the British government respond?

# Chapter Review

## Summary

| CHRONOLOGY OF MAJOR EVENTS | |
| --- | --- |
| 1754–1763 | French and Indian War |
| 1760 | King George III becomes ruler of England |
| 1763 | England passes the Proclamation of 1763 |
| 1764–1767 | England passes the Sugar Act, the Quartering Act, the Stamp Act, and the Townshend Acts |
| 1770 | Boston Massacre |
| 1773 | Boston Tea Party |
| 1774 | Intolerable Acts |
| 1774 | First Continental Congress |

- The French and Indian War was fought because France and England each wanted to control the Ohio Valley.

- After winning the war, England kept settlers out of the Ohio Valley, enforced new taxes to pay its war debt, and left its soldiers in America.

- England wrote new acts to further control the colonists. Many colonists felt they had no say in their government.

- The Boston Massacre resulted in the repeal of the Townshend Acts. The tea tax remained.

- At the Boston Tea Party, colonists dumped a shipload of British tea into the harbor. This resulted in even stricter laws from England.

- At the First Continental Congress, colonial leaders asked for a say in their government. Delegates sent a Declaration of American Rights to King George III.

## Chapter Quiz

Answer these questions on a separate sheet of paper.

1. What was the cause of the French and Indian War?

2. Who won the French and Indian War?

3. Why were the colonists angry about the acts England passed?

4. Tell what caused the Boston Tea Party.

5. Name four leaders at the First Continental Congress.

## Thinking and Writing

1. What did Samuel Adams do in 1772 that made him a leader? Why are men like Adams important when change is about to occur?

2. Explain the phrase "No taxation without representation."

3. What did the British government do after the Boston Massacre? What did it do after the Boston Tea Party? Compare the results of the two events.

## Chapter 5

# Americans Fight for Freedom

**1775**
Battles of Lexington and Concord

**1783**
America and Britain sign peace treaty

**Paul Revere**

## Chapter Learning Objectives

- Describe how the Americans organized an army to fight the British.
- Name two things the Second Continental Congress did.
- Tell why the Declaration of Independence is an important document.
- Explain how the Americans won the Revolutionary War against a larger, better-trained army.

## Words to Know

**equality** fairness; sameness

**Loyalists** Americans who supported the British in the Revolutionary War

**militia** a group of citizens who are not regular soldiers but who get some military training

**Neutralists** colonists who did not care which side won the Revolutionary War

**pamphlet** a thin booklet with a paper cover

**Patriots** Americans who wanted independence from Britain

**pursuit** the act of going after something, of seeking it

**retreat** to move back from; to escape

**surrender** to give up

**traitor** a person who helps his country's enemies

**unified** joined together as one

"The British are coming!" That's what Paul Revere cried in his famous night ride. In this chapter, you'll find out *why* the British were coming. And you'll share the drama of what happened once they got here.

## Liberty or Death!
## The Colonists Prepare To Fight

The First Continental Congress had tried to settle the problems between England and its American colonies. But things did not get better.

England's King George III was prepared for trouble. "I will make them give in!" he said.

But the Americans were not ready to give in to the king's demands. They wanted the tax on tea repealed. They wanted to be able to hold public meetings and to make laws. They wanted their freedom. "Give me liberty or give me death!" Patrick Henry cried.

War had not yet been declared. Still, Americans began preparing for conflict. Why?

Patrick Henry wasn't the only one who was ready to fight and die for freedom. In Massachusetts, groups called Minutemen were formed. These colonists, who were between the ages of 16 and 60, agreed to turn out at a minute's notice. They would be ready any time there was danger.

The Minutemen began to store guns and bullets in Concord, a town 20 miles outside of Boston.

All the angry feelings were about to explode.

## "If They Want a War, Let It Begin Here!"

The British General Thomas Gage knew about the American guns at Concord. He was worried. Gage decided to destroy the guns in a surprise raid.

Late on the night of April 18, 1775, about 1,000 British soldiers marched quietly out of Boston. They were on a secret mission to Concord. But someone was watching them.

The Boston colonists had thought of a way to warn of a British attack. They had a special signal. One flash of a lantern in the church tower meant the British were coming by land. Two flashes meant the British traveled by sea. Just one flash lit that dark, tense night.

Paul Revere is famous as the American patriot who made a midnight ride. Did you know he was also a great silversmith?

## "The British Are Coming!"

The Minutemen had to be warned of the British attack on Concord! And colonist Paul Revere would be the one to warn them. He rode 16 miles on horseback through the surrounding towns. In Lexington, people were sleeping peacefully, when out of the darkness came Paul Revere's cry. "The British are coming!" he shouted. He warned the colonists that General Gage and his soldiers were on the way.

In Lexington, Revere was joined by William Dawes. Together they rode toward Concord shouting the alarm.

Revere and Dawes were captured. But Samuel Prescott, another colonist, continued the ride. Prescott spread the warning.

When the British arrived in Lexington, 40 Minutemen were waiting for them on the village green.

American Captain John Parker gave his men orders. "Stand your guard. Don't fight unless fired upon. But if they want a war, let it begin here!"

**Words From the Past**

The poet Henry Wadsworth Longfellow tells about Paul Revere's ride in a famous poem.

*Listen my children, and you shall hear,*

*Of the midnight ride of Paul Revere,*

*On the eighteenth of April in Seventy-five*

*Hardly a man is now alive*

*Who remembers that famous day and year.*

*One if by land, and two if by sea;*

*And I on the opposite shore will be,*

*Ready to ride and spread the alarm*

*Through every Middlesex village and farm.*

## Lexington and Concord

The Battle at Lexington brought defeat for the Minutemen. Eight colonists were killed. Ten were wounded. Only one British soldier died.

The British soldiers were called "Redcoats" because their uniform coats were bright red. Imagine how they looked compared to the American soldiers, dressed for farm and field.

Then the British went on to Concord. There the Redcoats destroyed American guns and supplies.

But the Americans did not give up the fight. Four hundred and fifty Minutemen raced across North Bridge and began chasing the Redcoats back to Boston.

On the way, more and more Minutemen joined the fight. They hid behind trees and fired shot after shot. Many British soldiers simply threw down their guns and ran. By the time they reached Boston, 300 British and 90 Americans had been killed or hurt.

The army of Minutemen was made up mostly of farmers and storekeepers. Yet they had stood up to the powerful British army. And they had won! They'd proven that Americans were willing to die for a cause they believed in.

**North Bridge, Concord**

## Great Names in History:
## Ethan Allen and the Green Mountain Boys

After the Battles of Lexington and Concord, the Americans knew they needed guns and ammunition. They could get these things by taking British forts.

An American frontiersman named Ethan Allen gathered a group of settlers. These men wore long green coats and high boots and called themselves the Green Mountain Boys. The group rowed silently across New York's Lake Champlain. They surprised the British and captured Fort Ticonderoga. Then they took cannons and ammunition for the Minutemen.

The news spread. Americans were proud that they could capture such a powerful fort.

## History Practice

Answer these questions on a separate sheet of paper.

1. Who were the Minutemen?

2. How did the colonists know British troops were marching to Concord?

3. Which American captain surprised the British in Lexington?

# The Second Continental Congress

Less than a month after the Battles of Lexington and Concord, colonial leaders met again in Philadelphia. They called their meeting the Second Continental Congress.

You've read about the First Continental Congress. Remember that the delegates back in 1774 agreed to meet again in May of 1775. The Second Continental Congress was that next meeting.

War had not been declared. In fact, the delegates to the congress still did not want war. They decided to ask England for peace. But they felt that it wouldn't hurt to be prepared. So while they hoped for peace, they prepared for war.

A Virginia planter, George Washington, was chosen to lead the American army. Washington had bravely led a group of Americans during the French and Indian War.

## The Battle of Bunker Hill

While the Congress was meeting in Philadelphia, conflict was breaking out in Boston.

After Lexington and Concord, the colonists had forced the British to stay in Boston. A few months later, on June 17, 1775, the British decided to escape. But first they would need to break through the American militia on Bunker Hill and Breeds Hill.

After a bloody battle, the British took Bunker Hill. But they lost twice as many men as the Americans did. The colonists were proud of their effort. They felt that even though they had lost the battle, they might win the war.

King George III was shocked by the news of the heavy British losses. He ordered the Royal Navy to blockade shipping to the colonies. He also hired Hessians, soldiers from the German state of Hesse, to help control the colonists.

## The Declaration of Independence

The Second Continental Congress had sent King George III a petition that asked for peace. In answer, the king sent 30,000 new troops to America.

Now the Americans felt they had only one choice. It was time to ask for independence.

**Then:** "...Remember the ladies." That's what Abigail Adams wrote to her husband, John Adams. At the time of her letter, he was on his way to the Second Continental Congress. Abigail wanted the delegates to grant women more rights. She hoped they would "not put so much power in the hands of the husbands." Women, she wrote, "would not hold ourselves bound by any laws in which we have no voice."

**Now:** Today women do not have to ask their husbands to speak for them. In 1917, a woman named Jeannette Rankin became the first woman elected to the U.S. Congress. Now women speak for themselves.

In June of 1776, the Continental Congress gave an important job to Thomas Jefferson. They asked the young delegate from Virginia to write a declaration. The declaration would tell why the colonies should be independent from Britain.

In the declaration, Jefferson told what Americans believed. He said that Americans believed in **equality**. He said people have the right to life, liberty, and the **pursuit** of happiness.

The delegates read the declaration and agreed with most of it. Before they would accept it, however, they took out one of Jefferson's ideas. Jefferson had wanted to put an end to slavery in America. But the Congress would not agree to that part of the Declaration.

People around the world look to the Declaration of Independence as a symbol of freedom. When you celebrate the Fourth of July, think about what this holiday means.

**Thomas Jefferson**

On July 4, 1776, the Declaration was completed. The Americans who signed it gave notice that "These United Colonies are, and of right ought to be, free and independent States."

**Great Names in History:**
**Thomas Paine and Common Sense**

Thomas Paine was an American patriot. His writings stirred the American spirit toward independence. In 1776, Paine published a **pamphlet** called *Common Sense*. It advised independence from England. George Washington, Thomas Jefferson, and other leaders read *Common Sense*. Its simple and direct message soon spread throughout the colonies. Paine later served as a revolutionary soldier. But his greatest service to his country came from his written words.

## History Practice

Answer these questions on a separate sheet of paper.

1. Who did the Second Continental Congress choose to lead the American army?

2. What idea did the delegates remove from Jefferson's Declaration of Independence?

3. Why is July 4 considered America's Independence Day?

## Patriots and Loyalists

Not all Americans wanted independence. Some wanted to remain a part of Britain. These people were called **Loyalists**. They were loyal to England. Some of them even fought in the British army.

The colonists who wanted America to be free were called **Patriots**. Some joined the American army. Some patriots fought in their local **militia**. People in militias fought only when their own area was under attack. The rest of the time they worked on their farms.

Colonists who did not care which side won the war were called **Neutralists**. Some Neutralists just wanted to make money by selling supplies to both sides.

Think of reasons why some colonists would be Patriots. Think of reasons why some would be Loyalists. Do you think you would have been one or the other? Which one?

## The Americans Against the British

The Americans were not trained soldiers. They were farmers, store owners, and craftsmen who had taken up arms. Many of their leaders had never fought in a war. Yet the Americans had some things in their favor. The most important of these was that they were fighting for a cause they believed in.

The chart below shows other advantages the American army had during the Revolutionary War. It also shows the advantages the British army had.

| AMERICAN ADVANTAGES | BRITISH ADVANTAGES |
|---|---|
| The Americans. . . <br> • knew the land <br> • had learned Native American fighting methods <br> • had the support of many European nations <br> • had a strong leader in George Washington <br> • were fighting for their own homes and freedom <br> • knew Britain had to give attention to other parts of the world | The British. . . <br> • had a large, well-trained army and more money <br> • had the help of Cherokee Indians and German soldiers called Hessians <br> • controlled the seas and could stop trade in the colonies |

## Washington's Battle Plan

Washington figured his best hope of defeating the stronger British army was with surprise attacks. He did this in New Jersey at Trenton and Princeton. Other colonial leaders used surprise when attacking Saratoga. After each attack, the American army would **retreat**. Fighting and retreating, the American army battled its way to independence.

The Revolutionary War lasted five years. It began in the summer of 1776 and finally ended when the British **surrendered** at Yorktown, Virginia in the fall of 1781. The following are the major events of the American Revolution.

**Washington learned about surprise attacks during his service in the French and Indian War.**

*Summer of 1776, Battle of New York*

A powerful fleet of British ships sailed into New York harbor and attacked. General Washington led the retreat, saving his men. If not for Washington's wise retreat, the British might have won the war right there.

*December 25, 1776, Battle of Trenton*

On Christmas Day, Washington ordered a surprise attack on Hessian troops in Trenton, New Jersey. Hessians were German soldiers paid to fight for the British.

Washington and his troops rowed across the icy Delaware River. Then they marched to Trenton and captured a thousand Hessians. Only four of Washington's men were lost. Trenton was the first victory since independence had been declared.

Victory at Trenton raised American spirits. Many American soldiers signed up for another term in the army.

## Words From the Past

A colonial soldier named Nathan Hale spied on the British in New York. He was caught. Right before he was hanged, he said these famous words: "I only regret that I have but one life to lose for my country."

*October 17, 1777, Battle of Saratoga*

The British army surrendered to the American army at Saratoga, New York. The battle that took place there is thought of as the Revolutionary War's turning point.

The American troops were led by Benedict Arnold. Arnold was a hero at Saratoga, but a year later he became a **traitor** to America.

*Winter, 1778, Valley Forge*

This was the low point of the war. The American army lived in tents in the snow. They had no warm clothing, blankets, or shoes to replace their worn ones. About 2,500 Americans died from cold and sickness. Others simply went home.

"You can tell where the American army has been," General Washington said, "by the footprints of blood in the snow."

Meanwhile, the British army was safe and warm in Philadelphia.

**Valley Forge**

*February 1778, France enters the war*

The victory at Saratoga had shown the French that the Americans could win battles. The French were then ready to join the American fight for independence.

Benjamin Franklin went to France seeking friends for the colonies. A treaty of friendship was signed between France and America.

A rich French nobleman named Marquis de Lafayette led French soldiers against the British in Virginia. Lafayette had already joined the American cause earlier in the war. He proved to be a great friend.

*1778, America wins the West*

Patrick Henry, the Virginia governor, sent George Rogers Clark into the Ohio Valley in the spring. By the next winter, the British had lost their control of the West.

*1778, Other European nations support America*

Spain and the Netherlands both lent money to help the American effort. A German military leader named Baron Friedrich von Steuben served with the Americans. And Poland's Count Pulaski and Thaddeus Kosciusko also fought.

**American soldiers had courage and spirit. But they needed the military know-how of their foreign friends.**

*Spring, 1780, American defeat at Charleston*

Charleston, South Carolina, fell to the British. This was the biggest British victory yet.

*Fall, 1781, Battle of Yorktown*

This was the last battle of the war.

The British General, Lord Cornwallis, marched through the South. The American and French armies moved to Yorktown to trap the British. The French navy closed off the bay, which trapped the British. On October 19, 1781, Cornwallis surrendered.

**Cornwallis surrendering**

## A Free Country

Yorktown was the last battle of the American Revolution. King George III might have gone on fighting. But he saw that the British people were tired of war.

A group of American leaders went to Paris to work out a peace treaty with the British. It took almost two years to prepare the treaty. Finally, in 1783, the British and the Americans signed it. It was called the Treaty of Paris.

The colonies were now called the United States of America. The United States was a free and independent country.

The Americans had fought and defeated the world's most powerful country. They had won because they felt they had a cause worth fighting for. They had gained their freedom.

**Think of ways your life might be different today if the British had won the Revolutionary War.**

Now they had to form a government that would keep them free, strong, and **unified**. This would prove to be as hard as winning independence.

**Major Battles of the American Revolution**

## History Practice

Answer these questions on a separate sheet of paper.

1. What were the Americans who supported the British called?

2. Name two advantages the Americans had in the war. Name two advantages the British had.

3. Which country decided to join the American fight for freedom in 1778?

# Chapter Review

## Summary

| CHRONOLOGY OF MAJOR EVENTS | |
|---|---|
| 1775 | Battles of Lexington and Concord |
| 1775 | Battle of Bunker Hill |
| 1775-76 | Second Continental Congress meets |
| 1776 | Congress approves Declaration of Independence |
| 1778 | American army spends hard winter at Valley Forge |
| 1778 | France enters war on American side |
| 1781 | British surrender at Yorktown |
| 1783 | Americans and British sign final peace treaty in Paris |

- As problems between England and America continued, the colonists began preparing for war. The Minutemen were formed.

- The British planned a sneak attack on Concord to destroy American supplies.

- Paul Revere, William Dawes, and Samuel Prescott warned the colonists of the attack.

- Minutemen and Redcoats fired the first shots of the Revolution at Lexington and Concord.

- The Second Continental Congress chose George Washington to lead the American army. It sent a final letter to King George asking for peace. King George refused.

- Thomas Jefferson wrote the Declaration of Independence.

- Washington's battle plan used surprise attacks and retreats.

- The hard winter at Valley Forge was the low point of the war.

- France joined the American fight in 1778. Other foreign nations lent support.

- British General Cornwallis surrendered at Yorktown in 1781.

- The final peace treaty was signed in Paris in 1783.

## Chapter Quiz

Answer these questions on a separate sheet of paper.

1. What did Paul Revere do?

2. Who wrote the Declaration of Independence?

3. Which country, England or America, had a better army?

4. Which battle was the turning point of the war?

5. Name three countries that helped America win the war. Tell how each one helped.

## Thinking and Writing

1. At the start of the Revolutionary War, which side do you think had the best chance of winning? Explain your answer.

2. Jefferson wanted the Declaration of Independence to put an end to slavery in America. Can you think of reasons why some delegates did not like that idea?

3. Thomas Jefferson wrote that "all men are created equal." What did he mean?

# Unit Two Review

Use information you have learned in Chapters 4 and 5 to complete this page. Write your answers on a separate sheet of paper.

## A. Who did it?

1. He set up the Committees of Correspondence.
2. He warned the colonists that "the British are coming!"
3. He wrote a pamphlet called *Common Sense*.
4. He wrote the Declaration of Independence.
5. He said, "I am not a Virginian, but an American."
6. He led the American army in the Revolutionary War.
7. He was the first colonial to be killed in the Boston Massacre.
8. He captured Fort Ticonderoga.
9. He was a Frenchman who fought for the Patriots.

## B. Which came first?

1. the Boston Massacre *or* the Boston Tea Party?
2. the American Revolution *or* the French and Indian War?
3. Paul Revere's ride *or* the Battle of Bunker Hill?
4. the Battles of Lexington and Concord *or* the Battle of Yorktown?
5. the signing of a peace treaty in Paris *or* the Second Continental Congress?

## C. Explain....

1. ...why the American colonists got angry after the French and Indian War.
2. ...how the Committees of Correspondence helped unite the colonies.
3. ...the purpose of the Declaration of Independence.
4. ...why American soldiers were called "Minutemen."
5. ...the positions of the Loyalists, Patriots, and the Neutralists.

# Unit Three

# The Young Nation

# Chapter 6

# A Government for the Ages

| 1783 | 1800 |
|---|---|
| Independence for the United States | Thomas Jefferson elected President |

**John Adams**

## Chapter Learning Objectives

- Tell why the Articles of Confederation failed to provide a good government for the United States.
- Describe a compromise reached at the Constitutional Convention.
- Describe how power is divided among the different branches of the government.
- Tell why the Bill of Rights was added to the Constitution.

# Words to Know

**alien**   person from a foreign country who is not yet a citizen

**amendment**   a change or addition to a document

**bill**   an idea for a law

**cabinet**   a group of people chosen by the president to give advice

**constitution**   the law and plan of a country's government

**executive**   the branch of government having power to carry out laws

**houses**   groups of people who make laws

**judicial**   the branch of government that settles arguments about the meaning of laws and that punishes law-breakers

**legislative**   the branch of government that makes laws

**politics**   the art of running a government

**ratify**   to approve or accept

**sedition**   acts that stir up rebellion against the government

**Supreme Court**   the United States court that has final say on law disputes

**veto**   reject

George Washington was the first president of the United States. John Adams, shown at left, was the second. But right after the Revolutionary War, there was no president to lead the country. In this chapter, you'll read about how the country was first governed. You'll learn why the first form of government didn't work. And you'll find out how our government came to be what it is today.

## The Articles of Confederation

The Revolution had been won, and the 13 colonies were now free states. It was time for Americans to make their new nation strong. The first few years after the war were very important. Much of what America is today was decided then.

The Second Continental Congress had continued to meet throughout the war. During that time, the Congress drew up the Articles of Confederation.

This written agreement contained a plan for the new government.

The government was run by Congress. Congress was run by the states. Each state had one vote. Before Congress could pass any law, nine states had to agree on it.

The national government was very weak. There was no president to lead the country and carry out the laws. There was no **Supreme Court** to settle important arguments. Congress could ask for money from the states, but the states did not have to pay. The government could not collect taxes. It had no way of getting money for things it needed, such as an army.

Many Americans were afraid of a strong central government. They had seen what had happened under powerful British rule. In many ways, the states looked upon themselves as separate countries.

## Post-War Problems

Here are some of the problems America faced after the Revolutionary War:

- England closed its ports to America. The new country had to find new trading partners.
- Spanish-American relations were poor.
- The country owed money to soldiers who had fought in the war. Money that had been borrowed from France and the Netherlands could not be paid back. Because Congress could not collect federal taxes, the government couldn't pay its debts.
- There was no central money system. Some states printed their own money. It was worthless in other states.
- Congress could not control trade between the states.
- There were no courts to settle arguments between the states.

Under the Articles of Confederation, Congress made laws. But there were no government officials to carry out those laws. Do you think that kind of government can work for long?

The Spanish held Florida and the city of New Orleans. They interfered with trade on the Mississippi River. The United States was too weak to do anything about the problems with Spain.

It was becoming clear that a stronger government was needed.

## Shays's Rebellion

In 1786, a mob of Massachusetts farmers gathered in front of a courthouse. They were in debt, and they could not pay state taxes. Massachusetts courts had been taking away the farms from people who could not pay taxes. Daniel Shays and his group of farmers shut down the courts in protest.

Shays also made plans to attack an army post to get guns. The U.S. government knew about these plans but had no army to stop Shays. The soldiers who finally put down the revolt had to be hired by Massachusetts businessmen.

"Mr. Shays," a soldier said, "this army post is owned by the government of the United States. I order you to leave it."

"What government?" Daniel Shays asked. "There is no government that I can see!"

**Brawl between government supporter and rebel at time of Shays's Rebellion.**

Shays's Rebellion gave the country a shock. George Washington wrote, "If the government cannot protect its own posts from a group of farmers, how can our country protect itself from powerful foreign countries?"

America needed a stronger central government. Leaders feared that if it did not get one soon, there would be no United States at all.

What would become of the frontier?

## The Northwest Ordinance

**The Northwest Territory was bordered by the Ohio River, the Mississippi River, and the Great Lakes.**

You learned earlier that as the colonies grew, settlers moved to the frontier. The frontier to the northwest of the 13 states was called the Northwest Territory. After the Revolution, this area was not part of any state.

How would it be governed? How could the territory become part of the United States? In 1787, Congress answered these questions in a plan called the Northwest Ordinance. The plan had three parts:

1. At first, the territory would be ruled by a governor and three judges. All would be appointed by Congress.

2. When the population reached 5,000 free men of voting age, it could elect its own legislature. Congress would still appoint the governor.

3. When the population of any part of the territory reached 60,000, the people there would draw up a constitution. The constitution would be approved by Congress. That part of the territory would become a state. No less than three and no more than five states would be created.

The Northwest Ordinance said slavery was not allowed in the territory.

**History Practice**

Answer these questions on a separate sheet of paper.

1. Why did many Americans fear a strong central government?

2. Name three problems that faced America under the Articles of Confederation.

3. Why was the government unable to put down Shays's Rebellion?

# A Meeting in Philadelphia

In May of 1787, 55 men came together in Philadelphia. They met to think of ways to improve the national government. They had been sent by 12 of the 13 states. Rhode Island was the smallest state. It was worried that any changes would leave it with less power. Rhode Island did not send a delegate to the meeting.

The delegates met to change the Articles of Confederation. But they soon decided to write a whole new plan of government. They were going to write the **Constitution** of the United States. For this reason, the meeting in Philadelphia was called the Constitutional Convention.

Among those who went to the meeting were three very famous men: George Washington, Benjamin Franklin, and James Madison. Washington arrived in Philadelphia wearing his old army uniform. After leading the Revolution, he was deeply respected by Americans everywhere.

Benjamin Franklin was one of the most famous citizens in the United States. He was a scientist, a writer, and a statesman. Now, at the age of 81, Franklin was performing his last act of public service.

**We know a lot about what went on at the Constitutional Convention because James Madison kept notes. These notes were later published.**

Another well-known delegate was James Madison. He was highly respected for his quick mind. Madison felt strongly about the need for a more powerful central government. He became known as the "Father of the Constitution."

**James Madison**

## Big States vs. Small States

On the first day of the Convention, delegates agreed on everything that came before them. They all felt that George Washington should run the meeting. They also agreed, in spite of the summer heat, to lock the doors of the meeting room. And they would close the windows and curtains. This would keep their talks secret until the new plan was completed.

The first day, however, was the only one on which the delegates were of one mind. After that, they agreed on almost nothing. They argued throughout the summer and into early fall. Their most important question had to do with how the new Congress would be set up. How many votes would each state have? Would all the states have an equal say? Or would the states with more people have more votes?

Virginia put forward a plan giving more power to the large states than to the small ones. Each state would have votes in Congress according to its population. The states that had the most people would have the most representatives. The larger states liked this idea. The smaller states hated it.

The small states presented another plan. They wanted each state, no matter what its size, to have only one vote. The small states would have just as much power as the large states.

The argument went on for six weeks. It seemed that neither side would give in. At this point, the Convention might have fallen apart. Fortunately, a Connecticut delegate named Roger Sherman found a middle ground.

Under Virginia's plan for Congress, Virginia would have 16 votes and Georgia would have only one.

"Why not have two **houses** of Congress?" he said. "In one house, all states will have the same number of votes. In the other house, the number of votes will depend on the number of people in the state."

This would protect both the large and the small states. It didn't take long for all the delegates to go along with the idea. Sherman's plan was accepted on July 16.

Sherman's plan is still in effect today. The two houses of Congress are called the House of Representatives and the Senate.

The number of representatives a state has in the House of Representatives depends on that state's population. In the Senate, each state has two representatives.

**Roger Sherman**

Who are your Representatives in the House? Who are your Senators?

For three long months, the delegates argued about other parts of the government. Many times they seemed unable to reach agreement. But each time they worked something out. Finally, their new plan was written down as the Constitution of the United States of America. Thirty-nine of the 55 delegates signed it.

Now it was time to come out from behind the locked doors. The delegates brought the Constitution back to their states. Nine out of the 13 states had to approve, or **ratify**, the Constitution before it went into effect.

## Great Names in History: Benjamin Franklin

During the Convention, Benjamin Franklin had sat quietly, listening to delegates speak. Often he had looked at the tall chair in which George Washington sat. He had noticed that the back of the chair was carved with a large sun just above the horizon. Was it a rising sun or a setting sun? Franklin could not decide.

On the last day of the meeting, Franklin rose to speak. "This Constitution that we are about to sign will surprise our enemies. They are waiting for us to break up. They think we plan to cut each other's throat."

Then Franklin pointed to Washington's chair. "For many weeks I have looked at that sun behind Mr. Washington without being able to tell whether it was a rising sun or a setting sun. But now, seeing this Constitution we have before us, I am happy to know that it is a rising sun."

## Federalists and Anti-Federalists

Over the next few months, people in the 13 states discussed the new Constitution. Members of the convention tried to convince the citizens in their states to vote for it. Those in favor of the Constitution and a strong central government were called Federalists.

James Madison, Alexander Hamilton, John Jay, and others wrote letters to New York City newspapers praising the Constitution. These letters came to be called the "Federalist Papers." They are among the most famous writings in American history. The Federalists said that there would be less quarreling and confusion between states under the Constitution. They said the Constitution would keep the nation united.

People who feared a strong central government wanted more power for the individual states. These people were called Anti-Federalists. The Anti-Federalists worried that the new government would be too much like Britain's. They wondered what was to stop a president from becoming as powerful as a king. Anti-Federalists were especially concerned about one part of the Constitution. It gave Congress the power to "lay and collect taxes." The Anti-Federalists worried that Congress would pass high taxes that many Americans would not be able to pay.

One by one, the states approved the Constitution. And in time, a weak collection of 13 states became a strong country. It has changed some over the years. But the United States Constitution has remained the law of the land. It is the basis, or foundation, for all of our other laws.

**Alexander Hamilton**

## History Practice

Answer these questions on a separate sheet of paper.

1. Name three famous leaders who attended the Constitutional Convention.

2. Explain why the delegates decided on two houses of Congress.

3. What were the two houses of Congress called? How was each organized?

4. What did the Federalists believe? What did the Anti-Federalists believe?

## Checks and Balances

To keep government from becoming too strong, the Constitution provides for a system of checks and balances. This means that power is divided between three different branches of the federal government. The three are the **Legislative**, the **Executive**, and the **Judicial** branches.

The Legislative branch, also known as Congress, makes the laws. Congress is made up of the Senate and the House of Representatives.

The Executive branch is headed by the president. This branch sees that the laws are carried out. The president signs and approves the laws that Congress makes. Until the executive branch approves the laws, they are called **bills**.

If the president doesn't like a bill Congress has passed, he can refuse to sign it. That is called a **veto**. When a president vetoes a bill, it can still become a law. But two-thirds of Congress must then vote to override the veto.

The Judicial branch is the system of federal courts. The courts decide what different laws mean. They make sure people are treated fairly under them. The most powerful court in the land is the Supreme Court. It makes sure that the laws Congress passes are allowed by the Constitution.

Each branch of the government checks the power of the others. None has purpose without the other two. This is how the United States government keeps a balance of power.

Congress can remove the president from office. The House of Representatives can charge the president with a crime or some other form of misconduct. The Senate can then put the president on trial. This is another way that the Legislative branch checks the power of the Executive branch.

| THE CONSTITUTION | | |
| --- | --- | --- |
| **Congress** | **The President** | **The Supreme Court** |
| • Makes laws<br>• Can pass laws after a president's veto, with two-thirds vote<br>• Must approve president's choices for judges | • Enforces laws<br>• Can veto laws<br>• Appoints Supreme Court judges | • Decides if laws are constitutional |

## The Bill of Rights

Many Americans thought that the Constitution should list basic human freedoms. They wanted a Bill of Rights added. The Bill of Rights guarantees certain rights to every American. Some of these are:

- The right to express your opinions in books, newspapers, and magazines.
- The right to worship as you please.
- The right to a speedy trial by jury.
- The right to speak your opinions.

The Bill of Rights was added to the U.S. Constitution in 1791. The ten freedoms it outlines make up the first ten **amendments** to the Constitution.

Many amendments have been added to the Constitution since 1791 but none is more important than those first ten. Our American freedoms depend on the Bill of Rights.

Think of something that you did this week that involved a freedom granted you by the Bill of Rights. (Did you go to church or synagogue? Did you read a newspaper or watch television?)

## History Practice

Answer these questions on a separate sheet of paper.

1. Name the three branches of the federal government.

2. Give one example of how the president can check Congress. Give one example of how Congress can check the president. Give one example of how the Supreme Court can check Congress.

3. Why did some people feel that the Constitution needed a Bill of Rights?

4. Name three freedoms that the Bill of Rights protects.

## The First President

On April 6, 1789, George Washington was elected to be the first president of the United States. John Adams, as runner-up, became the vice-president.

Washington served two four-year terms. His job was not easy. He had to choose advisors, or as they are called today, a **cabinet**. He had to find money to pay war debts. He had to work out agreements with foreign nations.

Who is the president of the United States today? Who is the vice-president?

Washington chose his advisors wisely: Thomas Jefferson, Alexander Hamilton, Henry Knox, and Edmund Randolph. He also chose John Jay to be Chief Justice of the United States. Jefferson became Secretary of State. Hamilton became Secretary of the Treasury. Knox became Secretary of War. Randolph became Attorney General.

Washington settled money problems. He kept the United States out of foreign conflicts. The country grew stronger under his leadership. Washington would become known as "the Father of his Country."

After two terms, Washington announced that he would not again be a candidate for president. He was anxious to return to a more private life. Like many things Washington did, this decision set an example for the future. For more than 140 years, it remained the custom for presidents to step down after two terms.

---

**Then and Now**

**Then**: After the Revolutionary War, the United States owed money to its citizens and to other countries. Alexander Hamilton, Secretary of the Treasury, recommended an import tax and a whiskey tax to raise money. The nation paid off most of its debts and won the respect of countries around the world. The American people gained new confidence in their government. Hamilton also set up a national bank and a coin system.

**Now**: National debts are a concern today. As of 1990, America had a debt of hundreds of billions of dollars. That debt has been growing every year. How do you think this might affect our reputation in the world? Candidates in the 1992 presidential election promised to cut the national debt. What problems does a large national debt cause at home?

---

## A New Capital

George Washington first governed the United States from New York City. Then, between 1790 and 1800, Philadelphia served as the nation's capital.

In 1800, the capital was moved to the banks of the Potomac River. Virginia and Maryland had each given land for the city. The capital was called Washington, D.C. (District of Columbia).

The capital of the United States is in Washington, D.C. Where is the capital of your state?

Washington, D.C., is still the nation's capital. The District of Columbia is not a very large place. Yet it is one of the world's most important centers of power. The District of Columbia belongs to the federal government.

---

**Great Names in History:**
**Benjamin Banneker**

Benjamin Banneker was an African American farmer and scientist. He was chosen by President Washington to serve on the committee that planned the new capital.

The planning committee was led by Pierre L'Enfant. This French engineer had fought in the Revolutionary War. L'Enfant laid out beautiful plans for the new city. Then he had an argument with local landowners. L'Enfant quit in anger and took his plans with him.

But work on the capital was completed. Benjamin Banneker had memorized the plans.

---

## Hamilton, Jefferson, and the Two-Party System

Alexander Hamilton was Secretary of the Treasury in Washington's cabinet. Thomas Jefferson was Secretary of State. These two men were Washington's most important advisors.

Hamilton and Jefferson had different ideas about governing the nation. Hamilton believed in a strong national government. He also thought that only well-educated landowners knew enough to take part in government. He did not trust the average person.

Thomas Jefferson disagreed with Hamilton. Jefferson wanted everyone to have a voice, not only the rich. He worried about the government becoming too strong and about its spending too much money.

The people who supported Hamilton and his views were called Federalists. The people who supported Jefferson's ideas were called Democratic-Republicans. This was the beginning of the two-party system of **politics**. Every president since Washington has belonged to a political party.

## John Adams: The Second President

Washington was very popular, but he refused to accept a third term as president. John Adams of Massachusetts was elected to be the second president. Adams belonged to the Federalist Party. Adams and the Federalists in Congress passed laws that the Democratic-Republicans did not like.

**What are the names of today's two major political parties?**

## The Alien and Sedition Acts

Adams and the Federalists made their biggest mistake when they passed the Alien and Sedition Acts.

The Alien Act was passed in 1798. It said that an **alien**, or immigrant, had to wait 14 years to become a citizen. Before, the waiting period had been five years. The Alien Act certainly did not go over well with new immigrants.

**Today an alien must wait five years for citizenship.**

The **Sedition** Act made it a crime for anyone to write or print articles against the government. Angry citizens thought this limited the freedom of speech guaranteed in the Bill of Rights.

The Alien and Sedition Acts made Adams unpopular. In 1800, he lost the presidential election. Thomas Jefferson became the third president of the United States.

**The Bill of Rights**

## Learn More About It:
## The First National Census

Every ten years, a census is taken in the United States. A census tells how many people live in a place. The first national census was taken in 1790. Here's what it showed:

The population of the United States was about 4 million people. (Today, that number is over 220 million.) Almost one-fifth of the population were slaves. Only about one out of every 12 African Americans was free. In 1790, half the total population lived in the south. Philadelphia was the largest city. Next largest were New York, Boston, Charleston, and Baltimore. Most people lived in small towns. Only about 5 percent of the population lived in towns larger than 2,500 people.

## History Practice

Answer these questions on a separate sheet of paper.

1. Name three tasks Washington had to accomplish.

2. How did a two-party political system develop in America?

3. What was Alexander Hamilton's job in George Washington's administration?

4. How did the American people feel about John Adams as president?

# Chapter Review

## Summary

| CHRONOLOGY OF MAJOR EVENTS | |
| --- | --- |
| 1783 | Americans and British sign final peace treaty |
| 1783-1787 | Articles of Confederation are in effect |
| 1786 | Shays's Rebellion |
| 1787 | Constitutional Convention meets; delegates sign Constitution |
| 1789 | George Washington elected first president |
| 1790 | Constitution accepted by all states |
| 1791 | Bill of Rights added to Constitution |
| 1796 | John Adams elected second president |
| 1800 | Capital moves to Washington, D.C. |
| 1800 | Thomas Jefferson elected third president |

- The Articles of Confederation gave the United States a weak central government.

- Delegates from 12 states met at the Constitutional Convention. They decided to write a new U.S. Constitution.

- The delegates compromised on a law-making system. Congress would be made up of the House of Representatives and the Senate.

- After debate, the Constitution was accepted by all 13 states.

- The legislative, executive, and judicial branches of the government provide a system of checks and balances.

- The Bill of Rights protects individual freedoms.

- George Washington was elected the first president. He served two terms. Federalist John Adams became the second president. Thomas Jefferson was the third.

## Chapter Quiz

Answer these questions on a separate sheet of paper.

1. What was the main problem with the Articles of Confederation?

2. What did the Northwest Ordinance say about slavery in the Northwest Territory?

3. Describe the conflict between large states and small states at the Constitutional Convention.

4. How was the conflict resolved?

5. What do we call the first ten amendments to the Constitution?

6. Which class of people did Alexander Hamilton think should run the government?

## Thinking and Writing

1. Why do you think the Constitutional Convention did not allow presidents to be elected for life?

2. Under the Bill of Rights, people have the freedom to express unpopular opinions. Give a modern-day example of this.

3. Why is the Bill of Rights important today?

# Chapter 7

# A Time to Grow: New Frontiers and a Stronger Nation

| 1800 | 1823 |
|------|------|
| Jefferson's election | Monroe Doctrine |

**The Lewis and Clark expedition**

## Chapter Learning Objectives

- Describe Thomas Jefferson's political beliefs.
- Describe how the United States obtained the Louisiana Territory and Florida.
- Describe the Lewis and Clark expedition.
- Tell what the War of 1812 accomplished.

# Words to Know

**anthem**   the official song of a country

**chief justice**   the judge in charge of a court made up of several judges

**corps**   a group of people working together

**doctrine**   a set of beliefs or principles

**embargo**   an enforced halting of trade

**expedition**   a long journey of discovery

**foreign policy**   the way a country deals with other countries

**nationalism**   love of country, patriotism

**neutral**   not taking sides in a quarrel or war

**unconstitutional**   not allowed by the Constitution

---

In the early 1800s, this new young country, the United States, was growing quickly. The picture at left shows a daring journey that helped the country expand. In this chapter, you'll share the excitement of this trip and what led up to it. You'll discover the problems that came with growth. And you'll see how the new nation dealt with these problems.

## The Election of 1800

In 1800 there were two political parties in the United States. The Federalists wanted John Adams to be president again. The Democratic-Republicans supported Thomas Jefferson for president and Aaron Burr for vice-president. The Democratic-Republicans won the election.

According to the Constitution, the person with the most votes would be president. The person with the next highest number would be vice-president. But in the election of 1800, Burr and Jefferson tied. So the decision was left to Congress. The Congress voted for Jefferson to become president. Burr would be his vice-president.

Thomas Jefferson's name wasn't new to American politics. Jefferson had written the Declaration of Independence in 1776. In that document, he declared his own love of freedom and his belief in equality.

Jefferson had been governor of Virginia during the Revolution. He had been vice-president under John Adams.

Jefferson was not only a statesman. He was also a musician, scientist, inventor, and designer of buildings. He had high hopes and new ideas for the country's future.

Who is vice-president of the United States today?

---

**Then and Now: Electing Our Leaders**

**Then:** According to the U.S. Constitution, America's early voters did not vote directly for president and vice-president. Instead they voted for electors. These chosen electors voted for president and vice-president. The candidate who got the most votes became president. The candidate with the second largest vote was declared vice-president. In 1796 electors chose a president from one party and a vice-president from the other party.

**Now:** We do not use the "runner-up" system of electing a vice-president today. The presidential and vice-presidential candidates run for office together. The political parties decide who these candidates will be. They are nominated by the members of their parties.

---

Jefferson was wealthy. But he believed the "common" person should have a voice in the government. The farmer and the shopkeeper should have as much say as the rich landowner. Jefferson wanted to see every citizen educated. He believed everyone should be able to vote.

Thomas Jefferson died on the 4th of July, 1826. It was the 50th anniversary of the Declaration of Independence.

Jefferson insisted that the president should not be treated like a king. Instead of riding in fancy coaches, he walked or rode horseback. Many believe Jefferson did more for the idea of equality in America than anyone else.

## History Practice

Answer these questions on a separate sheet of paper.

1. Which political party did Thomas Jefferson represent?

2. Why did Congress decide who would be president and who would be vice-president in the election of 1800?

3. Tell two things Jefferson believed in or did that showed how he felt about equality.

# The Louisiana Purchase

Spain once controlled a large region west of the Mississippi River. It was called the Louisiana Territory. President Jefferson thought the United States could gain control of that land. The Spanish military was weak. But Spain made a secret treaty with Napoleon, ruler of France. In the treaty, Spain gave Napoleon the Louisiana Territory.

Jefferson, therefore, had to deal with Napoleon. And Napoleon's armies were strong. Jefferson now knew that the land could not be taken by force. So he thought of another way to get the Louisiana Territory.

Jefferson sent some men to France.

"Buy as much land as you can for 10 million dollars," Jefferson told them.

Jefferson was surprised when Napoleon offered the entire region for 15 million dollars.

Jefferson quickly got Congress's approval for the purchase. The United States then bought the Louisiana Territory.

Jefferson wrote that the Louisiana Territory would provide a "widespread field for the blessings of freedom and equal laws."

Fifteen million dollars sounds like a lot of money, but it was a bargain. The Louisiana Territory was about 823,000 square miles. That means the United States got the land for less than three cents an acre! Today, land in some big cities can cost over one million dollars an acre.

The Louisiana Territory became a part of the United States on December 20, 1803.

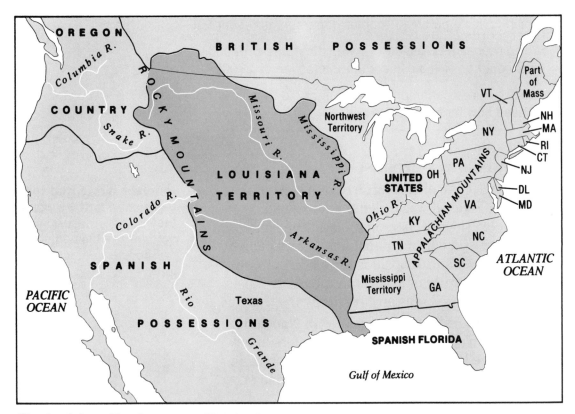

**The Louisiana Purchase**

**Map Study**

Study the map. Then answer the questions on a separate sheet of paper.

1. What river marks the eastern border of the Louisiana Territory?
2. What mountain range lies along the western border of the Louisiana Territory?
3. Was the Louisiana Territory larger or smaller than the Northwest Territory?

You can see from the map that purchase of the Louisiana Territory doubled the size of the United States. This area was later divided into states.

## The Lewis and Clark Expedition

When the Louisiana Purchase was completed, it was time to explore all that new land.

In 1804, President Jefferson met with Captain Meriwether Lewis. Jefferson told Lewis to keep careful records of the journey. He wanted maps of the area. But he also wanted information about the climate, and about the human, plant, and animal life there.

Meriwether Lewis chose an old friend from his army days to help lead the **expedition**. Lieutenant William Clark joined Lewis on the journey west. They called themselves a "**Corps** of Discovery." With a party of 40, they set off on May 14, 1804.

Along the way Lewis and Clark added to their party. A Native American woman, named Sacajawea, offered to guide the group through the mountains. Sacajawea was a Shoshone. But when she was a young girl another tribe had kidnapped her. Sacajawea had been living with the Mandan Indians.

Sacajawea means "Bird Woman" in the Shoshone language.

Lewis and Clark hoped to get horses from the Shoshone. But when they reached Shoshone land, the Indians greeted them in fierce war paint. The Shoshones knew what white men had done to other tribes. Native Americans had often lost their lands and their ways of life.

Sacajawea faced the group. She approached its chief.

"Hello, my brother," she said.

Sacajawea was the long, lost sister of the Shoshone chief!

Sacajawea pointed to Lewis and Clark. "These men are my friends," she said. "They only want horses."

**Sacajawea**

The Shoshone helped Lewis and Clark. They sold them horses and taught them to build birch-bark canoes. Then the Shoshone guided Lewis and Clark over the Rocky Mountains.

Lewis and Clark's group journeyed all the way to the Pacific Ocean. They became the first known white Americans to make the overland trip across the country. They spent the winter of 1805 in what is now Oregon.

Upon returning to Washington, Lewis and Clark gave President Jefferson valuable information. They had maps and pictures and stories about the people, plants, and animals of the West. Lewis and Clark had kept the records Jefferson wanted. Years later, settlers studied those records when they traveled through the Louisiana Territory.

## Learn More About It

Sacajawea was not the only unusual member who joined the Lewis and Clark expedition. Her husband, Toussaint Charbonneau, also joined the party. Charbonneau was a loud, boastful French trader who bought Sacajawea as his wife. Just months before the expedition started west, Sacajawea gave birth to a son. She called the baby Pomp. In Shoshone it meant "first born." As the Lewis and Clark party set forth, Pomp rode comfortably on a "papoose board" on his mother's back. As they journeyed west, Sacajawea and her baby rode along in the lead canoe with Lewis and Clark, and all their important papers, compasses, and medicines.

## History Practice

Answer these questions on a separate sheet of paper.

1. Describe how the United States gained the Louisiana Territory.

2. Why did President Jefferson ask Meriwether Lewis to lead a westward expedition?

3. How far west did Lewis and Clark travel?

## Problems with Britain
## Lead to Another War

Back when Washington was president, war had broken out between Britain and France. The United States remained **neutral** and continued to trade with both nations. But Britain began to cause problems for the United States.

Britain needed more sailors to help in sea battles against the French. So the British boarded American vessels looking for runaway English sailors. They took any Englishmen they found off the ships. And they took some American sailors, too. The United States was angry and demanded that Britain stop such actions.

At the same time, Englishmen in Canada began to stir up trouble between the Indians and the white American settlers. The Americans thought the British were helping the Indians attack American frontier settlements.

Jefferson wanted a peaceful solution to the problem with Britain. And he wanted to show England and France that the United States was neutral. Jefferson ordered an **embargo** on goods that were being traded with both countries. He figured this would hurt both countries because each needed U.S. products. And England would have more respect for America. The British would stop boarding U.S. ships.

The embargo did hurt England and France. But it hurt the United States the most. American businesspeople lost a lot of money. The embargo was considered a failure. It was repealed in 1809.

There was one positive result of the embargo. When trade was cut off, American companies began producing goods they had always bought from other countries. This helped American industry grow.

# War Is Declared

James Madison was elected president in 1808. At first, he wanted to continue Jefferson's policy of remaining neutral. But there was talk of war with Britain. Americans who favored a war were called "war hawks." One of the most outspoken of the hawks was a man named Henry Clay.

The hawks wanted Congress to declare war on Britain. As the problems with Britain continued, Madison lost patience. Finally, on June 1, 1812, President Madison asked Congress for a declaration of war. The votes were split, but enough yes votes were cast to begin the war.

The American army was poorly prepared. So was the American navy. Britain had to divide its efforts between war with the United States and war with France.

Both nations struggled along. The United States suffered some defeats and won some battles.

Perhaps the greatest blow to the Americans came when the British fleet landed soldiers near Washington, D.C. Madison and his cabinet left the capital just in time. The British captured the city. They burned the Capitol building and the White House.

The British marched from Washington to Baltimore. There they attacked Fort McHenry. An American named Francis Scott Key watched the battle at Fort McHenry from a warship on Chesapeake Bay. When the smoke of battle cleared, Key saw the American flag flying above the fort. He knew the battle had been won: "Our flag was still there!" he wrote.

The American victory had inspired Key to write the words to the "Star Spangled Banner." Later, his words were put to music. The song became the country's national **anthem**.

The U.S. Constitution says that only Congress can declare war. The president cannot order a war.

The War of 1812 has been called a "war of poor communications." Britain said it would stop bothering American ships, but it was too late. America had already declared war.

Do you know all the words to the "Star Spangled Banner"? Where do you hear this song sung?

Dolley Madison, the wife of President James Madison, was a calm, brave woman. When the British marched on Washington, D.C., President Madison was out of the city. "You must save yourself!" friends warned Dolley. "British soldiers are coming, and you must flee!"

However, Dolley Madison was not afraid. She calmly packed the president's important government papers. She even set the table for dinner. At last a message arrived from President Madison. It told his wife to leave Washington at once. Not long after Dolley escaped, soldiers marched into the White House. They ate Dolley Madison's dinner. Then they set the White House on fire.

## Peace and a Final Battle

**The Battle of New Orleans is another reason the War of 1812 is called the "war of poor communications."**

It was called the battle that never should have been fought. The Battle of New Orleans started on January 8, 1815. General Andrew Jackson led the Americans to victory. But Jackson didn't know that a peace treaty had already been signed.

Representatives from Britain and from America had met in Ghent, Belgium. On December 24, 1814, they had signed the Treaty of Ghent. The war was over.

Communications were slow in the early 1800s. It took until February, 1815, for news of the peace treaty to reach the United States. But even though peace had already been made, Jackson and his troops were thought of as heroes.

## Words from the Past

Captain Oliver H. Perry and a small naval force won control of Lake Erie in September, 1813. The British ships had more guns, but Perry's daring seamanship won the battle. He announced his success with a message that became famous. Captain Perry declared, "We have met the enemy and they are ours!"

# Results of the War of 1812

"All territory, places, and possessions . . . taken by either party during the war shall be returned."

So read the Treaty of Ghent. There were no big winners in the War of 1812, and no land was gained by either side. The treaty did set a clear boundary between Canada and the United States. Most importantly, the War of 1812 ended conflict between Britain and America. The United States never again went to war against Britain. And the United States had won new respect in the eyes of other countries. The war also stirred a united spirit. Americans were proud to be Americans, proud that they'd defended themselves. This feeling of **nationalism** grew.

## History Practice

Answer these questions on a separate sheet of paper.

1. What did England do that angered Americans and brought about the War of 1812?

2. What did the "war hawks" want?

3. Why shouldn't the Battle of New Orleans have been fought?

4. How did the War of 1812 change America's reputation around the world?

## President Monroe

Do you think that a one-party political system could work in a democratic nation? Why or why not?

Americans felt united after the War of 1812. As you read, the Federalists had been against the war. But from the popular point of view, the war had turned out well. So the Federalist party lost its popularity. America became a one-party nation of Democratic-Republicans.

In 1816, James Monroe was elected president. He was elected again in 1820. Monroe's two terms in office were marked by feelings of national pride and satisfaction. That's why those years are often called the "Era of Good Feelings."

## The United States Gains Florida

But even during the Era of Good Feelings there were some problems. One was that Florida still belonged to Spain. Runaway slaves were escaping from the southern states into Florida. Some of these former slaves and their Native American friends would then cross the border and raid U.S. settlements. Then they would flee back to Florida. The Spanish did not punish them.

President Monroe decided to deal with this problem by sending troops into Florida. Andrew Jackson led the march into the Florida Territory. Jackson and his troops captured two Spanish forts.

Revolutions for independence were brewing in Latin America, and the Spaniards were busy protecting their interests there. With the choice being lose Florida or sell it, the Spaniards sold.

In 1819, the United States signed a treaty with Spain. The treaty gave Florida to the United States. As payment for Florida, the U.S. government agreed to drop a 5 million dollar debt that Spain owed

**James Monroe**

America. The United States also agreed to give up any claim to Texas gained from the Louisiana Purchase. Now American settlers began to move south into Florida.

## The Monroe Doctrine

For a long time the United States was the only independent nation in the New World. Much of the rest of North and South America was made up of colonies that belonged to European nations. The time came when these colonies wanted freedom.

In 1801, people in the French colony of Haiti fought a revolution and won their independence. Between 1810 and 1825, most of the other Spanish colonies in Central and South America rebelled and became independent.

The United States wanted to see those new countries remain independent. It wanted the western hemisphere to be free of control or strong influence by European governments. In a speech before Congress, President Monroe promised the free nations on the American continents America's support. He did this on December 2, 1823.

The **foreign policy** presented in that speech was called the Monroe **Doctrine.**

The Monroe Doctrine warned Europe not to start new colonies or try to get back old ones. The colonies still there could not be enlarged. It also said that the United States would not interfere with concerns in Europe. The Monroe Doctrine guided U.S. foreign policy for years to come.

## Words From the Past

From *The Monroe Doctrine* (1823)

*The American continents...are henceforth not to be considered as subjects for future colonization by any European powers...we should consider any attempt on their part to extend their system to any portion of this hemisphere as dangerous to our peace and safety...*

The Monroe Doctrine continued with a warning. It said that any attempt by a European country to set up colonies in the New World, or to take control of any American country, would be looked upon as an unfriendly act toward the United States. The Monroe Doctrine showed the growing spirit of strength in the United States.

## Then and Now: The Supreme Court

**Then:** In 1801, President John Adams appointed John Marshall of Virginia as **chief justice** of the Supreme Court. Marshall served as chief justice for 34 years. His court made decisions that strengthened the federal government. The court ruled that what the Constitution said was more important than what individual states said. Marshall also determined that the Supreme Court had the right to decide if state and federal laws were **unconstitutional**. This power to review laws has made the Supreme Court a very strong branch of the government.

**Now:** The Supreme Court still uses its power to make sure state governments follow the U.S. Constitution.

## History Practice

Answer these questions on a separate sheet of paper.

1. Why were President Monroe's terms in office called the "Era of Good Feelings"?

2. How did Andrew Jackson help the United States gain Florida?

3. Why did Spain so easily agree to sell Florida?

4. What were the main points of the Monroe Doctrine of 1823?

# Chapter Review

## Summary

| CHRONOLOGY OF MAJOR EVENTS | |
| --- | --- |
| 1803 | United States buys Louisiana Territory from France |
| 1804 | Lewis and Clark expedition begins |
| 1809 | James Madison becomes fourth president |
| 1812 | United States declares war on Britain |
| 1814 | British and Americans sign peace treaty in Ghent, Belgium |
| 1817 | James Monroe becomes fifth president |
| 1819 | United States buys Florida from Spain |
| 1823 | Monroe Doctrine |

- Democratic-Republican Thomas Jefferson became the third U.S. president. Aaron Burr was Jefferson's vice-president. Jefferson believed in the equality of all people.

- Under Jefferson, the country expanded westward. It doubled in size when the Louisiana Territory was purchased.

- Problems with Britain led to the War of 1812. The British were boarding American ships.

- President James Madison and war hawks convinced Congress to declare war. Many other people thought there was no need for war. America won the war but didn't really gain much. The War of 1812 did inspire American nationalism.

- James Monroe's years as president were called the "Era of Good Feelings."

- The United States expanded again when it bought Florida from Spain.

- The Monroe Doctrine warned foreign nations against trying to set up colonies in the Americas.

## Chapter Quiz

Answer these questions on a separate sheet of paper.

1. Which country sold the Louisiana Territory to the United States?

2. What was the purpose of the Lewis and Clark expedition?

3. What was the result of the War of 1812?

4. Name two policies stated in the Monroe Doctrine.

5. Describe how the Supreme Court became stronger under Chief Justice John Marshall.

## Thinking and Writing

Think about the following questions. Then write your answers on a separate sheet of paper.

1. Today we do not call the land involved in the Louisiana Purchase the "West." Why was it called the "West" in the 1800s?

2. Why did Lewis and Clark ask Sacajawea to join their expedition? Name two ways she helped them.

3. In what ways could you compare Lewis and Clark's expedition through the West with modern expeditions into space?

## Chapter 8

# The Age of Jackson

| 1824 | 1839 |
|---|---|
| John Quincy Adams elected president | Cherokees driven out of Southeast |

**Andrew Jackson's inauguration**

## Chapter Learning Objectives

- Tell how Andrew Jackson was different from presidents before him.
- Explain why many people moved to the cities during the Age of Jackson.
- Name three groups of people who did not enjoy democracy in the Age of Jackson.
- Tell how Jackson treated Native Americans.

## Words to Know

**candidate**   a person running for political office

**Electoral College**   group of people elected by voters to choose the president and vice-president

**inauguration**   the swearing in of a president

**industry**   the making of goods on a large scale

**majority**   more than half

**nominated**   named to run for office

**tariff**   a tax on goods brought in from another country

**urban**   relating to a city

The picture on the left shows President Andrew Jackson on his **inauguration** day. In this chapter you'll learn why Jackson was so popular. You'll find out how he made life better for many people during his term of office. You'll also learn about the people who still were not treated fairly.

## Adams, the Unpopular President

In 1824, John Quincy Adams was elected president. The Era of Good Feelings with its one-party system had ended. The nation's spirit was more divided. Each region was developing its own interests.

In the North, **industry** was growing rapidly. The main business in the South was growing crops, especially cotton. In the West, the goals were exploration, expansion, and freedom.

During the 1824 elections, each region had its own candidate. The New England states **nominated** John Quincy Adams as their **candidate** for president. Adams was from Massachusetts. He had been serving as Secretary of State under President Monroe.

John Quincy Adams was the son of John Adams, the second president. They are the only father and son to both become president.

Kentucky, in the West, nominated Henry Clay. William Crawford of Georgia and John C. Calhoun of South Carolina were southern candidates. Frontiersmen had their candidate in Andrew Jackson.

When the electoral votes were counted in 1824, no one man had a **majority** of votes. There were 99 for Jackson, 84 for Adams, 41 for Crawford, and 37 for Clay. Calhoun had withdrawn.

What happens when no one receives a majority of votes? The Constitution says the House of Representatives must then choose the president from the top three candidates. Clay, who was out of the race, gave his support to Adams. Adams then had a majority. He became the sixth president of the United States.

Jackson's supporters were angry with the outcome of the race. Jackson was a much-loved war hero. He was a hardy frontiersman. Adams was a quiet man who never knew how to please the crowds.

**John Quincy Adams**

# Learn More About It: The Electoral College

Each state in the United States sends representatives to the **Electoral College**. These representatives, or electors, elect the president and vice-president. The number of electors for each state is equal to the number of that state's senators and representatives in Congress. Electors are expected to vote for the candidate who wins the popular election in their state. So if a candidate does not win in a state, he will receive no electoral votes from that state. If the candidate wins more than half the state's popular votes, he should get all its electoral votes. The map below shows the number of electoral votes allowed each state. How many electoral votes does your state have?

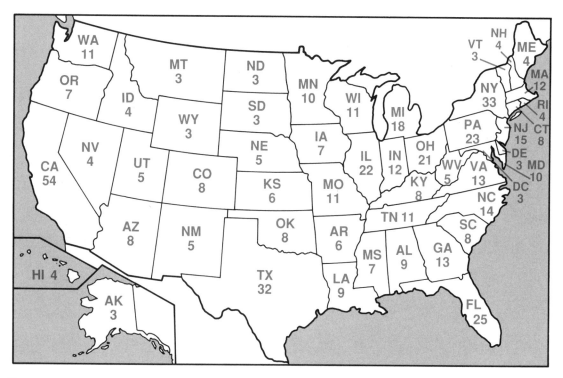

**Electoral Votes**

# The Tariff of 1828

A bill, passed in Congress in 1828, put a higher **tariff**, or tax, on goods coming from foreign countries. The idea was to raise the price of foreign goods. This would encourage Americans to buy manufactured goods from home.

What products do you use that are imported from other countries?

The North was the manufacturing center of the United States. The northern states liked the tariff. But the South and the West did not like it. Most of the people there were farmers. All the tariff did for them was raise the cost of the manufactured goods they needed from Europe.

The Tariff of 1828 made Adams even less popular in the South and West than he had been. That same year, 1828, was an election year. Jackson and Adams were again the two major candidates. But this time, a big change was about to take place.

## History Practice

Answer these questions on a separate sheet of paper.

1. Explain why John Quincy Adams was named president even though Andrew Jackson received more electoral votes.

2. The Tariff of 1828 raised the tax on what goods? What was the purpose of this tax?

3. Why did the northern states favor the Tariff of 1828?

4. Why didn't states in the South and the West support this tariff?

## Inauguration Day

In the election of 1828, Andrew Jackson received twice as many electoral votes as John Quincy Adams. He was sworn in as President on March 24, 1829.

Washington had never seen anything like that inauguration day. Excitement filled the city as Jackson became the seventh president of the United States.

Thousands of people watched Andrew Jackson take office. Later, they crowded around him, trying to shake his hand. Most of these toughened men were from the frontier. Their clothes were made of animal skins. They chewed big plugs of tobacco.

At a party in the White House, the frontiersmen stood on fancy velvet chairs. They wanted to get a better view of their hero. Others pushed to the tables to get something to eat. Food and drink spilled on the beautiful carpet. Some rooms were so crowded that people could not get to the door. They had to climb out the windows to leave the White House.

Andrew Jackson would be the most popular president since George Washington. But not everyone was pleased on his inauguration day. Massachusetts Senator Daniel Webster looked on the celebration unhappily. In a letter to a friend, he later wrote, "There are thousands of frontier people in the city. I never saw anything like it before. Some of them have come 500 miles to see Jackson. They look on us, the people of wealth and power, as the enemy. They think Jackson will save the country from us!"

Jackson had separated from the Democratic-Republican party. He formed the Democratic party. Adams's supporters were called National Republicans. They were later called Whigs.

# A Hero to the People

Who was Jackson, and why were people so excited about him?

Andrew Jackson was very different from anyone who had been president before him. Some earlier presidents, such as George Washington, had come from very rich families. Others, like John Adams, had received very good educations. And others, like Thomas Jefferson, were both rich and well educated. In addition, all the presidents before Jackson had come from either Virginia or Massachusetts.

Andrew Jackson, like most Americans, was born very poor. Yet he had grown up to become rich and to be elected president. That made him a hero. He proved that a poor person born in a log cabin could rise to power in the United States. In most other countries, that could never have happened.

The log cabin where Andrew Jackson was born was in North Carolina. His mother and father had both died by the time he was 14. As a boy, he was too poor to go to school for very long. Mostly, he taught himself.

Jackson moved to Tennessee and became a lawyer. As one of the first lawyers in that state, he became quite wealthy. He was elected to Congress. Later, voters made him a judge. People called him the toughest, bravest, hardest-working man in Tennessee. But no matter how high he rose, Jackson remained a man of the frontier.

# The Spoils System

There is a saying that goes, "To the victor belong the spoils." This means that the winner can do what he wants with what he has won. Andrew Jackson practiced what some people called a "spoils system" of handing out government jobs. He gave many of these jobs to his friends. Jackson was not very concerned with the experience or education of the people he chose. Instead, he picked those who were loyal to him and to the Democratic Party.

Jackson also believed that it was important to keep changing officeholders. He felt that government workers who stayed too long in office might forget that they were there to serve the public. He wanted as many Americans as possible to learn by experience how their government worked.

The spoils system is still in use today. Presidents usually appoint people from their own political parties. This has made the parties stronger.

## The Kitchen Cabinet

Andrew Jackson did not always turn to his Cabinet for advice. Instead, he often discussed government problems with old friends. These friends helped him make important decisions.

Jackson's helpful friends usually walked into the White House through the kitchen door. They met with the president informally. They became known as Jackson's "Kitchen Cabinet."

## The Nominating Convention

Jackson believed that the common people should have a voice in choosing political candidates. Candidates for president and vice-president had always been chosen by congressmen at secret meetings. Americans voted, but only after the candidates had been picked by others.

Many people thought that this was not democratic. They felt they really had no voice in choosing their leaders. During Jackson's term, a new system of choosing presidential candidates was set up. Political parties now held nominating conventions. At these conventions delegates from each party came together. They represented people from all parts of the country. These delegates chose the candidates for their party.

Now we can watch nominating conventions on TV. At their last convention, whom did the Democrats nominate for president? Whom did the Republicans nominate?

## History Practice

Answer these questions on a separate sheet of paper.

1. In what way was Andrew Jackson different from the presidents before him?

2. What is the spoils system?

3. Who were the members of Jackson's Kitchen Cabinet?

4. Who attends a nominating convention? What do they do there?

## Growing Cities

America was changing. The country was spreading westward. Jackson was elected largely because westerners wanted to have one of their own as president.

But it wasn't only the frontier that was behind Andrew Jackson. He was also a hero to the workers in America's growing cities.

As the country grew, it had more and more **urban** laborers and fewer farmers. Back in 1800, when Thomas Jefferson was elected, this was a nation of farmers. Only six out of every 100 Americans lived in cities. But by 1828, when Jackson was elected, America was changing into a nation of city people.

By 1980, 79 out of every 100 Americans lived in urban areas. Why do you think the number of people moving to the cities continued to grow?

Why did people go to the cities? They went because there were jobs there. Rich people were building factories in the Northeast. Many workers were needed. Large numbers of people in Pennsylvania, New York, and Massachusetts left the farms to work in factories. By 1845, the year Jackson died, more than 20 percent of America lived in cities.

As industry in the North grew, more and more products were made by machine. Before, many things had been made by hand. The growth of industry and the change from hand-work to machine-work was called the Industrial Revolution. The Industrial Revolution took place mainly in the North. In the South, much of the farming, such as picking cotton, was still done by hand. Slaves did it.

## More People Come to America

As America grew, more and more people were drawn here. Often the immigrants came in order to escape terrible living conditions. In the early 1800s, many European farmers had trouble growing enough food to feed their families. This "Great Hunger" drove people to the United States.

In 1980, 21 of every 100 people in New York City were born in a foreign country.

Most of these immigrants were forced to work at low-paying jobs and to live in run-down buildings. Still, a low-paying job was better than no job at all.

In America, people could work hard and improve their lives. And they had rights that they did not have in Europe. The most important of these was the right to vote. Citizens could choose the people they thought would best look after their interests. This was something new.

## "They'll Ruin Our Country"

But even in America, not everyone had a say. When the Constitution was written, many leaders did not believe that poor Americans would use their votes wisely. In the nation's early years, only white men who owned property could vote. Poor white men, women, and Native Americans had no say in

**The "Great Hunger" forced many people to leave Europe.**

the government. Slaves had no rights at all. Free black men could vote in just a few states. As the United States grew, more people were allowed to vote. By 1828, when Jackson was elected president, almost all white men were permitted to vote.

Some people were frightened by this. Many rich people feared that poor people would elect leaders who would steal their wealth. The country would be ruined, they said.

The poor saw things differently. By getting the vote, they were able to elect leaders who worked for them. These leaders passed laws that made life better for the average person.

In the early 1800s, progress came in several areas. Many states passed laws that set up free public schools for both boys and girls. Before this, the schools were costly and open only to boys. Now there were states that even set up schools for blind people. In some places, state hospitals were built for the mentally ill.

Horace Mann is called the "Father of America's public education." Thanks to his efforts, free public schooling became a reality.

We shouldn't get the idea, however, that the United States was a perfect democracy. Some Native Americans and African Americans still had very few rights. Women were not allowed to vote or to own property. And if a woman earned money at a job, she had to give it to her husband.

In the 19th century women were treated very differently than they are today. This example of attitudes toward women comes from 1837:

A British navy captain named Frederick Marryat came to America. He wrote a book about his trip. While visiting Niagara Falls, Marryat went out with a young woman. The woman slipped and fell.

"Did you hurt your leg?" Marryat asked.

The woman was shocked.

Marryat didn't know that the word leg was never spoken in front of a lady. Instead, people used the word limb. In the presence of a woman some people even said that a table had four limbs!

## The Native Americans Lose More Lands

Andrew Jackson was a great believer in democracy and equality. He wanted to do away with slavery. Still, he drove the Native Americans from their lands.

Many Native Americans lived east of the Mississippi River. Frontiersmen wanted their lands. They especially wanted the lands that were good for farming. Andrew Jackson sided with the frontiersmen. He wanted the Native Americans moved west of the Mississippi. During the Age of Jackson, Native Americans lost much of their eastern lands.

## The Cherokees and the Trail of Tears

Many eastern tribes had accepted the white man's ways. They had farming communities and schools for their children. One such tribe was the Cherokee. Cherokees grew cotton on their land. A Cherokee leader named Sequoyah developed an alphabet.

In 1830, Congress passed the Indian Removal Act. Now President Jackson could order the Cherokees and other tribes off their southeastern lands. Within ten years, U.S. soldiers had forced more than 70,000 Native Americans to the West. These people had to walk many hundreds of miles. The government gave them no shelter. Thousands died along the way. Their journey came to be known as the Trail of Tears.

The government also drove the "Sac and Fox" tribes from their lands in Illinois. Black Hawk, a tribal leader, returned with a band of warriors to fight for their homeland. The U.S. Army was called in to aid the settlers. The army trapped and killed Black Hawk and his men.

## History Practice

Answer these questions on a separate sheet of paper.

1. Why did many people move to the cities during the Age of Jackson?

2. Who had the right to vote in the 1828 election?

3. How did education change when Jackson was president?

4. In what ways did Andrew Jackson's America fall short of perfect democracy?

5. Why was the journey of Native Americans out of the Southeast called the "Trail of Tears"?

# Chapter Review

## Summary

| CHRONOLOGY OF MAJOR EVENTS | |
| --- | --- |
| 1824 | John Quincy Adams elected sixth president |
| 1828 | By now most states have done away with laws that say only property owners can vote |
| 1828 | Congress passes tariff on foreign goods |
| 1828 | Andrew Jackson elected seventh president |
| 1832 | Andrew Jackson elected to second term |
| 1830-40 | Forced movement of American Indians to west of Mississippi River |

- In 1824, Adams ran against Jackson in the national election. Neither won a majority of votes. The House of Representatives chose Adams to be president.

- The Tariff of 1828 raised the prices of foreign goods.

- Manufacturing developed rapidly in the Northeast. The Southeast and West remained farming regions.

- Elected in 1828, Jackson was a very popular president.

- Jackson chose loyal supporters for government jobs. This was called the "spoils system." Jackson often asked his friends, rather than his cabinet, for advice.

- Jackson made sure all white men, rich or poor, had a voice in government. African Americans, Native Americans, and women still had few rights. Jackson approved laws pushing Native American tribes west of the Mississippi.

- Many people moved from farming regions to cities. Europe's "Great Hunger" brought many immigrants to the United States.

## Chapter Quiz

Answer these questions on a separate sheet of paper.

1. Name two things that made John Quincy Adams unpopular.
2. What does the Electoral College do?
3. What kind of people liked Andrew Jackson?
4. What was the Industrial Revolution?
5. Why did immigrants come to America in the early 1800s?
6. How did Native Americans lose their lands in the Southeast?

## Thinking and Writing

Think about the following questions. Then write your answers on a separate sheet of paper.

1. How was Andrew Jackson's background different from the backgrounds of earlier presidents?
2. Explain how different regional interests led to different opinions about the Tariff of 1828.
3. Was there democracy for all during the Age of Jackson? Explain your answer.

# Unit Three Review

Use the information you have learned in Chapters 6 through 8 to answer the questions on this page. Write your answers on a separate sheet of paper.

## A. Who did it?

1. He led a rebellion of farmers protesting state taxes.
2. He was the "Father of the Constitution."
3. He said that the president should not be treated as a king.
4. He was Jefferson's secretary and led an expedition to the Pacific.
5. She was a guide on the Lewis and Clark expedition.
6. He was president during the War of 1812.
7. He wrote the "Star Spangled Banner."
8. He was president during the "Era of Good Feelings."
9. He said foreign countries could not form new colonies in the Americas.
10. He became the "frontier president."

## B. Explain . . .

1. . . . the weakness of the Articles of Confederation.
2. . . . how the Constitution keeps one part of government from becoming too powerful.
3. . . . why the Bill of Rights was added to the Constitution.
4. . . . why the years after the War of 1812 were called an "Era of Good Feelings."

## C. Think about what you have learned. Then answer the following questions on a separate sheet of paper.

1. Neither John Adams nor John Quincy Adams was a very popular president. Give one reason for each man's unpopularity.
2. Name two major points of the Monroe Doctrine.
3. Describe democracy as it existed during the Age of Jackson.

# "A House Divided Cannot Stand."

# Chapter 9:

# Nationalism and Further Growth

**1825**
Erie Canal Completed

**1860**
Pony Express

**Heading west in covered wagons.**

## Chapter Learning Objectives

- Name the new methods of transportation that helped the United States expand.
- Explain how a need for faster communication was met.
- Describe how Texas, California, and the Oregon Territory joined the United States.
- Tell what caused the war between the United States and Mexico. Explain the results of that war.

# Words to Know

**canal**   a waterway dug across a stretch of land

**communication**   the passing along of information, the exchange of messages

**destined**   bound to happen

**expansion** growth outward

**immigrants**   people who come into a country not of their birth in order to settle there

**parallel**   one of the imaginary lines around the Earth that runs in the same direction as the equator

**territory**   the land ruled by a nation. A territory does not have the full rights of a state.

**transportation**   the moving of goods and people from one place to another

The mid-1800s were exciting times. Rugged Americans were heading west in covered wagons. New ways of **communication** were changing American life. The United States was expanding from coast to coast. In this chapter, you'll learn about these booming years of American history.

## New Roads

As **transportation** improved, the West grew quickly.

In 1811, the government started building the Great National Pike. It went westward from Maryland. It came to be known as both the Cumberland Road and the National Road. Thousands of men worked on the road. Every few years, a new section was opened. By the 1830s, the road stretched almost to the Mississippi. Its main part reached from Columbia, Maryland, to Vandalia, Illinois.

Stagecoaches and covered wagons traveled along the National Road. The stagecoaches carried mail

The National Road was also known as the Cumberland Road. It started in Cumberland, Maryland.

and passengers. The covered wagons were loaded with people who were making the long, tough move west.

Western farmers used the road to transport sheep and cattle to the big markets in the East.

But farmers faced a problem. They could move cattle, but how could they get their crops east? The trip along the road was so long that the crops might rot. And they couldn't go by river because the rivers flowed to the south and west.

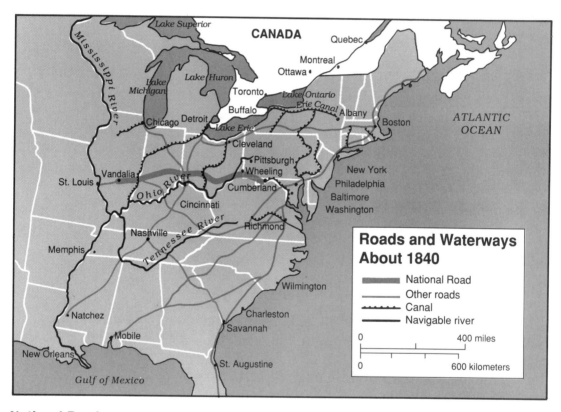

**Roads and Waterways About 1840**

National Road

# The New Canals

One answer to the problem of transporting goods was to build **canals**. The Erie Canal was the longest and best known canal. It was the first important waterway in the United States. It stretched all the way from Lake Erie to the Hudson River. From there, goods could be moved down the Hudson to New York City. It joined the entire Great Lakes system with the Atlantic Ocean.

The Erie Canal was finished in 1825. It was the best way to move crops from the farms to the cities. The Erie Canal also carried factory goods and thousands of new settlers from east to west. Passengers on the heavy canal boats paid a penny and a half per mile to travel on the waterway.

Still, canals were not the perfect means of transportation. Though travel by canal was faster than by road, it was still quite slow. Canal boats could only go about five miles per hour. In winter when the canals filled with ice, boats moved even slower. But the worst problem was that the canals could not pass over mountains. What was to be done?

It took eight years to build the Erie Canal.

# The Railroad

A man named Peter Cooper was going to help answer America's transportation needs. He'd do it with a steam-powered train.

It was April of 1830. Two coaches stood side by side on the rails. One was hitched to a horse. The other was hooked up to a strange-looking steam boiler on wheels. Black smoke puffed from the boiler's smokestack. The words "Tom Thumb" were written on the side of this "iron horse." Peter Cooper crawled over the Tom Thumb. He made sure everything was ready. A group of men in black clothing watched with interest.

Then the race began. At first, the horse pulled far ahead. Then the Tom Thumb caught up with the horse-drawn coach. Now the Tom Thumb pulled ahead! It was far in the lead when suddenly there was a loud pop. The Tom Thumb rolled to a stop. And the horse-drawn coach won the race.

Cooper's steam-powered train had failed its first test. However, all was not lost. The men watching the

**The Tom Thumb**

race were owners of the new Baltimore and Ohio Railroad. Until now, all their coaches had been pulled over the rails by horses. After seeing the Tom Thumb, they knew where the future lay. On the spot, they ordered two steam engines from Peter Cooper. The age of the railroad had begun.

It now seemed that a solution had been found to America's transportation problem. Railroad trains ran in almost any weather. They were much faster than canal boats. And the trains could go wherever tracks could be put down. Trains even ran along the sides of mountains.

During the 1840s, "railroad fever" swept the country. By the 1850s, Cleveland, Detroit, Chicago, and St. Louis were linked by rail to the East. As transportation improved, the spirit of nationalism grew stronger.

## The Telegraph Changed Communication

Remember reading about poor communications during the War of 1812? A huge battle was fought after a peace treaty had already been signed. Communication was so slow that the soldiers did not know the war had ended.

Mail traveled by horseback, by boat, and later, by rail. It took days to send messages across the miles.

An invention by an American artist, Samuel Morse, solved the problem of slow communication. Morse invented the telegraph. He used electricity to send signals over wires. In this way, he could send messages in just a few seconds. Morse used short and long signals to represent each letter of the alphabet. This system of signals was called the Morse Code.

Soon telegraph wires were strung from city to city. On May 24, 1844, a crowd gathered to watch while Morse tapped out a message on his new invention.

Why do you think the steam locomotive was called the "iron horse"?

The Tom Thumb sped along at 18 miles per hour. Some of today's trains can travel at over 100 miles per hour.

**Pony Express rider**

The telegraph was a success. By 1861, the telegraph connected the West Coast with the East.

## The Pony Express

"Expert young riders wanted. Must be willing to face death daily. Orphans preferred." Advertisements like this one appeared in 1860. They were asking for Pony Express riders.

These young men carried mail across the country. They galloped at full speed. Every 10 miles or so the riders changed to fresh horses. The job offered adventure and good wages. Young riders faced storms, Indians, and bandits. The Pony Express ran mail from St. Joseph, Missouri, west to Sacramento, California. The trip took ten days. Stagecoaches could make the trip in two weeks at best.

The Pony Express carried mail for 18 months. When the telegraph reached California in 1861, messages could be sent in minutes. This ended the need for the Pony Express.

## History Practice

Answer these questions on a separate sheet of paper.

1. Name the two bodies of water linked by the Erie Canal.

2. What was the "iron horse"?

3. Name three ways railways were better than roads and canals.

4. What did Samuel Morse invent? How did this invention change communications?

# Texas Faces Trouble With Mexico

Texas had always been a part of Mexico. And Mexico belonged to Spain.

But in 1821, Mexico won its independence from Spain. Mexicans then allowed Americans to settle in Texas. The Americans had to obey Mexico's laws. It was thought that the new settlers would become good citizens.

Many American settlers traveled on the Santa Fe Trail. It ran from Independence, Missouri, to Santa Fe, New Mexico.

A man named Stephen Austin led more and more American settlers into Texas. These settlers began to think of themselves as a special group of people. Twice, the United States offered to buy Texas from Mexico. Mexico refused both offers.

Texans became more independent. They no longer obeyed the Mexican laws. They wanted to break away from Mexico and set up the Republic of Texas. Texans knew then they'd have to fight for their independence. An experienced soldier named Sam Houston led an army of Texan rebels.

Mexican president Santa Anna wanted to remind Texans they were under Mexican rule. On February 23, 1836, he brought 6,000 soldiers to San Antonio, Texas.

It was the beginning of one of the most famous battles in American history.

The Republic of Texas had its own flag. On it was a single star. Texas is still known as the "Lone Star State."

Santa Anna surrounded 200 Texans at a fort in Texas called the Alamo. After days of fighting, the Texans were defeated. Only four people were left alive inside Fort Alamo. Jim Bowie and Davy Crockett, two famous frontiersmen, died in the battle.

Santa Anna thought the war had been won. But he was wrong. "Remember the Alamo!" became the battle cry of Sam Houston and the Texans. On April 21, 1836, they attacked the Mexican army at the San Jacinto River.

In victory, Texas soldiers took Santa Anna prisoner. Finally, Santa Anna agreed to give Texas its independence.

Texas became a separate nation. Sam Houston was its first president. Texas even had its own constitution. Texas remained independent for nine years.

In 1845, Texas joined the United States as the 28th state.

## Manifest Destiny

Many Americans thought Texas should be part of the United States. Democrat James K. Polk was one of them. Polk was a candidate in the 1844 presidential election.

Polk's wish to expand America did not stop with Texas. He thought the United States was **destined** to stretch from the Atlantic to the Pacific. He said such **expansion** was the "manifest destiny" of the United States. Manifest Destiny became part of the American spirit.

When the votes were counted, Polk had won the election of 1844. Americans wanted the rapid expansion President Polk would give them.

As Polk gave his inauguration speech, Samuel Morse sat nearby and tapped it out on his telegraph.

## The Mexican War

Even after Texas became a state, fighting with Mexico did not end. Mexico and the United States could not agree on a southern border for Texas. President Polk said the Rio Grande should be the boundary. Mexicans said that this river was inside their country. Mexico refused an American offer to buy land.

At last President Polk sent American troops to take the borderlands. The troops were led by General Zachary Taylor. On May 13, 1846, the United States went to war with Mexico. The war soon expanded beyond Texas. The United States invaded California. In the next year, 1847, U.S. troops marched into Mexico City.

Mexico asked for peace in 1848. It had already lost California, Nevada, and Utah to the United States. A final treaty was signed in the village of Guadalupe Hidalgo, near Mexico City. The Treaty of Guadalupe

In other parts of the country there were less serious things happening. On June 19, 1846, the first official baseball game was played in Hoboken, New Jersey.

Earlier in this chapter, you read about "railroad fever." The United States wanted the land in the Gadsden Purchase for an important railroad route.

Hidalgo also gave the United States parts of Colorado, Arizona, and New Mexico. All those lands became known as the Mexican Cession. The United States now held land from the Atlantic to the Pacific Oceans.

In 1853, the United States bought more land from Mexico. That land deal was called the Gadsden Purchase. It was named after the U.S. agent who arranged the sale. The Gadsden Purchase gave the United States the lands that make up the southern parts of Arizona and New Mexico.

## The Oregon Territory

At one time or another, four nations claimed the forested region known as the Oregon Country. Russia, Spain, Great Britain, and the United States all had interests in the Northwest. By 1818, Britain and the United States had agreed to share the land.

After the Lewis and Clark expedition, more American settlers came to the Oregon Country. Polk no longer wanted Britain to jointly occupy the land. It was time for the United States and Britain to reach a new agreement.

Pioneers traveled the Oregon Trail from Independence, Missouri, to the Oregon Country. Which other famous trail began in Independence?

In 1846, a treaty was signed without any fighting. A boundary dividing Canada and the Oregon **Territory** was marked at the 49th **parallel**. Britain received land to the north of the 49th parallel, in Canada. The United States took the land to the south. This land later became the states of Washington, Oregon, Idaho, and parts of Montana and Wyoming. The land in Canada became British Columbia.

The only ones who wanted to fight over the decision were the Native Americans. They were losing their lands. After many battles between Native Americans and settlers, the natives were forced onto reservations.

## Westward Expansion

### Map Study

Study the map. Then answer the questions on a separate sheet of paper.

1. When was the Mexican Cession added?
2. Which three regions are farthest west?
3. When we say the country stretched from "sea to shining sea," which oceans are we talking about?

**Forty-niners pan for gold.**

## The California Gold Rush

"Gold!"

Believe it or not, that simple cry led to statehood for California.

In 1848, James Marshall was building a sawmill in California. One day he spotted some small gold stones in a nearby river. He took them to John Sutter, his boss. A new era for California began with Marshall's discovery.

It was the era of the gold rush. People from all over hurried to California to get rich quick. The largest number of them came in 1849. Towns boomed. In January, 1849, the population of San Francisco was around 2,000. By December, 1849, it had grown to 20,000. Some of the forty-niners, as the gold rushers were called, did strike it rich. But more gave up the hunt for gold and turned to farming or ranching.

The California boom made some people rich. Not everyone got rich by finding gold. Can you think of other ways a person could make money during a population boom?

Waves of people entered California seeking fortune, adventure, and jobs. The forty-niners included thousands of South Americans and Mexicans. They also came from as far away as China. Many of the Chinese **immigrants** went to work building the railroads. The population was soaring, and in 1850 California became the 31st state.

---

### Great Names in History: Levi Strauss

Not everyone came to California to dig for gold. Some people had other ideas for getting rich.

Levi Strauss was a German merchant. He came to California to sell canvas for tents. But he quickly saw that there was something the miners needed more than tents. They needed pants! They needed rough, sturdy pants that would stand up to a lot of hard use. Strauss began making pants out of tent canvas. He called his pants "Levi's."

Thanks to Levi Strauss and the California gold rush, blue jeans were born. They became one of the world's most popular items of clothing.

---

## History Practice

Answer these questions on a separate sheet of paper.

1. Which country did Texas belong to in the early 1800s?

2. Which Texas leader won independence for Texas?

3. In what year did U.S. soldiers march into Mexico City? How many years after this did the United States gain the Mexican Cession?

4. Which two nations settled the Oregon Territory boundary?

5. What caused the population of California to grow so quickly?

# Chapter Review

## Summary

| CHRONOLOGY OF MAJOR EVENTS | |
|---|---|
| 1825 | Erie Canal completed |
| 1836 | Texas wins independence from Mexico |
| 1837 | Samuel Morse invents telegraph |
| 1844 | James Polk elected eleventh president |
| 1845 | Texas becomes a state |
| 1846-48 | War with Mexico |
| 1848 | Mexican Cession |
| 1848 | Gold discovered in California |
| 1860-61 | Pony Express |

- Roads, canals, and railroads improved transportation.

- Pony Express riders raced across the country carrying mail.

- The invention of the telegraph improved communication.

- American settlers moved onto the Mexican land known as Texas. Before very long, they wanted to break with Mexico. Texas fought for and won independence. Later it became a U.S. state.

- President Polk wanted the United States to reach from sea to sea. This belief in the rapid expansion of the United States was called Manifest Destiny.

- War with Mexico broke out. Mexico lost and gave the United States land that stretched to the Pacific.

- A peaceful agreement with Britain gave the Oregon Territory to the United States.

- The gold rush and a booming population led to statehood for California.

## Chapter Quiz

Answer these questions on a separate sheet of paper.

1. Why weren't canals the best possible means of transportation?

2. What was "railroad fever"?

3. What was the purpose of the Pony Express?

4. What happened at the Alamo?

5. What part of the Oregon Territory did the United States receive in 1846?

6. Who were the "forty-niners"?

## Thinking and Writing

1. Explain how the National Road and the invention of the telegraph encouraged nationalism.

2. Explain the meaning of James Polk's term "Manifest Destiny." How did the Mexican Cession accomplish Polk's goal?

3. Mexico allowed U.S. settlers to make homes in Texas. But many of the settlers were not law-abiding citizens. Mexico did not allow slavery, yet many of the Texas settlers brought slaves. Some settlers were outlaws. Do you think Santa Anna was right in trying to rule with a strong hand?

# Chapter 10

# A Nation Divided

**1820**
Missouri Compromise

**1860**
Abraham Lincoln elected president

## N. B. FOREST,
## DEALER IN SLAVES,
## No. 87 Adams-st, Memphis, Ten.,

HAS just received from North Carolina, twenty-five likely young negroes, to which he desires to call the attention of purchasers. He will be in the regular receipt of negroes from North and South Carolina every month. His Negro Depot is one of the most complete and commodious establishments of the kind in the Southern country, and his regulations exact and systematic, cleanliness, neatness and comfort being strictly observed and enforced. His aim is to furnish to customers A. 1 servants 'and field hands, sound and perfect in body and mind. Negroes taken on commission.                    jan21

**A slave dealer's advertisement**

## Chapter Learning Objectives
- Describe conflicts between the states.
- Identify the invention that strengthened slavery.
- Describe life on a plantation.
- Explain the Missouri Compromise.
- Explain the Compromise of 1850.

# Words to Know

**abolitionists**  people who worked to end slavery

**secede**  to separate from the rest of a country

**sectionalism**  an interest in only one section or region of a country

In the last chapter, you read how new forms of transportation and communication helped link the country together. In this chapter, you'll read about some of the things that divided the country. Different areas fought to keep the power they said was theirs. Slavery was tearing the country apart.

## Sectionalism

The North and the South had very different ideas about how the government should be run. The North wanted a strong central government. The South wanted each state to have more of its own power.

The North and the South had always been at odds over the slavery issue. The disagreements about slavery became more bitter. Also, the North continued to develop manufacturing while the South built larger farms. This led to different ways of life and different needs.

And the West had ideas and problems all its own.

The differences in interests, problems, and opinions between the regions led to **sectionalism.** People became more concerned about their own areas than about the country as a whole.

The chart below shows how these three regions of the United States felt about different issues.

Differences between regions would lead to bigger problems in the years ahead.

| | North | South | West |
|---|---|---|---|
| Tariffs | For. Tariffs meant that northern goods could be sold at a lower price than foreign goods. | Against. Southern farmers wanted to buy low-priced foreign goods. | For. Westerners used money from tariffs to build railroads and roads. |
| Immigrants | For. The North needed factory workers. | Against. Most immigrants moved to the North. This meant more votes for the North in Congress. | For. There was plenty of land to settle in the West. |
| Transportation | For. Manufactured goods needed to be shipped. | Against. Farmers in the South didn't need more roads or canals. | For. Large areas needed good transportation. |
| Slavery | Against. Slaves were never widely used in the North. | For. The South wanted plantation workers. | Undecided. Would new states enter the Union as slave states or free states? |

## North and South Disagree

They had conflicts, but the North and South needed each other. The North needed the South to supply raw materials and cotton and other crops. The South needed the northern markets for its cotton. But the two sides just could not get along. Their ways of life had become so different.

Their conflicts heated up. Each side fought to protect its own interests in Congress. In 1856, Senator Charles Sumner of Massachusetts gave a speech in the Senate. He said some angry words about the South. Preston Brooks, a southern member of the House of Representatives, got very angry. He hit Senator Sumner with his cane! Some southerners were proud of this attack. Senator Sumner was seriously hurt. Southerners sent more canes to Preston Brooks. They told Brooks to use the canes over more northern heads.

## History Practice

Answer these questions on a separate sheet of paper.

1. What is sectionalism?

2. More people were coming to the United States from foreign lands. How did the North feel about the newcomers? How did the South feel?

3. Look at the chart on the previous page. What question was left to be answered? How do you think this question caused conflict between the North and the South?

# Slavery and the South

Today, most people would say that slavery was an evil system. But in the 1800s, it was the way of life in many parts of the South. Southern whites had come to believe that the South simply could not survive without slavery. They also thought that other Americans would stop at nothing to end slavery.

**Picking cotton**

Slavery had grown when many people were needed to work on the South's cotton plantations. But after a while, cotton became less important. The crop wore out the soil. If cotton were grown in the same spot for too many years, that land could not be farmed. Also, cotton was not worth anything until the seeds were removed from the fuzz that grew around them. This took a lot of time. It made cotton very expensive. By the 1790s, many cotton farmers were turning to other crops.

## "Cotton Is King!"

Then, in 1793, a new machine saved the future of cotton farming. And slavery became more important than ever.

The machine was the cotton gin. It separated the seeds from the fuzz. The cotton gin worked much faster than any person could work. With the gin, farmers could again make money growing cotton. Soon, cotton again became the South's most important crop.

As "King Cotton" spread, so did slavery. Slaves were used to clear new fields. They grew and picked cotton and hauled it to the gins.

Louisiana, Mississippi, Alabama, Florida, and Texas joined the United States as slave states. In these states, slavery was allowed by law. By 1850, slaves made up nearly one-third of the people of the South. There were about five times as many slaves in 1850 as there were in 1790.

Eli Whitney invented the cotton gin. Its use made the United States the largest cotton producer in the world.

**The cotton gin**

# A Slave's Life on the Plantation

It was four o'clock in the morning.

At the plantation of James Rutherford, a horn sounded. In the big white house, family members heard the horn. They turned over and went back to sleep. But in the small wooden cabins nearby, the slaves were rising from their straw beds. In the darkness, they headed out to the cotton fields.

For the slaves of the Rutherford plantation, another day had begun.

Gabriel Prosser was one of those slaves. He was 19. Prosser had been born on the Rutherford plantation. He expected to die there. Six days a week, 52 weeks a year, he worked in the fields. Prosser would probably have to do the same thing all his life. It was against the law to teach a slave skills such as reading and writing.

As grim as that sounds, Prosser could still feel lucky. At least he had never been beaten. On many plantations, slaves were beaten harshly just for talking back to their masters. And they were also beaten for not working as hard as their owners demanded.

Prosser's parents lived with him on the plantation. His father, who had a heart problem, worked in the Rutherford's big house. His mother worked in the fields.

Prosser had a brother and sister, but he no longer saw them. Two years earlier, Rutherford did not have money to buy seed. To get the money he needed, Rutherford sold a group of young slaves.

**Why do you think it was against the law to teach a slave to read and write?**

**What are the differences between a "slave" and a "servant"?**

Prosser's brother and sister were in that group. His parents cried when their children were sold. His father begged Rutherford to stop the sale.

The owner said he needed the money.

## Words from the Past

Solomon Northup was a free man until he was kidnapped in Washington, D.C., and sold into slavery. For twelve years he was a slave on a plantation. Finally he won his freedom. The following is from his book *Twelve Years a Slave*. Here he is describing cotton picking on a Louisiana plantation in the month of August.

"An ordinary day's work is two hundred pounds. A slave who is accustomed to picking is punished, if he or she brings in a less quantity than that. . . .

"The hands are required to be in the cotton field as soon as it is light in the morning, and, with the exception of ten or fifteen minutes, which is given them at noon to swallow their allowance of cold bacon, they are not permitted to be a moment idle until it is too dark too see, and when the moon is full, they often times labor till the middle of the night. They do not dare to stop even at dinner time, nor return to the quarters, however late it be, until the order to halt is given . . . . "

## Plans for Rebellion

Slaves in the South were very tightly controlled. But sometimes they fought back.

Gabriel Prosser was one of these "fighters." In 1800, he planned a rebellion. Prosser spoke to fellow slaves in areas around Richmond, Virginia. He told them to rise up against their masters. He put together a force of about a thousand slaves who were ready to follow him.

Prosser's plan called for the capture of Richmond. Then the nearby towns would be taken. When Virginia was under control, all slaves would be freed.

But the revolt never took place. Prosser was betrayed. Also, a violent rainstorm had washed out the roads and bridges into Richmond.

Prosser was arrested. He did not deny his plans. He was quickly brought to trial and sentenced to die. In August of 1800, Prosser and 36 others were hanged. Before he was killed, Prosser made a powerful speech. "I have nothing more to offer," he said, "than George Washington would have had to offer had he been taken by the British and put to trial by them." Gabriel Prosser gave his life in the hope that others might have freedom.

**Prosser compared himself to George Washington. Washington had fought to free Americans from English control. Prosser was fighting to free slaves from the control of other Americans.**

## Nat Turner's Rebellion

There were other slave rebellions throughout the early 1800s. The most violent of the revolts took place in Virginia in 1831. A slave named Nat Turner led this revolt. Turner believed that God had chosen him to lead his people to freedom. Turner and his men went from plantation to plantation, killing slaveholders. When news of the revolt spread,

**Nat Turner**

thousands of soldiers were called in from surrounding areas. Nat Turner and 19 of his followers were arrested, tried, and hanged.

By the time Nat Turner's revolt had ended, about 55 whites and 100 slaves had been killed.

All the slave rebellions failed. In fact, the rebellions sometimes made life even worse for slaves. That's because southerners became scared. In an effort to gain more control over their slaves, they'd become even stricter.

But there was one thing the rebellions made clear. Slaves hated the system that kept them in chains.

## Abolitionists

The **abolitionists**, who were mostly northerners, wanted to end (abolish) slavery. Black and white, they traveled around the country speaking out against it. And many abolitionists did more than just talk about slavery. Sometimes they risked their lives by helping slaves escape.

Unfortunately, not everyone in the North was against slavery. It had been accepted as a normal part of American life. The abolitionists were attacked in both the North and the South.

## Harriet Tubman and the Underground Railroad

It was a warm summer night in 1851. Outside the slave cabins, a woman sang a song called "Steal Away." The men, women, and children in the cabins heard the song. It was a signal to wrap the few things they owned and make their escape.

The woman singing the song was Harriet Tubman. She was born a slave, but she had escaped to the North, promising to return one day to help others.

She made good on her promise. Harriet Tubman went back to slave country 19 times. She helped lead more than 300 African Americans to freedom. Slave catchers tried to capture her, but they never could. Tubman always managed to get away. At one time rewards for her capture totaled about $40,000.

Harriet Tubman was a conductor on the Underground Railroad. This was not really a railroad, and it was not really under the ground. It was a secret means of escape for slaves.

Abolitionists set up "stations"—places of safety—along different routes. Most underground railroads led through Ohio and Pennsylvania. There the slaves, called "passengers," could hide. They were given food and rest before moving on. Brave people called "conductors" helped lead the slaves to the North. From one stop to another they were kept moving until they reached safety. Some of the slaves were taken all the way to Canada. At least 50,000 slaves escaped to freedom along the Underground Railroad.

**The Underground Railroad**

## Great Names in History: Frederick Douglass

Frederick Douglass was born into slavery. Douglass never went to school, but he did learn one lesson very well. He learned that black people were treated as if they belonged to white people. And he knew that was wrong.

As a slave he was called Frederick Bailey. When Frederick was caught reading, his master was angry. When the master caught young Frederick teaching other slaves to read, he was furious. He took Frederick to a "slave breaker." There, Frederick was beaten again and again. But the cruel slave-breaker only made Frederick's beliefs stronger. Frederick was determined to gain his freedom.

When he was 21 years old, Frederick Bailey made his escape. He had been working on the docks. He dressed as a sailor and boarded a rail car that took him out of Maryland. He then changed his name to Frederick Douglass. Soon he became a leader in the Massachusetts Abolitionist Society. He started his own abolitionist newspaper, called The North Star.

Frederick Douglass was a tall, handsome man with a deep, warm voice. When he talked, people listened. He told about his experiences in the South. He let the whole country know that slavery was evil.

## History Practice

Answer these questions on a separate sheet of paper.

1. What invention strengthened slavery in the South?

2. Describe the results of slave rebellions.

3. Who were the abolitionists?

4. What was the Underground Railroad?

## New States

The West was fast becoming an important area for farming and ranching. Both the North and the South had a strong interest in the West. Everyone realized that some day the western lands would become states in the Union. Would those new states be slave or free?

The answer was important because every state had votes in Congress. Those votes could be either for or against slavery.

As each western territory asked to become a state, arguments raged all over the land.

## The Missouri Compromise

In 1819 both Maine and Missouri had asked to become states. Missouri wanted to enter the Union as a slave state. Slavery was legal in the Territory of Missouri. About 10,000 slaves already lived there. But northerners wanted Missouri to be a free state. Congress would decide.

Because Maine was also joining the Union, Congress made a compromise. Maine would join as a free state. Missouri would join as a slave state.

There would then be 12 slave states and 12 free states. It was thought that this would create a balance of power.

The southern states depended on slave labor to grow their huge cotton crops. They were afraid that federal law might soon put an end to slavery. The South felt that its only safety was in keeping an even balance.

There were other terms of the Missouri Compromise. A line was drawn at the southern border of Missouri. The line extended across the West.

Any new states north of this line would be free states. And any new states south of the line would be slave states.

## The Compromise of 1850

In 1850, another slavery conflict arose. California was about to become a state. At that time there were 15 slave states and 15 free states. People in California wanted their state to be free. But that would destroy the balance of power.

Congress tried to settle the bitter fighting between the anti-slavery North and the pro-slavery South. Daniel Webster, Henry Clay, and Stephen A. Douglas led the fight for a series of new laws. John C. Calhoun led the southern forces.

Finally, the Compromise of 1850 settled the issue. It allowed California into the Union as a free state.

You learned earlier that in a compromise, each side gives up part of its demands. In the Compromise of 1850, what did the South give up? What did the North give up?

However, in the future, Congress would no longer decide if a new state would be free or slave. Rather, the people who lived in the new state would decide for themselves, by voting. Also, the North had to guarantee that it would strongly enforce the runaway slave law. In return, the District of Columbia would stop its slave trade.

In other terms of the compromise, Texas sold some land to New Mexico for 10 million dollars.

## The Kansas-Nebraska Act

The Kansas Territory was just west of Missouri. Southerners wanted slavery to move westward. They thought Kansas was a good place for this to happen.

But Kansas Territory was north of the line drawn by the Missouri Compromise. Northerners thought Kansas was a good place for slavery to be stopped.

The Kansas-Nebraska Act was passed in 1854. It created two new territories, Kansas and Nebraska from native lands west of the Mississippi River. It opened the area for settlement and it did away with the Missouri Compromise. The imaginary line between slave states and free states no longer existed.

The territories would decide the slavery issue for themselves. This meant that slavery would now be legally possible in a huge new area.

Northerners were angry. The Kansas Territory itself was divided on the slavery issue. Violence broke out. John Brown, an abolitionist, led a raid on a small settlement of southern sympathizers in 1856. This raid focused the country's attention on the conflict between pro- and anti-slavery forces.The territory became known as "Bleeding Kansas."

Compromises no longer kept the peace. The nation was moving toward civil war.

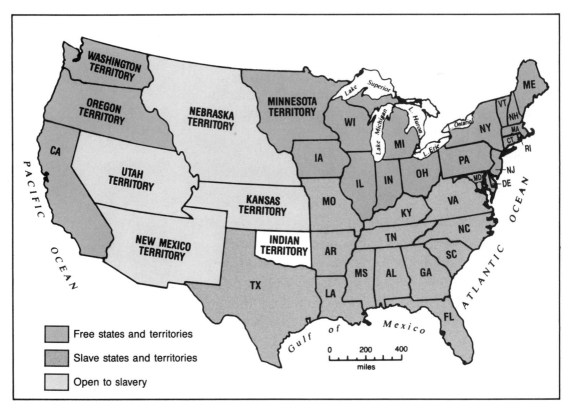

**Slavery, 1854**

## A House Divided

In 1858, a tall man in Illinois was a candidate for the United States Senate. He took note of the nation's sectionalism. He said, "A house divided against itself cannot stand. I believe our country cannot last half-slave and half-free."

That man was Abraham Lincoln. Lincoln did not win that election. But his words made him known in all parts of the country. Northerners looked to Lincoln to hold the United States together and to keep slavery from spreading west. Southerners saw Lincoln as a dangerous enemy of slavery and of the South. Many southerners said they would **secede** if Abraham Lincoln ever became president.

**Abraham Lincoln**

## History Practice

Answer these questions on a separate sheet of paper.

1. Why were new states important to the North and the South?

2. What was the purpose of the imaginary line drawn by the Missouri Compromise?

3. How did the southern states feel about Abraham Lincoln?

# Chapter Review

## Summary

| CHRONOLOGY OF MAJOR EVENTS | |
| --- | --- |
| 1793 | Invention of the cotton gin |
| 1820 | Missouri Compromise |
| 1831 | Nat Turner's Rebellion |
| 1850 | Compromise of 1850 |
| 1851 | Harriet Beecher Stowe writes *Uncle Tom's Cabin* |
| 1854 | Kansas-Nebraska Act |

- Sectionalism developed between North and South.

- The North became an industrial area. The South became an agricultural area.

- The South needed slaves to work on the large plantations. The North did not need slaves.

- Slavery became more important again in the South after the cotton gin was invented.

- Some slaves rebelled against cruel plantation life.

- Abolitionists fought slavery in the North and South.

- The Missouri Compromise and the Compromise of 1850 were made to keep a balance between free and slave votes in Congress.

- The Kansas-Nebraska Act ended the Missouri Compromise.

- Abraham Lincoln warned that the Union could not last if it were divided over slavery.

## Chapter Quiz

Answer these questions on a separate sheet of paper.

1. Who invented the cotton gin?

2. What did it do that had been done before by hand?

3. The Missouri Compromise was signed in 1820. In 1819, how many slave states were there? How many were free states?

4. How many slave states were there before the Compromise of 1850? How many free states were there?

5. What was the name of the act that did away with the Missouri Compromise?

6. What did Gabriel Prosser, Nat Turner, Harriet Tubman, and Frederick Douglass have in common?

## Thinking and Writing

1. What is sectionalism? Explain how northern industrial growth and the invention of the cotton gin encouraged it.

2. Why was it so important whether a new state joined the United States as a slave state or a free state?

3. Why would a conductor on the Underground Railroad need to be very brave?

# Chapter 11

# The Civil War

**The Battle of Fort Sumter**

## Chapter Learning Objectives

- Tell why the North expected the Civil War to end quickly.
- Explain why the Civil War was called a "war between brothers."
- Describe where most of the fighting took place.
- Tell two things the Civil War decided.

## Words to Know

**blockade**   to keep supplies from getting in or out of a place

**charity**   kindness; good will

**Confederacy**   the southern side in the Civil War

**malice**   ill will; anger; hatred

**proclamation**   a public statement

**Union**   the northern side in the Civil War

Fort Sumter was the scene of the first fighting of the Civil War. The war would not end until four terrible years had passed. During that time, hundreds of thousands of lives would be lost. The hatred that arose then would affect life in the United States for many, many years to come.

## The First Shots

Abraham Lincoln won the presidential election of 1860. Shortly after the election, seven southern states announced they were no longer a part of the United States. In February of 1861, leaders of these states met to form their own country. They elected Jefferson Davis president of the Confederate States of America. Four more states soon joined the **Confederacy.**

South Carolina was the first state to secede from the Union.

Tension mounted. Lincoln felt he could not permit the South to secede. War seemed impossible to avoid.

It began at Fort Sumter on an island in the harbor of Charleston, South Carolina. The South had already left the **Union.** But this fort remained under northern control.

Leaving the Union was not a new idea for the South. Southerners had considered it since 1832. They thought that if they could make their own laws, they could preserve slavery.

The southern forces had gathered across the water. They were waiting for the signal to attack. On April 12, southern cannons began firing. All day, they pounded the fort. Finally, Fort Sumter surrendered. Southerners took control and raised the flag of the Confederacy.

The Civil War had started.

**The Battle of Bull Run**

# Battle of Bull Run

It was a bright sunny day in July of 1861. In Washington, D.C., smiling men and women climbed into horse-drawn carriages. They were carrying baskets of food. They looked as though they were going to a picnic.

But these people were not off to picnic in the country. They were going to a battle. The people of Washington were following the Union army as it marched down the road. At a stream called Bull Run, not far from the city, the Confederates were waiting. The people had come out to watch the North win a victory. It was supposed to end the South's rebellion.

Northerners believed the Union would quickly end the war. They had some good reasons for their beliefs. The North had a far larger population than the South. It had more people who could fight as soldiers, work in factories, and grow food. The North also had many more factories. It could make more guns and cannons. The North had many more miles of railroad. It could get soldiers, guns, cannons, and food to the front lines faster than the South could.

The war would be over soon. The South would be punished. Or so the people of Washington believed.

It didn't turn out that way. At Bull Run, the North suffered a crushing defeat. The southern army sent the northerners fleeing back to Washington. The people with their wagons became part of the retreat. Everyone rushed to escape as cannon fire roared overhead.

The South won this battle. People on both sides now saw that it would be a long, hard war.

| THE CIVIL WAR | |
|---|---|
| **Northern Advantages** | **Southern Advantages** |
| <ul><li>more people to fight and work</li><li>more factories to produce military supplies</li><li>more railroads, canals, and roads to transport goods</li><li>ships to block supplies from reaching the southern coast</li></ul> | <ul><li>shorter supply lines</li><li>excellent leadership in the army</li><li>determination to protect their way of life</li><li>knowledge of the land in which they were fighting</li></ul> |

**Abe Lincoln's wife, Mary Todd Lincoln, knew about families torn apart by war. Her youngest brother and three half-brothers fought in the Confederate army.**

**Do you have any relatives living in other parts of the country? Think about what a war within a country might mean.**

## Brother Against Brother

The smoke hung heavily after the battle of Shiloh. For two days in April, 1862, the armies had fought and killed. Thousands lay dead. A northern general walked over the field and wondered how it could have come to this. Why did Americans have to spend years fighting and killing one another? The general passed a northern soldier dressed in his blue uniform. He was slowly digging a grave. The general nodded to the man sadly. The man must have been burying a friend. Then the general looked at the body the man was burying. The dead man was wearing the gray colors of the Confederacy. The general was surprised. "Private," the general asked, "with so many of our side dead, why do you bury this man?" Tears were running down the face of the soldier as he answered the general.

"Sir, this man here, I know he was a rebel. But, sir, he was also my brother."

All wars are terrible. But the Civil War was terrible in a different way. It was not a war between different countries. A civil war is one which is fought between groups of people within the same country. The

American Civil War caused families to be torn apart. It set cousin against cousin, brother against brother, and father against son.

**Can you think of any other countries that have fought civil wars?**

## Major Civil War Battles

### Map Study

Study the map. Then answer the questions on a separate sheet of paper.

1.  How many battle sites are shown on the map?
2.  In which state of the Confederacy were the most battles fought?
3.  In which two Union states were battles fought?

## Squeezing the South

To defeat the South, the Union used what it called the 'Conda Plan. The South American snake called the anaconda coils itself around its prey. It slowly squeezes the life out of it. In the same way, the North tried to squeeze the South to death.

The South did not have many factories. It needed to trade cotton for guns and cannons. But northern ships **blockaded** southern harbors on the Atlantic and Gulf coasts. These ships kept out goods from other countries.

The northern army and navy captured towns along the Mississippi River. This separated the western part of the Confederacy from the eastern part. The South could not move armies and supplies from one part to the other.

Northern armies set about destroying roads, bridges, and railways in the South.

Northern generals believed that the South could not hold out for long.

## Confederate Plans

The South planned to wage a defensive war. Southerners reasoned that if they could hold out long enough, the North would grow tired of fighting. The South also hoped to get help from Britain and France. It believed that these nations needed Southern cotton enough to come to the aid of the Confederacy.

In the beginning, the Confederacy had far better leaders than the Union did. Generals such as Robert E. Lee and Stonewall Jackson outsmarted the Union generals. The Union didn't start to get the upper hand until Lincoln named Ulysses S. Grant to lead the northern armies.

## The Emancipation Proclamation and an End to Slavery

Another problem for the North was that it did not always seem to know why it was fighting. Was the purpose of the war to end slavery? Was it to save the United States? Was it to allow for the growth of business?

Lincoln hated slavery. He wanted to see it stopped. "If slavery isn't wrong," he once said, "then nothing is wrong." But Lincoln had been afraid that ending slavery might divide the country. When the South seceded, Lincoln felt forced to go to war to keep the country whole. As the war went on, he saw that doing something to end slavery would encourage the northerners.

On January 1, 1863, Lincoln signed an order called the "Emancipation **Proclamation.**" It prohibited slavery in the states still fighting the Union at that time. When he signed the order, Lincoln said, "I never in my life felt more certain that I was doing right than I do in signing this paper."

The proclamation helped lead to the passage of the Thirteenth Amendment to the Constitution. On December 18, 1865, this legally abolished slavery throughout the country.

One part of the Emancipation Proclamation invited African Americans to fight with the northern forces. Many thousands signed up in the Union's army and navy. By the end of the war, more than 200,000 African Americans had fought in some of the war's bloodiest battles. Twenty black soldiers won the Medal of Honor, America's highest award for bravery. About 38,000 black soldiers died in the fighting.

Lincoln was most interested in keeping the nation together. "My paramount object in this struggle is to save the Union, and is neither to save or to destroy slavery."

## Learn More About It: The 54th Regiment

The 54th Massachusetts was a Union regiment made up of African American soldiers. These men led several attacks into South Carolina. They faced a danger that white soldiers did not. If captured in the South, they would be treated according to Confederate law. They would be considered outlaws and killed or sold into slavery.

On a July evening in 1863, the 54th launched a daring attack on the fort that guarded Charleston harbor. The regiment, led by Colonel Robert Gould Shaw, scaled the walls and fought in hand-to-hand combat inside the fort. More than half the members of the 54th were killed that night. The fort did not fall, but the soldiers of the 54th showed remarkable courage.

## History Practice

Answer these questions on a separate sheet of paper.

1. What advantages did the North have in the Civil War? What advantages did the South have?

2. How did the North plan to beat the South?

3. What did the Emancipation Proclamation do?

## Battle at Sea

The Confederacy tried to break the Union's blockade of Southern harbors. They sent an unusual ship to attack the Union navy. Warships at that time were made of wood. The Confederacy covered a wooden ship called the *Merrimac* with iron plates. They renamed the ship the *Virginia,* but it was still known by its earlier name. When the iron-clad

*Merrimac* sailed into battle, Union shells just bounced off its sides. The *Merrimac* sank two ships from the Union navy.

The next time the *Merrimac* sailed, the Union navy was ready. A northern engineer named John Ericsson had built a new ship called the *Monitor*.

**While thousands of soldiers died in battles, others died in prison camps and hospitals. Medical care was very poor. Three thousand women became army and navy nurses. Often unpaid, they aided the sick and wounded.**

The *Monitor* was covered with iron, too. It was an odd vessel that looked like a round box on top of a raft. It had two large cannons. On March 9, 1862, the *Monitor* met the *Merrimac* in America's first battle between iron-clad ships. By the end of the day, neither ship had won. But the battle ended the Confederacy's hopes of breaking the blockade. It also ended the era of wooden warships.

## The Turning Point

The turning point of the Civil War came in 1863. General Lee had decided to invade the North. He knew the North didn't have many good generals. He expected victory.

In July, Lee and the Confederates met the Union army at Gettysburg, Pennsylvania. It was a fierce, three-day battle. There were 90,000 Union soldiers and 75,000 Confederate soldiers fighting at Gettysburg. More men died there than in any other battle of the war.

The battle ended when the South had to retreat. It was running out of supplies and could not attack again.

In 1863 another battle turned the tide of war in favor of the North. At Vicksburg, Mississippi, General Ulysses S. Grant and the Union army surrounded the Confederate army. Union forces kept food and supplies from getting through to the Confederates. Victory at Vicksburg gave the Union control of the Mississippi River.

## Sherman's March to the Sea

The battlefields of the Civil War were mainly in the South. Southerners felt the greatest damage and loss.

The year 1864 brought a time of destruction that

would become known as Sherman's March. On March 9, 1864, General Ulysses Grant became supreme commander of all Union armies. Two months later he sent General William T. Sherman and 100,000 troops to invade Georgia. General Sherman and his troops attacked Atlanta, Georgia. Sherman ordered his soldiers to torch the city. Their attack left Atlanta a heap of ashes.

After victory in Atlanta, Sherman marched 60,000 of his men across Georgia to Savannah. General Sherman believed the quickest way to win the war was to completely destroy the South. He wanted to break the South's spirit and let civilians feel the sting of war. He wanted to leave the enemy without food or

## Learn More About It:
## Young Soldiers of the Civil War

Many of the Confederate troops who faced General Sherman's march through Georgia were very young. Most southern soldiers were serving in regiments outside the state. The Confederate army had to turn to new recruits. Often, these were boys no more than 15 years of age.

Both the Union and Confederate forces included young soldiers. Nearly 60 percent of the troops on both sides were less than 26 years old. It was common to find soldiers in battle under the legal enlistment age of 18.

Young drummer boys of only 10 or 12 faced enemy fire. They carried gunpowder to the men firing the cannon. Soldiers of 13 or 14 received no special treatment because of their age. Sometimes these young soldiers rose in rank to become officers. They led men into battle who were twice their age.

During the Civil War, women were not allowed to serve as soldiers. More than 400 women disguised themselves as men so that they could join the troops. Some were discovered when they were wounded in battle.

supplies. Sherman gave his men an order: "Destroy everything in sight! Leave nothing the Confederate soldiers can use." For sixty miles, the Union soldiers followed Sherman's order. They burned bridges and barns and houses. They killed livestock and destroyed crops. Sherman's men tore up more than 300 miles of railroad track.

Sherman's army met little resistance from Confederate troops. Most southern regiments were fighting outside the state. Only about 13,000 poorly trained Confederate troops faced Sherman's army. On December 22, 1864, the Union army took Savannah. General Sherman sent President Lincoln a telegram. It said: "I beg to present to you, as a Christmas gift, the city of Savannah..."

Sherman's march to the sea helped bring a quick end to the war. Some people considered General Sherman a hero. Other's thought of him as a cruel villain. Sherman himself felt that his march through Georgia was a "hard" kind of fighting.

When Ulysses Grant ordered Sherman's march of destruction, he also ordered General Philip Henry Sheridan to raid the Shenandoah Valley. The valley was one of the main sources of food for the hungry Confederate army. Sheridan was sent to burn all fields and farmlands. These burn and destroy tactics were known as Grant's "scorched earth policy."

**Chart Study**

Look at the chart on page 189. Then answer the questions on a separate sheet of paper.

1. Where was the first naval battle of the war fought?
2. Who won the battle at Antietam?
3. Vicksburg and Gettysburg were important victories for which army?
4. Why was the battle of Chattanooga important?

## SOME MAJOR BATTLES OF THE CIVIL WAR

| Battle | Date | Battle Site | Description |
|---|---|---|---|
| Fort Sumter | July 12–14, 1861 | South Carolina | Opening shots; Civil War declared |
| First Bull Run | July 21, 1861 | Virginia | First Civil War battle; Confederates show strength |
| Hampton Roads | March 8, 1862 | Virginia | First major naval battle; *Monitor* vs. *Merrimac* |
| Battle of Shiloh | April 6–7, 1862 | Tennessee | 23,000 soldiers die in Union victory |
| Second Bull Run | Aug. 27–30, 1862 | Virginia | Confederate army forces Grant's army to retreat to Washington |
| Antietam | Sept. 17, 1862 | Maryland | 23,000 soldiers die in bloodiest one-day battle; Lincoln claims victory for the North, but outcome of battle unclear |
| Vicksburg | May 19–July 4,1863 | Mississippi | Union victory; opens Mississippi River as Union supply route |
| Gettysburg | July 1–3, 1863 | Pennsylvania | Union victory; more soldiers killed than at any other battle |
| Chickamauga | Sept. 19–20, 1863 | Georgia | Confederate victory; Union army retreats to Chattanooga |
| Chattanooga | Nov. 23–25, 1863 | Tennessee | Union sends more troops and wins control of key railway center of Deep South |

## Surrender at Appomattox

By early 1865, the 'Conda Plan had achieved its goals. The South lay in ruins. The Union army had taken the Confederate capital of Richmond, Virginia. Surrounded and outnumbered by Union soldiers, Lee now saw that the southern cause was hopeless. At a small house in the town of Appomattox Courthouse, Virginia, Lee surrendered his army to Grant. It was April 9, 1865.

General Grant showed respect when accepting Lee's surrender. Grant took no Confederate prisoners. He allowed the southern officers to keep their swords and their horses. The two generals shook hands.

All over the North people celebrated the end of the bloodshed. When General Grant heard Union gunshots fired in celebration, he turned to his men. "Stop the firing," General Grant said. "The Rebels are our countrymen again."

## Lincoln's Assassination

The celebrations did not go on very long. Five days after the war's end, Abraham Lincoln was shot as he sat watching a play. His killer was a man named John Wilkes Booth. John Wilkes Booth was a well-known actor. He wanted the South to win the Civil War. On the night of April 13, 1865, Booth arrived at Ford's Theater in Washington, D.C. He went up to the president's box. No one was guarding the door. Booth went in, put a pistol to the back of Lincoln's head, and fired. Then he jumped down to the stage, breaking his leg in the fall. He escaped on horseback. Twelve days later soldiers captured Booth in a barn in Virginia. When Booth tried to escape, he was shot and killed.

Abraham Lincoln died on the morning of April 15. John Wilkes Booth thought he was helping the South. What he had done was kill the one person who could best help the South recover. It had been Lincoln's hope that the South would come back into the country as a full partner with the North. In the last days of the war, he'd said, "With malice toward none, with charity for all, let us work to bind up the nation's wounds." Lincoln thought of southerners as Americans who had suffered greatly from war.

## Words from the Past: The Gettysburg Address

In July, 1863, at the site of the Battle of Gettysburg, President Lincoln honored the soldiers who died there. His Gettysburg Address began with these words:

*Four score and seven years ago our fathers brought forth on this continent a new nation.*

The address ended with a pledge to remember those who fought for the Union:

*... we here highly resolve that these dead shall not have died in vain; that this nation, under God, shall have a new birth of freedom; and that government of the people, by the people, for the people, shall not perish from the earth.*

## A Stronger Country

The Civil War was the most terrible war the United States had ever fought. It killed more than 600,000 people and destroyed cities and farms.

Yet the war decided two important questions, slavery and secession. Never again would the law allow one person to own another as property. And never again would one state be able to have its way by removing itself from the nation. The United States had paid a great price with the Civil War. But it would become a stronger country.

## History Practice

Answer these questions on a separate sheet of paper.

1. What happened to the South during Sherman's March to the Sea?

2. What was the purpose of Sheridan's raid on the Shenandoah Valley?

3. Where and to whom did General Lee surrender?

4. Why did John Wilkes Booth shoot President Lincoln?

5. What two important questions did the Civil War decide?

# Chapter Review

## Summary

| CHRONOLOGY OF MAJOR EVENTS | |
| --- | --- |
| 1861 | Lincoln elected 16th president |
| 1861 | Civil War begins at Fort Sumter |
| 1861 | Battle of Bull Run |
| 1862 | Battle of Shiloh |
| 1863 | Emancipation Proclamation |
| 1863 | Battles of Vicksburg and Gettysburg |
| 1864 | Sherman's March to the Sea |
| 1865 | Lee surrenders to Grant |
| 1865 | Thirteenth Amendment to the Constitution abolishes slavery |
| 1865 | Lincoln assassinated |

- Lincoln was elected president in 1860.

- The Confederacy seceded from the Union. It wanted to make its own laws and preserve slavery.

- The fighting began at Fort Sumter, South Carolina.

- Most of the fighting took place in the South.

- General Robert E. Lee and Stonewall Jackson were Confederate leaders. Ulysses S. Grant led the Union army.

- Lincoln's Emancipation Proclamation outlawed slavery in the Confederacy. It also invited blacks to join the Union army.

- Battles at Gettysburg and Vicksburg turned the war toward a Union victory.

- Lee surrendered to Grant at Appomattox Courthouse, Virginia, in April, 1865.

## Chapter Quiz

Answer these questions on a separate sheet of paper.

1. Who was the president of the Confederacy?

2. How did the Battle of Bull Run change the way northerners thought about the South's rebellion?

3. How does a civil war differ from other wars?

4. What was Abraham Lincoln's chief concern?

5. Why was the Battle of Vicksburg important?

6. The Emancipation Proclamation outlawed slavery in the South. Which law outlawed it throughout the country? How much time passed between the signing of the two laws?

## Thinking and Writing

1. The North had better supplies and equipment. The South had more good leaders. Which do you think is more important, supplies or leadership? Explain your answer.

2. Some black soldiers were former slaves. How do you think they felt about the war?

3. The people rushing off to watch the Battle of Bull Run were caught up in the excitement and glory of war. Do you ever see that attitude today? Do war movies make war look exciting?

# Chapter 12

# A New South

**Atlanta railroad depot destroyed during the war.**

## Chapter Learning Objectives

- Describe the purpose of Reconstruction.
- Tell how Andrew Johnson and Congress disagreed over plans for Reconstruction.
- Explain why the 14th and 15th Amendments were added to the Constitution.
- Tell how African Americans were denied their rights after the Civil War.

# Words to Know

**Carpetbaggers**   northerners who came south after the Civil War. They took power and used southern problems for their own gain.

**facilities**   places, such as buildings or rooms, for certain activities; a school is a facility for learning

**impeach**   to accuse a public official of doing wrong and to send that official to trial

**lynchings**   killings by mobs, usually by hanging, without trial

**poll**   a place where people vote

**Reconstruction**   the time after the Civil War; the rebuilding of the South and the bringing of the southern states back into the Union

**Scalawags**   southerners who helped northern Republicans and southern blacks gain public office

**segregated**   separated by race

**sharecropping**   farming someone else's land while paying a share of the crop as rent

---

Four years of Civil War had left a nation torn in two. The southern states needed rebuilding. Four million freed slaves had to shape new lives. The end of the Civil War did not mean the end of the Union's problems. In this chapter, you will read about Reconstruction, the effort to rebuild the South.

## Lincoln's Plans for Reconstruction

President Lincoln had been making plans for the **reconstruction** of the South before the war was over. Lincoln's plans treated the South very generously. He did not want to punish the southern states. He wanted to forgive them. He wanted to help them rejoin the Union.

**Some people wanted to punish the South for their part in the war. Others wanted to forgive the South. How do you think you would have felt about people who had been your enemies?**

Not everyone agreed with Lincoln. There was a group of Congressmen who were known as Radical Republicans. They thought Lincoln was too easy on the South. They wanted stricter rules for the states that were rejoining the Union. They wanted more rights for blacks. Most southern states weren't willing to let blacks have their rights.

## The Freedmen's Bureau

**Think about problems facing the freed slaves. Where would they live? Where would they work? Whose responsibility do you think it was to help them?**

In March, 1865, just before the war ended, Congress passed a new law. It set up a Freedmen's Bureau. The Bureau gave food, clothing, and medicine to freed blacks and to poor southern whites. It set up schools and helped people find jobs. The Freedmen's Bureau was the first federal organization set up to help people in need.

**Andrew Johnson**

## Andrew Johnson Becomes President

Lincoln did not live to see his Reconstruction plans carried out. Five days after the war ended, he was assassinated.

Andrew Johnson, the vice president, took over as President of the United States. This was in keeping with Constitutional law. Rebuilding the South became the new president's job.

Johnson planned to follow Lincoln's reconstruction ideas. He wanted to make it as easy as possible for the southern states to rejoin the Union.

The Radical Republicans found even more fault with Johnson than they had with Lincoln. Johnson was a southern Democrat himself. He had even owned slaves at one time.

The Radical Republicans accused Johnson of favoring the southern states.

## Black Codes

Under President Johnson's plans, men who had been Confederate leaders could still hold high government jobs. The 13th Amendment had outlawed slavery in 1865. But these men passed state laws known as the Black Codes.

The Black Codes were like the old slave laws. In many ways, it was simply as if the word "Black" had replaced the word "slave."

The Black Codes took away many of the rights of the free blacks. Among other things, they kept blacks out of schools and off juries.

Black Codes also kept former slaves out of good jobs. In South Carolina, for example, a law required African Americans to pay $10 to $100 for a license to hold any job other than that of servant or farmer.

# The Radical Republicans vs. Andrew Johnson

What problems might be caused by former Confederate leaders in government positions?

The Radical Republicans were in an uproar during the next session of Congress. They felt Johnson was too easy on the South. They said the Black Codes were hardly better than slavery. They said that former Confederate leaders had no right in government jobs.

Congress set up its own plans for Reconstruction. It was different from the president's. In 1866, Congress passed the Civil Rights Act. It said that black people should have the same rights as whites.

President Johnson refused to sign it. He vetoed the Civil Rights Act.

The Constitution said that Congress could pass the bill over the president's veto. Two-thirds of Congress would have to vote in favor of the bill. A vote was taken. The Civil Rights Act became law.

# The 14th Amendment

President Johnson's power was limited by the system of Checks and Balances.

Republicans in Congress wanted something stronger than the Civil Rights Act. They wrote a 14th Amendment to the Constitution. The 14th Amendment gave former slaves citizenship. It also said that former Confederate leaders could not hold office or vote.

President Johnson was against the amendment. But, by 1868, it was approved by most states. Southern states had to approve it before they could come back into the Union.

Federal troops were sent into the South to make sure the states followed Congress's rules.

# Learn More About It: Reconstruction Acts

In 1867 Radical Republicans passed these acts over President Johnson's veto.

1. Federal troops would maintain law and order in the South.

2. Former Confederate soldiers and leaders could not vote or hold office.

3. Freed slaves had the right to vote and hold office.

4. New state constitutions must be written and approved by Congress.

5. To rejoin the Union, southern states must approve the 14th Amendment.

How do you think southerners felt about federal troops in their states?

## History Practice

Answer these questions on a separate sheet of paper.

1. Why was Lincoln unable to carry out his plans for reconstruction?

2. Who were the Radical Republicans?

3. How did Andrew Johnson become president of the United States?

4. What did Black Codes do to the rights of freed blacks?

5. What did the 14th Amendment say? How did President Johnson feel about this amendment?

## Sharecropping in the South

The days of the rich plantations and of slavery were gone. The South had been very nearly destroyed. Both blacks and whites had to build new lives.

What would happen to the freed slaves? Most had little or nothing of their own. They had no education and no jobs.

Some blacks stayed with their former owners. Some looked to other white farmers for jobs. But the war left many of the white farmers poor, too. They could not pay workers.

A system called **sharecropping** developed. Farmers let workers live on their farms and work a part of their land. The farmers gave the workers tools, seed, and work animals. In return, the black workers did the labor. Most of the crops went to the landowners. A small portion went to the black workers.

The system allowed the black sharecroppers to survive. But it kept them poor.

Some blacks hated the idea of staying on the white man's farms. They moved to cities in both the North and the South. Suddenly there were thousands of unskilled people looking for work. They took what they could find. A few did well and found ways to get jobs and education. Most, however, had a very hard time.

**The sharecropping system was used in America in later years too. Why was it difficult for sharecroppers to get ahead?**

**Many blacks finally had a chance to attend schools. Some even went to college. Tuskegee Institute, in Alabama, was founded by Booker T. Washington, a famous black leader.**

## Scalawags and Carpetbaggers

The South needed leaders. Congress, the Radical Republicans, and the 14th amendment made sure that old southern leaders had no official power. Where would the new South get its government officials?

Northerners arrived to help the South solve its problems. Politicians and businessmen came to the South. Some really wanted to help. But many saw a chance for easy money and quick power. They gained public office and began reorganizing the local governments.

The southerners did not like most of these northern newcomers. They scornfully called them **Carpetbaggers**. The name described the suitcases made of carpet material that the northerners carried south with them.

**Carpetbaggers**

These northerners did some good things. They started schools and rebuilt roads. They helped blacks protect their rights. But others worked merely for their own gain.

Many southerners disliked the **Scalawags** as much as the Carpetbaggers. The word *scalawag* means scoundrel or rascal. Scalawags were white southerners who helped put African Americans and northerners into public office. Most black officeholders had no experience in politics. Many did whatever the white Scalawags told them.

Some Scalawags did try to help the South. But there were too many of them who simply were after power and money for themselves.

## Black Southerners in Office

Northern Carpetbaggers controlled most of Reconstruction government. Some southern Scalawags held office, too. Remember, southern leaders from the days of the Confederacy could not vote or hold office. This left offices open to new black leaders. Mississippi sent two black senators to Washington. They were Hiram Revels and Blanche K. Bruce.

Most African Americans who held office during Reconstruction were more than fair to the white southerners. They were not after revenge for the hard days of slavery. Many even favored returning the vote to the whites who had once kept them as slaves.

**Hiram Revels, left, and other black Reconstruction-era members of the House of Representatives**

## History Practice

Answer these questions on a separate sheet of paper.

1. How did sharecropping work?

2. Who were the Carpetbaggers?

3. Who were the Scalawags?

## Republicans Impeach President Johnson

President Johnson and the Radical Republicans in Congress continued to disagree. The Republicans worried that Johnson would not back laws passed in Congress. They wanted Johnson out of office.

The only way to remove him was to **impeach** him. Johnson would be accused of crimes against the nation. Then he would face trial by the Senate. If found guilty, he would lose his job.

The Radical Republicans waited for Johnson to do something wrong. One day, he fired one of his cabinet members without Senate approval. The Republicans quickly accused him of an unconstitutional act. Then they impeached him.

The president's impeachment roused public curiosity and interest. Would the U.S. Senate remove Andrew Johnson from office? More than 1,000 Americans bought tickets to come watch the trial.

Thirty-six of the 54 senators (two-thirds of the Senate) would have to find Johnson guilty. Thirty-five Senators voted against him. Johnson finished his term of office.

**Andrew Johnson was the only U.S. president to be impeached. Richard Nixon, in 1974, resigned from the office of president.**

**Johnson was found not guilty by one vote!**

## The Election of 1868

In 1868, the people of the United States elected Ulysses S. Grant president. The people remembered him as a great war leader. He was the brave, northern general who had accepted Lee's surrender at Appomattox. Grant had no political experience. But, like George Washington, he was a national hero.

Over 500,000 freed slaves cast votes in the 1868 election. This helped Grant win the race. People began to see the importance of the African American vote.

**Ulysses S. Grant**

President Grant was an honest man. But many of the politicians who served him were not. His time in office was also a time of Carpetbaggers, Scalawags, and others who used the government for their own gain.

## The 15th Amendment

The 14th Amendment made blacks citizens in 1868. The amendment did not actually guarantee them a vote.

The 15th Amendment passed in 1870. It said that "the rights of citizens of the United States to vote shall not be denied . . . on account of race, color, or previous conditions of servitude." The 15th Amendment gave all male citizens the vote.

### History Practice

Answer these questions on a separate sheet of paper.

1. Why did the Republicans impeach Johnson? How did he manage to stay in office?

2. Why did the majority of people vote for Ulysses S. Grant for president?

3. What did the 15th Amendment guarantee? Which group of people was left out of the 15th Amendment?

## The End of Reconstruction

By 1870, all 11 southern states had rejoined the Union. Northerners began to lose interest in the South's problems. They were ready to forget the Civil War.

The South was about to stand on its own. In 1872, Congress passed a law letting many former Confederate leaders vote again.

Industry was growing in the South too. Hayes promised the South more railroads. More railroads were built.

In 1876, Rutherford B. Hayes became president. In a bitter election, Democratic candidate Samuel J. Tilden won more popular votes than Hayes. By the end of election day, Tilden had 184 electoral votes. But he needed 185 to win. There had been cheating by both sides at the polls. There was no way to know for sure who had won the electoral votes of three southern states. Each side claimed victory. Finally Congress set up a committee to decide the election.

To win the support of angry southern Democrats, Hayes and the Republicans agreed to end Reconstruction. Hayes promised to take northern soldiers out of the South. He also promised to put a Southerner in the cabinet. Rutherford Hayes was elected president.

In 1877, all federal troops left the southern states. This left southern blacks without federal protection. The era of Reconstruction was over.

In the North, industry was growing rapidly. Northerners were ready to turn to their own business. They would let the South take care of itself.

The rights of black Americans faded into the background.

**Great Names in History: Clara Barton**

The 15th Amendment ignored one whole group of people—women. In 1870, women could not vote. They could not hold public office. In some cases, they could not own property. The nation did not see the important roles that women played. It ignored women like Clara Barton, who'd given so much to her country and her fellow human beings.

Clara Barton had risked her life during the Civil War. As a nurse, she took care of wounded soldiers and carried supplies into battles. She was known as the "Angel of the Battlefield."

When the war ended, Clara Barton formed a group to search for missing men. She later founded the American Red Cross. It was Barton's idea to give care and money to victims of floods, earthquakes, and other disasters.

Yet Clara Barton could not vote.

## "Jim Crow"

After Reconstruction, white southerners took back control. The new southern leaders drew up state laws. Many of the new laws kept whites and blacks apart, or **segregated**. Some laws said that blacks and whites had to ride on separate railroad cars. Others kept blacks from eating in white restaurants and sleeping in white hotels. They kept blacks from seeking treatment in white hospitals and attending white schools. These segregation laws were called "Jim Crow" laws. (The name Jim Crow may have come from an 1830s song.)

Blacks challenged the segregation laws. But the results of this were a blow to civil rights. In 1896, the Supreme Court ruled that "separate but equal" was

Racism was by no means confined to the South. It took until 1954 for Congress to rule that segregation in the nation's schools was unconstitutional.

Do you see segregation existing anywhere today?

**Rutherford B. Hayes**

lawful. Blacks could be kept apart from whites as long as blacks had **facilities** of their own. Black children could be kept out of white schools as long as schools were set up for blacks. Would the all-black schools really be "equal" to the white schools? How well could such a system work?

## State Constitutions Limit Rights

After Reconstruction, the southern states wrote new constitutions. The 15th Amendment had given blacks the right to vote. That right was slowly taken away.

"A person must be able to read or write to vote," new state constitutions said. This literacy law required voters to pass a test before they could vote. Many blacks could not pass the test.

Some states required poll taxes. Every voter had to pay a small amount of money. Many blacks did not have the money to pay. They were not allowed at the polls.

White southerners used every trick they could think of to keep blacks from voting. Why do you think they were afraid to let blacks vote?

Other states said a voter had to have paid taxes on property worth $300 or more. Most blacks did not own property. They could not vote.

What about southern whites who did not own property or who could not read or pay the poll tax? A "Grandfather law" was written to protect them. The Grandfather law said that if a man's father or grandfather had voted, then that man could vote, too. This gave most whites the right to vote. It did nothing to help the blacks. Most of their fathers and grandfathers had been slaves.

Black Americans were losing their newly gained voice in state government.

## Murder

Southern blacks lived with segregation. They lived without a voice in government. And, many lived with fear.

There were **lynchings**. African Americans were charged with crimes, judged guilty without trials, and hanged by angry white mobs. Black neighborhoods were burned. Innocent people were killed.

A group called the Ku Klux Klan, which still exists today, terrorized blacks. Men wearing white sheets and pointed hoods burned crosses in front of blacks' homes. They carried out secret killings. They made sure many black people were too afraid to vote.

## Happy Anniversary

In 1876, America celebrated the 100th anniversary of the Declaration of Independence. What was the nation like on that anniversary?

Rutherford Hayes had just become the 19th president.

Segregation was dividing the South into powerful whites and have-nothing blacks.

Women could not vote.

Industry was growing rapidly, both North and South. Birmingham, Alabama, had become the industrial center of the South. Atlanta, Georgia, had become the southern business center.

A fair called the Centennial Exposition was held in Philadelphia, Pennsylvania. America showed its pride in its fine factories and new inventions. But it was an America that had not yet met its promise of justice and equality for all.

In what ways have we made good on our promise of equality? What still needs to be done?

## History Practice

Answer these questions on a separate sheet of paper.

1. What promises did Rutherford B. Hayes make to win the support of southern Democrats?

2. How did Jim Crow laws affect the lives of southern blacks?

3. How did southern states keep black men from voting?

4. What problems faced the United States on the 100th anniversary of the Declaration of Independence?

# Chapter Review

## Summary

| CHRONOLOGY OF MAJOR EVENTS | |
|---|---|
| 1865 | Andrew Johnson becomes 17th president |
| 1865 | Freedmen's Bureau set up |
| 1866 | Congress passes Civil Rights Act |
| 1867 | Congress passes Reconstruction Acts |
| 1868 | 14th Amendment makes blacks citizens |
| 1868 | President Johnson impeached |
| 1869 | Ulysses S. Grant becomes 18th president |
| 1870 | 15th Amendment guarantees men of all races can vote |
| 1872 | Confederate leaders allowed to vote and hold office again |
| 1876 | Rutherford Hayes becomes 19th president |
| 1877 | Federal troops leave the South |

- Johnson clashed with Radical Republicans in Congress. They thought he was too easy on the South.

- The Reconstruction Acts passed over Johnson's veto. Federal armies moved into the South. Former Confederate leaders could not hold office or vote.

- The 14th Amendment gave former slaves citizenship.

- Many freed slaves became sharecroppers.

- "Carpetbaggers" from the North took positions of power in the South. Some helped the South grow stronger; others only wanted to help themselves. Many southern "Scalawags" were after power and money, too.

- When Reconstruction ended, southerners wrote new laws that kept whites and blacks segregated. They also kept blacks from voting.

- Racist groups terrorized black citizens.

## Chapter Quiz

Answer these questions on a separate sheet of paper.

1. What event caused Andrew Johnson to become president?

2. Name two things the Black Codes did.

3. In what way were some Carpetbaggers and Scalawags alike?

4. If a president is to be impeached, where does the trial take place?

5. When did the nation see the importance of the black vote?

6. How did America celebrate the 100th anniversary of the signing of the Declaration of Independence?

## Thinking and Writing

1. President Lincoln hoped that Reconstruction would "bind the nation's wounds." What do you think he meant?

2. Describe at least two ways white southerners tried to limit the rights of blacks.

# Unit Four Review

## A. Who might have said it?

Nat Turner

Sam Houston

James K. Polk

Abraham Lincoln

John Sutter

1. "Remember the Alamo!"
2. "The United States should stretch from sea to sea."
3. "There is gold on my land!"
4. "I will lead my people to freedom from slavery!"
5. "A house divided against itself cannot stand."

## B. Decide if you agree or disagree with each of the following statements. If you disagree, write the statement so that you can agree with it.

1. Texas fought for independence from Spain.
2. Conflicts with Britain over the Oregon Country were settled peacefully.
3. The North was an agricultural region. The South was an industrial region.
4. The invention of the cotton gin almost ended slavery.
5. Most southern plantation owners had schools to teach their slaves to read.
6. Northerners thought the war would be a quick victory.
7. The North had more soldiers than the South.
8. John Wilkes Booth thought he was helping the South by shooting Lincoln.
9. President Andrew Johnson did not agree with Congress's reconstruction plans.

# A Changing America

**Chapter 13:**

# The Last Frontier

**East meets West**

## Chapter Learning Objectives

- Describe how people traveled west during the 19th Century.
- Explain what life was like for the pioneers who settled the West.
- Describe how the railroads changed the lives of the Native Americans.
- Tell where the Native Americans went as the white men took their lands.

# Words to Know

**ambush**   a surprise attack

**nomads**   people who wander about from one area to another

**pioneers**   people who go first, who open the way for others to follow

**prairie**   large area of flat or rolling grassland

**reservation**   an area of land set aside for American Indians

**transcontinental**   going across a continent

**treaty**   a written agreement

**wagon train**   a line of wagons that carried settlers westward

The movement of people in the United States has followed the sun. "Going west," they called it. Americans had been doing it long before Lewis and Clark. When the East Coast became crowded, people had packed up and traveled to the frontier. The photo on the left shows the completion of the first rail line to link the eastern and western parts of the country. In this chapter, you will learn how this connection was made in the 19th Century.

## Wagons West

How did families go west? There were few roads. Most of them were in terrible shape. In dry weather, the dust was so thick it coated travelers' bodies. In wet weather, the roads became rivers of mud. When a horse or wagon got stuck, it could take all day to get it out.

Still, wagons rolled west. **Pioneers** usually waited until enough wagons were ready to travel to make a **wagon train**. It was safer to travel in large groups. The wagon train offered some protection against Indian attacks. The pioneers could help one another face sickness, wild animals, and rough country.

The covered wagons were usually pulled by mules or oxen. A 2,000 mile journey would take about six months. The road west included the rough trail through the Rocky Mountains.

In 1836, the first white women crossed the plains. They were Narcissa Whitman and Elizabeth Spalding. Soon entire families were following the cry of "Westward Ho!"

Such a distance could be covered today by plane in about three hours.

## Pioneer Life

Nearly everyone in the West lived on a farm. Families worked long, hard hours. They had settled in land with thick forests. Their first job was to clear the land. For months, a family might live under a piece of cloth tied to the trees.

After the land was cleared, a family would put up a log cabin. Inside, it was likely to be dark, dusty, and crowded. Cold air blew through the walls. When it rained, the dirt floor turned to mud. The cabin's single room served as bedroom, kitchen, living room, and dining room.

There was always plenty of work to do. Family members planted crops in the fields. They hunted and collected firewood in the forests. There was usually something to prepare in the kitchen.

There were very few stores. If people needed tools, they either made them or traded for them. They spent their evenings making soap, cloth, and shoes.

How does this compare with how you spend your time?

Life on the frontier could be lonely. The families got together for long parties. People played as hard as they worked. The dancing, eating, drinking, and singing went on through the day and night.

## Rails West

It was one of the greatest races in American history. For six years, two railroad companies laid track. They worked toward each other. One company headed west and the other east. The plan was to meet somewhere along the route. Each side was racing to put down the most track before they met. They were building America's first **transcontinental** railroad.

In December of 1863, the crews of the Central Pacific Railroad began working near Sacramento, California. Most of the workers were Chinese immigrants. They had made the long trip to America for a chance to earn a decent living. For six years they pushed east. Sometimes they had to blast tunnels through solid rock, with workers hanging out over the edges of cliffs to set dynamite.

While the Central Pacific laid track from the West, the Union Pacific Railroad worked on America's Great Plains. Its crews had started in Omaha, Nebraska. These workers were mostly African Americans and Irish and German immigrants. They pushed their way across the Plains and up through the Rockies. In the summer, many fainted from the heat. In the winter, many died from the cold.

The railroad's path was sometimes blocked by 40-foot snowdrifts.

The heat and cold were not the only worries. As the railroads crossed the country, they cut through many native hunting grounds. Angry tribes began attacking railroad crews and supply trains.

The work did not stop. On May 10, 1869, the two companies met at a place in Utah called Promontory Point. The president of the Central Pacific Railroad was Leland Stanford. He pounded a solid gold spike into the ground. That spike would hold together the last two sections of rail. One had been laid by a Union Pacific crew, the other by a Central Pacific Crew. A message flashed over the telegraph lines: "From the Atlantic to the Pacific, the country is linked by rail."

The event was celebrated in Chicago with a seven-mile-long parade.

## Settling In

It wasn't until after the Civil War that large numbers of people began settling between the

**Leland Stanford**

Mississippi River and the Rocky Mountains. This large **prairie**, known as the Great Plains, became the last frontier.

By the 1890s, five rail lines ran across the Great Plains to the West Coast. Hundreds of towns sprang up along their paths. The land between the Mississippi and the Rockies became filled with farmers, ranchers, miners and townspeople. Beef cattle were brought to the cattle towns. Crops were brought to the farm towns. From the towns the cattle and crops were shipped east.

In the 250 years between 1620 and 1870, Americans had settled about 400 million acres of land.

In the 30 years between 1870 and 1900, another 400 million acres were settled. The central and western prairies and woodlands were "tamed" with

Today the Great Plains is a major source of the country's food.

Space can still be thought of as a frontier. So can Earth's oceans, especially their deeper parts.

the machines of the East.

By 1900, the "last frontier" had disappeared.

## Learn More About It: The Homestead Act

In 1862 the United States government passed the Homestead Act. This law encouraged people to settle the frontier. It offered 160 acres of land free to anyone who farmed it for five years. Thousands took advantage of the offer. Swedes, Norwegians, and Germans, as well as settlers from the eastern United States, made new homes on the Plains.

Plains settlers had to adapt to the dry, treeless country. Winds roared across the flat land, blowing dust in the summers and snow in the winters. Because there were so few trees for lumber, the settlers built their houses out of the hard, top layer of the earth, called sod. The sod houses stayed cool during the blazing summers and warm during the freezing winters.

Homesteaders found ways to solve other problems of the Plains. They built windmills to pump water from deep beneath the ground. They put up barbed wire fences to protect their crops from cattle ranchers' wandering herds. They built America's plains into a great farming region.

## History Practice

Answer these questions on a separate sheet of paper.

1. Why did pioneers travel in wagon trains?

2. What is the land between the Mississippi River and the Rocky Mountains called?

3. What were some of the difficulties faced by those who built the transcontinental railroad?

## Follow the Buffalo

The railroads brought many good things to the white settlers of the Great Plains. But they brought little good to the Plains Native Americans, many of whom were **nomads**. They followed roaming buffalo herds and hunted them from horseback.

To the natives of the Plains, the buffalo was life itself. No part of the animal was allowed to go to waste. The Native Americans ate buffalo meat. They used the skins for clothing and for coverings for their tents. They made tools and weapons from the bones. Buffalo droppings became fuel for their fires.

What would happen if the buffalo should disappear? It had always lived on the Great Plains. It seemed it always would.

## The End of the Buffalo

The railroad companies, however, saw things in a different light. They thought of the buffalo as a cheap source of food for their workers.

But the railroad companies also saw the buffalo as a cause of trouble. The animals needed large areas of ground on which to graze. Sometimes the buffalo tore up track as they moved from one place to another.

To deal with this, the railroad companies began hiring hunters. One of the hunters hired was "Buffalo Bill" Cody.

In one 18-month period, Cody killed more than 4,000 buffalo. He did this while working for the Kansas Pacific Railroad.

And Cody was only one of the hunters who were helping make more and longer rail lines possible.

But even after the railroads were built, the killing continued.

Shooting buffalo became a popular sport. Bored travelers would lean out of train windows and blast away at them.

In the 1860s, there had been 15 million buffalo on the Great Plains. It is interesting to note that in 1865, the *human* population of the United States was only 36 million.

In 1868, a Kansas Pacific train had to wait eight hours for a single herd to cross its tracks.

By the 1890s, there were no more than a few thousand of the animals left.

## Great Names in History: Sitting Bull

He had earned his name when he was 12 years old and had forced a buffalo calf to sit back on its haunches. His father taught him to be a Sioux warrior. But Sitting Bull became more than just a warrior. He was wise. Many saw the light of great spirits in his eyes. Sitting Bull became a powerful medicine man.

When white men came to the plains, Sitting Bull did not understand their ways. He told his people to follow the animals far into the hills and leave the strangers alone.

The white men kept coming. They built forts, and they stayed. "The Great Father in Washington wants to make peace with all the tribes," a soldier said. "Each tribe will have its own lands. Everything will be fair for all."

Other tribes agreed to the white man's **treaties**. Sitting Bull would not agree. If the white men left his people alone, they had nothing to fear. If not, then his tribe must protect itself.

Sitting Bull became Chief of all Sioux. He kept his tribe clear of the white men and away from trouble until 1864. Then white men began killing whole tribes of Native Americans. Sitting Bull knew they must fight back. He sent his war chief, Crazy Horse, into battle against General Custer. It was a Sioux victory, but Sitting Bull knew it was not the end. The angry government would force the Sioux onto a reservation. Sitting Bull felt he could not live on a reservation. He took his people to Canada.

There was no food in Canada. The hunting was poor. The weather was cold. The people had to return or starve. Sitting Bull decided not to move

*(continued on page 227)*

*(continued from page 226)*

onto the reservation. Instead he spent several years traveling with Buffalo Bill Cody's Wild West Show. The show billed him as a "real, live Indian Chief!"

But Sitting Bull was forced at last to live on a reservation. Reservation agents feared the power he seemed to have over his people. They were afraid that Sitting Bull would lead an uprising. When Sitting Bull was 60 years old, soldiers and police came to arrest him. "I am not going with you!" Sitting Bull shouted. He turned away from them. The police shot him in the back. Sitting Bull, Chief of all Sioux, died on the reservation. The days of the great tribes were over.

**Sitting Bull**

## Broken Treaties

The Native Americans lost more than the buffalo, their main source of life. The settlers built fences. This made travel across the Plains very difficult. The land itself was being taken from the natives.

The United States wrote treaties which forced the Native Americans onto reservations. The government had set aside for them areas it thought no one else would want.

The treaties promised the Native Americans that the white men would leave them alone "for as long as the grass grows or the water flows." However, most of the treaties were soon broken. One of the reasons for this was that gold and silver were discovered on **reservation** lands.

The Native Americans began to believe they had to fight to keep their way of life. Some, such as the Sioux and the Cheyenne, began attacking groups of miners and farmers.

The Indians had one great victory. In 1876, thousands of Sioux gathered in Montana along the Little Big Horn River. An American army force led by Colonel George Custer rode into an **ambush** and was wiped out.

The Sioux did not enjoy their victory for long. The army had too many soldiers and too many modern arms. In a few months, it defeated the Sioux. They were forced back onto the reservations.

One American general said, "We took away their country and their means of support. We broke up their way of living, their habit of life. It was for this that they made war. Could anyone expect less?"

## Then and Now: Alaska, A New Frontier

**Then:** The western United States was no longer an unexplored mystery. But farther north lay a land most Americans knew very little about. That land was Alaska, and it belonged to Russia.

In 1867, Russia offered to sell Alaska. President Andrew Jackson left the Alaskan purchase to his Secretary of State, William Seward. Seward wanted the United States to buy Alaska. He was able to get the Senate to approve the purchase. The United States bought Alaska for $7,200,000. Most Americans thought Seward was crazy. Many called Alaska "Seward's Folly" and "Seward's Icebox." They thought buying the frozen land was a terrible idea. They were wrong.

**Now:** Some people still call Alaska "The Last Frontier." In 1896, gold was discovered in Alaska. People then thought that William Seward had a pretty good idea after all. Alaska is rich in minerals, fish, timber, and oil. A huge pipeline brings crude oil out of the far north to the Alaskan coast for shipment in tankers. In 1959, Alaska became the 49th state. It was the first state that did not share a border with any other state. Alaska is the largest state in the Union.

## History Practice

Answer these questions on a separate sheet of paper.

1. Why was the buffalo so important to the Native Americans?

2. How did the railroad companies look upon the buffalo?

3. What is one of the reasons treaties between Native Americans and whites were broken?

# Chapter Review

## Summary

| CHRONOLOGY OF MAJOR EVENTS | |
| --- | --- |
| 1840 | Pioneers travel the Oregon Trail |
| 1849 | California Gold Rush |
| 1865 | End of Civil War |
| 1865-86 | Indian wars; U.S. battles Plains Indians |
| 1867 | United States buys Alaska from Russia |
| 1869 | Transcontinental railroad completed |
| 1874 | Gold discovered on Sioux land in South Dakota |
| 1876 | Sioux fight General Custer at Battle of Little Big Horn |

- Pioneers traveled west in wagon trains. Later a transcontinental railroad was built. The Central Pacific and the Union Pacific Railroads met in Utah.

- Farmers, ranchers, and miners of the Great Plains made their livings from the West's natural resources.

- Native Americans depended on the buffalo for food, clothing, tools, and weapons. The coming of the white man and the railroad meant the end of the buffalo.

- The white man took the good land. Native Americans were moved to reservations. Treaties were broken when the reservation lands proved valuable. That land was taken away, too.

- The Native Americans fought for their lives and their land but they were no match for the white man's numbers and arms.

## Chapter Quiz

1. List three hardships pioneers faced on the trail.

2. List three hardships settlers faced in the West.

3. What form of transportation made settlement of the Great Plains easier?

4. How long did it take to build the transcontinental railroad between Sacramento and Omaha? In which states are these cities?

5. The U.S. government wrote treaties with the Native Americans. The treaties sometimes included the phrase "for as long as grass grows or water runs." What did this mean?

6. Which event changed people's minds about the value of Alaska? What had they thought before this?

## Thinking and Writing

1. Describe at least three ways your life differs from the life of a pioneer. In what ways is your life easier? In what ways is your life more difficult?

2. Most people would agree that the U.S. government did not treat the Native Americans fairly. Describe what you think might have been a fairer way to settle the West.

3. What kind of problems faced a 19th century Native American chief? What decisions did he have to make?

4. Chief Joseph of the Nez Perce once said, "All men were made by the same Great Spirit Chief . . . . Whenever the white man treats the natives as they treat each other, then we shall have no more wars." Explain what Chief Joseph meant.

**Chapter 14:**

# A New Age for Industry

| 1860 | | 1920 |
|---|---|---|
| | era of invention and rapid industrial growth | |

**On December 17, 1903, Wilbur and Orville Wright flew the first heavier-than-air flying machine.**

## Chapter Learning Objectives

- Tell how the inventions of Thomas Edison, Henry Ford, and Alexander Graham Bell changed life in America.
- Describe the problems faced by America's rapidly growing cities.
- Explain how the growth of big business affected American workers.
- Tell why workers formed labor unions.

# Words to Know

**aqueducts**   large pipes that bring water from one place to another

**assemble**   to build

**building codes**   sets of laws and requirements that buildings must meet

**corrupt**   dishonest

**mass production**   the manufacturing of goods in large numbers at low cost

**patent**   the right given to someone by the government to be the only one who can make and sell a new invention

**phonograph**   a record player

**skyscraper**   a very tall building

**tenements**   run-down, crowded apartment buildings

**refinery**   a factory where something like oil or sugar is broken down into a purer form

**zoning laws**   rules that control building in certain parts of a city

---

When Orville and Wilbur Wright were born, the West was still wild. Pioneers were still heading for the frontier.

By the time they were young men, the frontier had vanished. There didn't seem to be any place left for pioneers.

But the Wright brothers lifted their eyes and saw a different territory. The air above would be their frontier.

This was the spirit that fired the new industrial age. In this chapter, you will learn how this new age affected life in America.

## Thomas Edison

He had already invented the **phonograph**. Now Thomas Edison wanted to light up America's cities. Some of the world's greatest minds had been trying for years to use electricity to make light. Edison was sure he could do what no one else had done. He would make small lights for use in homes and offices.

Think about how much we depend on the electric light bulb today. When something causes the electricity to go off, what do you miss the most?

Edison wanted to run a current through a thin thread set in a glass bulb. He spent two years searching for the right kind of thread or wire. He tried everything he could think of—gold, silver, cloth, wool, animal hair, human hair. No matter what he put in the bulb, it wouldn't stay lit. He sent people to Japan and to the jungles of the Amazon. Nothing they brought back worked.

Everyone was ready to give up. Everyone, that is, but Edison. One December night in 1879, he tried putting some cotton thread in the bulb. It worked! When the current was turned on, the bulb lit up the workshop. And it stayed lit. It burned through the night and into the next day. It went out only when Edison put extra current through the wire.

Something that looked almost like magic was about to affect people everywhere.

Edison did not want his invention to be only for the rich. He wanted as many people as possible to be able to light their homes. He built a power station in New York in 1882. It sent electricity to homes and businesses. "We'll make electric light so cheap," he said, "that only the rich will be able to burn candles."

By the early 1900s, many homes, offices, and stores had electric lights. No longer did families have to use candles at night. No longer did students have to read by oil lamps. Now they could flick a switch to get bright, steady light.

Thomas Edison had a talent for coming up with new ideas. He believed in try, try, and try again. When a new idea didn't work, he just kept trying until he succeeded. In his lifetime Edison applied for nearly 1,100 **patents** for new designs and products. His ideas changed the lives of Americans and made him known as the "wizard" of invention.

# Henry Ford

It was 1876 when Henry Ford first saw a horseless carriage. He was just 13 and was on a trip to Detroit with his father. A huge, black, iron machine clanked along the road before them. The machine was noisy and ugly. It scared the horse that pulled the Fords' wagon. But, the machine moved along under its own power. Henry Ford thought it was wonderful.

By the 1890s, several horseless carriages were on the market. But they were all expensive. Very few were built and each took a long time to make. Only the rich could buy them.

Henry Ford believed he could make a car that most families could afford. He worked on his ideas in a little shop behind his house. One evening in 1893, he called his wife Claire to the shop. "It is ready!" he exclaimed. Henry took Claire for a ride in his own invention.

In time, Ford developed a gas-powered car that people could afford. His car was strong. It was easy to drive. Best of all, the new "Ford" sold for only $850. Other automobiles of the day sold for up to $8,000. None cost less than $1,000.

By 1908, Ford had produced his biggest seller, the Model T.

How did he do it? How did Ford produce cars quickly and at low cost?

Ford used **mass production**. Many automobiles were produced at once in a factory. Workers stood along moving **assembly** lines. Each worker had a separate job. Ford was the first to use this process on a large scale. He became known as the "father of the assembly line."

Henry Ford was a good man to work for. "Every man has a right to live well," he said. Ford raised wages and shortened work weeks.

**The Model T Ford**

**Some U.S. inventions that boosted business and changed life in America:**

| INVENTION | DATE | INVENTOR |
|---|---|---|
| sewing machine | 1846 | Howe |
| railroad sleeping car | 1865 | Pullman |
| typewriter | 1867 | Sholes, Soule, Glidden |
| refrigerated railroad car | 1868 | David |
| telephone | 1876 | Bell |
| phonograph | 1877 | Edison |
| electric light bulb | 1879 | Edison |
| cash register | 1879 | Ritty |
| zipper | 1891 | Judson |
| gasoline automobile | 1892 | Duryea |

# New Inventions Lead to New Industries

At one time, nearly everything had been made of wood or iron. Power came from humans or animals. Or it came from steam. In the new America, there were railroads, bridges, and factories. They were made with steel. The energy that kept everything running came from coal, oil, and electricity.

In the 1850s, inventors found cheaper ways to make steel from iron and coal. This led to the birth of new industries. One industry was started to dig more iron ore and coal out of the ground. Another industry melted these two together to produce steel.

Steel and oil are basic products in modern life. Name some other industries and products that depend on steel and oil.

# Growth of Cities

Wherever there was a large group of factories, a city grew up around it. The cities attracted people seeking jobs. Older cities became larger. New cities sprang up where there had been only small towns. People needed food and clothing and homes. New businesses supplied these needs. America was becoming a land of big cities.

Some of the cities specialized in a certain industry or product. Pittsburgh, Pennsylvania, for example, became known for its steel yards. In Cleveland, Ohio the main industry was building locomotives for the nation's railroads. Chicago, Illinois became a transportation center, the hub of America's railways.

Exciting things were happening in the cities. Edison's electric light lit up the outdoors as well as the indoors. People could stay out later at night. Theaters, restaurants, circuses, and concerts made city life interesting and different.

Did any industries lead to the growth of your city or town?

All over America, new inventions were changing people's lives. Alexander Graham Bell had wondered if electricity could carry the human voice over a wire. In 1876, after years of work, he had come up with something he called the telephone. Service began in New Haven, Connecticut, in 1878 with 21 customers. Thirty years later, millions had phones.

The manufacture of steel beams meant that the cities could grow upwards. The first **skyscraper** was built in Chicago in the 1880s. It was ten stories high. With the invention of electric elevators, the buildings soon went even higher.

The cities stretched out as well as up. Electric streetcars and railroads were built. People could then live farther from their jobs.

The Sears Tower in Chicago, Illinois is the tallest building in the world. It is 110 stories high. What is the tallest building in your city or town?

**Thomas Edison**

The growth of big cities meant new problems. This chart lists some of those problems and some of the solutions that were found for them.

How does your city handle these problems?

| PROBLEMS | SOLUTIONS |
|---|---|
| water | Cities built **aqueducts** to bring water from lakes and rivers. |
| garbage | Cities collected garbage and burned it. |
| fire fighting | Small towns had volunteer fire departments. Bigger cities had fulltime firemen. |
| crime | Cities hired policemen. |
| transportation | Electric streetcars, bridges, and elevated railways helped people move about. Boston opened the first subway system in 1897. |
| housing | People crowded into **tenements**. **Building codes** and **zoning laws** helped control overcrowding. |

## History Practice

Answer these questions on a separate sheet of paper.

1. How did Ford cut costs and make his product more widely available?

2. How is steel produced?

3. What invention by Alexander Graham Bell improved communication in the United States?

4. What were three problems that rapidly growing cities faced?

## The Oil Industry

For years, people in Pennsylvania had noticed an oily liquid that dripped from between the rocks. The Native Americans and some pioneers had used it for medicine. Oil was once called "black glue." Many thought it was worthless. The first oil well in America was drilled in 1859. It was in Titusville, Pennsylvania. "Black glue" soon became "black gold."

In the 1860s, people started using oil for heating and lighting. This was the start of another industry.

Thousands of people rushed to the oil fields. They were all trying to strike it rich.

One of them was a young man named John D. Rockefeller. He saw, as few others did, just how important oil would become. Working out of Cleveland, Ohio, he started his own **refinery**. Things went well, and Rockefeller started buying other refineries in the country. He also owned drilling fields, pipelines, and tank cars. His company was Standard Oil.

It was one of the largest in the United States. John D. Rockefeller became one of the wealthiest men in the world.

## Workers' Rights

Rockefeller often said, "Don't be afraid to work." He took his own advice. He worked days, months, and years without a break. However, not everyone gained by this advice as Rockefeller did. Most people worked long and hard at their jobs for very little money.

Many people worked 12 or 13 hours a day, six days a week. The factories were dark, dirty, and often unsafe. Children also worked, sometimes for as little as 25 cents a day. Those that did had little time to study or play.

Later, laws were made to protect children. But the factories remained terrible places. There was no such thing as a vacation. Workers who were hurt on the job were not paid. Workers who got sick were not paid. Anyone who asked for higher pay or better working conditions could be fired.

One worker alone had little power to change things for the better. But many acting together might bring about changes. Labor unions were formed for this purpose. These were groups of workers who fought for better conditions and higher pay.

The unions did help many workers. But the struggles were hard. And the unions did not always win.

Sometimes dark, dirty factories were called "sweatshops." How do you think they got that name?

**Factory worker**

## Great Names in History: Alice Hamilton

Alice Hamilton, a young doctor from Indiana, was a pioneer of work safety. She visited factories around the country looking for problems. She showed the owners how to make their factories safer. She pointed out the need for federal and state safety laws.

## Some Big-Business Terms to Know

**corporation**   a group of people joining together in one business. Small businesses may join together to make one large one. Carnegie Steel became part of United States Steel in the early 1900s.

**stock**   shares in a business. People can buy stock in a corporation. Depending on how many shares they own, they receive a certain amount of the profits.

**trust**   a group of businesses joined together to control production and prices. In 1870, John D. Rockefeller formed the Standard Oil Company of Ohio. In the 1800s the Standard Oil Trust was formed. It controlled most of the oil in the United States.

**monopoly**   complete control of a product or service by a single person or company. A monopoly can set prices as it chooses (as a trust can).

Samuel Gompers came to America from London, England. When he was just 13, he joined his father working in a cigar making shop. Sam was a good speaker. When the cigar makers had problems with their boss, Sam was their spokesman.

Sam Gompers wanted to see the workers treated fairly. When a fellow cigar maker was cheated, Sam said he would quit. He encouraged other workers to do the same. The boss backed down. Sam saw that the workers had power if they stood together.

In 1886, one of the largest national labor unions was formed. It was called the American Federation of Labor (the AF of L). Samuel Gompers was its first president. Gompers and the AF of L wanted better hours, wages, and working conditions. They did not want strikes. Gompers always tried to work things out first. A strike was his "last weapon." A strike was called only if all else failed. "A fair day's wage for a fair day's work," said Gompers and the AF of L.

## The Steel Industry

After the Civil War, steel began taking the place of iron as America's basic building material. It was stronger than iron and didn't rust as quickly. The new city skyscrapers were made of steel. Bridges were made of steel. The wire that fenced in America's farms and ranches was made of steel.

Andrew Carnegie was an immigrant from Scotland. He became the king of steel in America. As a young man, Carnegie worked hard. Making money was the most important thing in his life. In 1865, he went into the iron business. Later he went into steel. He opened the first steel mill in Pennsylvania. Then he bought more mills. By 1892, Carnegie had steel mills all around Pittsburgh. He was making from two to twenty million dollars a year.

Carnegie bought coal mines. He bought ships and railroads to carry his products and equipment. Carnegie owned the steel business from beginning to end.

He became a very rich man. Carnegie did give much of his money to help others. He spent over 60 million dollars building 2,811 libraries. He gave money to colleges and churches, and set up a fund for world peace.

But Andrew Carnegie could also be a hard man. His Homestead Steel Works in Pennsylvania was one of the toughest places a person could work. Men worked within inches of melted steel. Often they were badly burned. Those who were hurt were taken off the payroll.

**Some people called Andrew Carnegie a very kind man. Others said he tried to make up for treating his workers poorly by giving away gifts and money.**

## Violence at Homestead

In 1892, the Homestead workers were told that the company was going to cut their pay. They decided to go out on strike.

The owners of the mill were not going to give in. A 12-foot high fence was put up around the mill. New workers were hired. Guards were brought in to keep the mill going. When the guards tried to enter the mill, a bloody fight broke out. Nine strikers and seven guards were killed. The state government sent troops to Homestead to keep the mill open and arrest strikers. Many workers could not get their jobs back. They had to seek work in another town in the middle of winter. Those who could return found that their pay had been cut almost in half.

**In 1892, workers at the Homestead plant made 14 cents an hour. What is the minimum wage today?**

The union movement suffered from this defeat. Factory owners all over America held out against the unions. It would be years before the government and the owners were willing to accept unions. Only then were workers able to win fair wages and safer working conditions.

Cities have faced strikes by police, firefighters, street cleaners, and teachers. Have you ever been affected by a strike?

## New Regulations Control Business

Some people feared that big business could become a threat to democracy. The owners of large companies could get the government to pass certain laws. They could destroy small businesses. They could charge any price they wanted for their goods. Prices were going up and the quality of goods was going down.

Ohio Senator John Sherman told Congress that it must limit the power of big business trusts. In 1890, the federal government passed the Sherman Anti-trust Act. It said that trusts and monopolies were against the law. Big business hired lawyers to find ways around the new regulations, but the act helped small businesses survive.

Do you remember reading about protective tariffs? The government taxed foreign goods to get people to buy American goods. In this way the government helped American businesses.

How does the government encourage people to "buy American" today?

The government also helped by controlling shipping costs. The powerful railroad companies were taking advantage of the small businesses. Some railroad companies charged higher prices to the small farmer than to big manufacturers. Large shippers sometimes received secret discounts for giving their business to the railroad companies. The Interstate Commerce Act of 1887 allowed the government to control the cost of shipping goods between states.

## Corrupt Politicians

Some businessmen were **corrupt**. They cheated the government and the citizens out of millions of dollars.

In New York City, William Tweed cheated the city through "improvement schemes." Tweed charged the city more for goods and services than they were worth—a lot more. Tweed had a great deal of power. He controlled the mayor and other city officials. Tweed paid them to do what he said. His schemes earned him close to 200 million dollars.

People like Tweed were called "Bosses." Boss Tweed and his group of businessmen were called Tammany Hall.

A man named Thomas Nast drew cartoons for New York newspapers. His cartoons showed Boss Tweed and Tammany Hall for what they were. In 1871, Tammany Hall was taken apart. Boss Tweed died in prison.

October 7, 1871

"Stop Thief!"

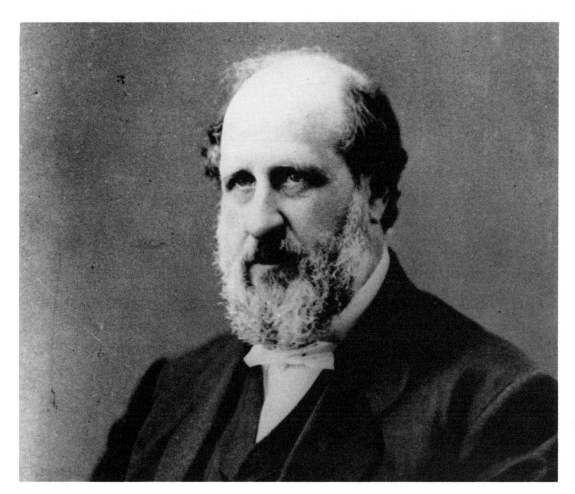

**Boss Tweed**

## History Practice

Answer these questions on a separate sheet of paper.

1. When did steel become such an important product?

2. What was the purpose of the trusts?

3. Why did the government place tariffs on foreign goods?

# Chapter Review

## Summary

| CHRONOLOGY OF MAJOR EVENTS | |
|---|---|
| 1867 | First elevated railway opens in New York City |
| 1876 | Bell invents telephone |
| 1877 | Edison invents phonograph |
| 1879 | Edison invents electric light |
| 1886 | Samuel Gompers starts AF of L |
| 1887 | Interstate Commerce Act |
| 1890 | Sherman Anti-Trust Act |
| 1892 | Homestead Steel Mill strike |
| 1897 | First subway system opens in Boston |
| 1903 | Orville and Wilbur Wright make first successful airplane flight |
| 1908 | Ford manufactures Model T |

- Thomas Edison's invention of the electric light changed American life.

- Henry Ford began mass producing automobiles.

- The oil and steel industries grew. America became a leading industrial nation. The growth of industry meant the rapid growth of cities.

- John D. Rockefeller gained control of the oil business. Andrew Carnegie gained control of the steel industry. Huge corporations were formed. Trusts and monopolies destroyed small businesses.

- Many factories were unsafe and unhealthy.

- Labor unions were formed to protect workers' rights.

- The federal government passed laws to protect small businesses.

## Chapter Quiz

1. Of what historic importance is Titusville, Pennsylvania?

2. Why did workers form unions?

3. What did Alice Hamilton and Samuel Gompers have in common?

4. How many years passed between the founding of the Standard Oil Company and the outlawing of trusts?

5. When and how was the cost of shipping goods from one state to another controlled?

6. Who ran Tammany Hall?

## Thinking and Writing

Think about the following questions. Then write your answers on a separate sheet of paper.

1. Tell five ways Americans' lives changed after Edison invented the electric light.

2. Name three inventions mentioned in this chapter other than the electric light. Explain how each affects your life today.

3. Choose a 20th century invention. Explain how it has changed Americans' lives.

## Chapter 15:

# A Nation of Immigrants

| 1840 | | 1929 |
|------|--|------|
| | years of large-scale immigration | the Golden Door closes |

**European immigrant**

## Chapter Learning Objectives

- Tell why people immigrated to America.
- Describe problems faced by newcomers to the United States.
- Explain why some native-born Americans did not like the new immigrants.
- Explain what a quota system is.

# Words to Know

**ghettos**  poor neighborhoods where people from one or more ethnic backgrounds live apart from others

**opportunity**  chance; a "land of opportunity" is a place where people have a chance to improve their lives

**prejudice**  hatred of a group of people, usually because of their race or religion

**quota system**  an immigration plan passed by Congress in the 1920s; it let in only a certain number of people from each country

**refugees**  people who have fled to a new country

**Scandinavia**  a part of northern Europe; it includes Denmark, Norway, Sweden, and Finland

**steerage**  the part of a ship where passengers paying the lowest fares stay

---

In 1912, in her book, *The Promised Land*, Mary Antin wrote: " . . . at last I was going to America! Really, really going, at last! . . . The winds rushed in from outer space, roaring in my ears, America! America!"

The United States is a land of immigrants. People have been coming here for many years. They still are today. In this chapter you will read about the years when the wave of immigration was at its peak.

## One Woman's Story

For two stormy weeks, the *Polynesia* had been steaming across the Atlantic. On the morning of May 18, 1893, Mary Antin had her first view of America.

First she saw trees. As the ship got closer, she saw the tops of buildings. The ship steamed slowly into the New York harbor. In Russia, the old country, Mary Antin had never seen a building taller than four

**Many immigrants came to America alone. Then they saved enough money to send for their families.**

stories. Before her were buildings that were 25 stories high. There were boats everywhere in the busy harbor. On Liberty Island was the Statue of Liberty. It was now eight years since the statue had been built. To Mary, it seemed a perfect sign of the powerful and free new country she was entering.

Everyone crowded to the rail to get a better look. It was a sight they would never forget.

The ship docked, and Mary saw her father. He had left Russia three years ago and settled in Boston. There he had saved enough money to send for Mary, her mother, two sisters, and a brother. He threw his arms around his family and smiled happily. "So now you are all Americans," he said.

Like many others, Mary Antin was an immigrant to the United States.

## Learn More About It: The Statue of Liberty

Since 1886, the Statue of Liberty has welcomed ships to New York Harbor. It was a gift of friendship from France to the United States. The Statue also has stood for the liberty enjoyed by free nations around the world. The Statue of Liberty arrived from France in 214 pieces. It was put together on Bedloe's Island. Later the island was renamed Liberty Island. In 1908, a poem by Emma Lazarus was carved at the statue's base.

*"Give me your tired, your poor,*
*Your huddled masses yearning to breathe free,*
*The wretched refuse of your teeming shore.*
*Send these, the homeless tempest-tossed to me,*
*I lift my lamp beside the golden door!"*

# Old Immigrants and New Immigrants

This is a "nation of immigrants," of people born in other places. In the last 200 years, more people have come to this country to live than to any other. More than 35 million entered the United States between 1840 and 1920.

In 1845, the potato crop in Ireland failed. Potatoes were the main food of the Irish peasants. Hunger drove a million Irish people from their country. They hoped to find a way to feed their families in America.

Before 1885, the immigrants came mainly from northern and western Europe. These people are known as the "Old Immigrants." They were from such places as Germany, England, and **Scandinavia**. They often settled in the central and western parts of the United States. Many Irish also arrived then. Most settled in Boston and New York and in other eastern cities. Africans, as we have learned, had been forced into slavery in the South.

During the 1880s the numbers of immigrants greatly increased. Many came from the countries of southern and eastern Europe. They were from Greece, Italy, Hungary, Austria, Poland, and Russia. By the 1890s, millions of "New Immigrants"—those who came after 1885—were flowing into the United States each year.

Like the Old Immigrants, the New Immigrants came for several reasons. They came to escape poverty and hunger. They came because they were ruled by unjust governments. The Old Immigrants worked mostly at farming. Many New Immigrants worked in the factories and mines of a growing America.

It is very likely that you have relatives who immigrated to America. Find out where they came from. What is the story of their journey here? What were their new lives here like?

**Passage to America**

### The Golden Door

The New Immigrants came by steamship. Most were poor and they spent the ocean trip in **steerage**. Their quarters were dark and dirty. Many people got sick. Some died.

Most immigrants stopped at Ellis Island in New York Harbor. Here doctors made sure they were healthy. Anyone found sick had to return home. The immigrants had to answer such questions as: "Do you have any family in America? Do you have a skill or a job?"

**Where do you think the phrase "the golden door" comes from?**

Ellis Island was often a scary place. The newcomers were tired from their long trip. They did not know what would happen to them here. Many worried that they would be sent back on the next ship. Few spoke English. Some people called Ellis Island the "Island of Tears."

From 1892 to 1954 more than 6 million people passed through Ellis Island. They brought their hopes and their dreams with them.

## The Strange and the New

It would be awhile, however, before their dreams could become real. The new land seemed very strange. In the cities, everything moved quickly. People spoke and dressed in ways the newcomers hadn't known before. Even the churches, schools, and stores were different from those in the old country.

The immigrants usually moved into parts of the cities where other people from their homelands lived. Neighborhoods like these were called **ghettos**. They had names like Little Italy, Little Poland, and Little China. The neighborhoods held some of the spirit of the immigrants' native lands. Customs, diets, and languages were kept alive.

Most of America's immigrants were poor. Many did not speak a word of English. Often they had come from farming villages. They weren't used to living in crowded apartments.

Some historians described the waves of immigrants as creating a "melting pot" in America where different cultures and traditions melted into one. But more recently the United States has been described as a "salad bowl." Each culture adds its distinct flavors and traditions to the mix.

Are there any neighborhoods in your city where a lot of people of one nationality or race live together?

Today Americans eat foods from Italy, Greece, China, France, Japan, Thailand, and many other lands. What is your favorite "foreign" food?

More and more immigrants entered the cities. Before too long, there were not enough places for them to live. Old buildings soon became crowded. Tenements were built quickly and cheaply. These buildings were often dark and narrow. Landlords crowded families into small rooms.

In one block of New York City in the 1890s, 577 people lived in just 97 rooms. If things were so bad, why did people continue to come here? America was the land of **opportunity**. The immigrants had lost the hope of bettering themselves in their homelands, where strict lines were drawn between social classes. A person who was born a peasant would most likely always be a peasant. They came to escape injustice, poverty, and disease. They came because of land shortages. They wanted homes and farms of their own. They wanted to make a better living in America. They wanted to be free to practice their religion as they pleased. They wanted education. America was the place where they and their children would have a new start in life.

Why was an education so important to the immigrants and their children?

## History Practice

Answer these questions on a separate sheet of paper.

1. What kind of work did most of the Old Immigrants do? What kind of work did most of the New Immigrants do?

2. What happened at Ellis Island?

3. What were three reasons people came to America?

4. What were some of the difficulties faced by the newcomers?

# A Cold Welcome

Immigrants faced many problems. For years, the United States had welcomed them. Workers had been needed to clear the frontier, build the railroads, and work in the new factories. But as time went on, a lot of Americans changed their minds. The immigrants were willing to work longer hours for lower wages. Some Americans worried that the immigrants would take their jobs.

Others did not like the new citizens because they found their ways of life strange. People forgot that the United States was built up by immigrants—by "outsiders."

Sometimes the immigrants faced so much **prejudice** it was hard to stay hopeful. The Irish Americans, as Catholics, faced prejudice. The Jews and the Italians could not buy houses where they wanted. Signs in shop windows and ads in newspapers showed this prejudice against the immigrant minority groups: "Help Wanted—No Irish need apply," and "Job Available—wages: $1.30–white, $1.25–colored, $1.15–Italian."

People from Asia often settled along the Pacific coast. They went to Washington, Oregon, and California. Many of the Chinese found work building the railroads. Others worked in the gold fields of the West. The Japanese worked hard in America, too. Many saved their money and bought farms. When jobs on the railroads and in the gold fields ended, some Asians returned to their original home. Others took jobs in the West Coast cities and towns. Because they needed the money so badly, Asians sometimes worked for lower wages. This made many white Americans angry. White farmers also talked about a "yellow danger." Chinese and Japanese immigrants were sometimes driven from their homes. Shopkeepers and landowners were beaten and even killed.

Some forms of prejudice still exist in the United States. Have you ever felt it yourself?

Do you know of any
cities that have a
Chinatown?

At one time cities had special areas where Chinese
were forced to live. Some of those areas have
remained home to Chinese people and are still called
"Chinatown."

## The Golden Door Closes

In the 1880s, anti-immigrant groups were formed.
Congress passed laws to stop the heavy flow of
immigrants. An 1881 law said that people could not
move to America without a certain minimum amount
of money. In 1882, the Chinese Exclusion Act
stopped Chinese workers from coming into the
country. It remained in force until 1943. Beginning
in 1917, only people who could read and write were
allowed to immigrate. During the 1920s, new laws
were passed to control the number of people coming
into the country. This was a **quota system**. Only
about 350,000 immigrants a year were allowed in. In
1929, the number was cut to 150,000. People from
northern and western European countries were
permitted before other people were. Those countries
were given higher quotas. Most Africans and Asians
were kept out entirely.

The golden door was being pulled shut.

## The Strength of Our Differences

Immigrants still come here, though not in the
same huge numbers they once did. In the early
1960s, President John F. Kennedy worked to make
fairer immigration laws. In 1965, the old quota
system was ended. New quotas were set. The new
system favored immigrants who had relatives in the
United States and those who had special job skills.

In recent years, many people from Mexico and Central America have come to live here. **Refugees** have come from Cuba, Southeast Asia, and the Soviet Union. Like the immigrants of 100 years ago, they have brought new ways to these shores. They have made our life richer. America's mix of cultures, talents, and skills is one of our greatest sources of strength.

The flow of immigrants into the United States peaked between 1900 and 1910. Then new immigration laws and quotas caused the numbers to fall.

## History Practice

Answer these questions on a separate sheet of paper.

1. Why did prejudice toward immigrant groups grow?

2. In what area of the United States did many Asian immigrants settle?

3. By the 1920s, which groups of people were kept out of the country almost entirely?

4. What did the quota systems mentioned in this chapter control?

# Chapter Review

## Summary

| CHRONOLOGY OF MAJOR EVENTS | |
|---|---|
| 1840–1885 | "Old Immigrants" come to America |
| 1845 | Potato famine hits Ireland |
| 1870–1910 | Heaviest wave of immigrants |
| 1882 | Chinese Exclusion Act |
| 1885–1929 | "New Immigrants" come to America |
| 1886 | Statue of Liberty set up in New York Harbor |
| 1892 | Ellis Island opened as receiving station |
| 1917 | Literacy laws passed to control immigration |
| 1921 | Congress begins quota system |

- The first wave of immigrants came from Germany, England, Ireland, and Scandinavia. They were called Old Immigrants. Most worked as farmers. After 1885, the New Immigrants came from Greece, Italy, Hungary, Austria, Poland, and Russia. Many worked in factories and mines.

- Many Americans worried that immigrants would take away their jobs. Some feared the newcomers different ways of life. Most immigrant groups have faced prejudice.

- Congress set up a quota system to control immigration.

- People still immigrate to the United States. They flee war, poverty, and cruel treatment from harsh governments. Most immigrant groups have faced prejudice.

## Chapter Quiz

1. Which parts of Europe did the "Old Immigrants" come from? Which parts of Europe did the "New Immigrants" come from?

2. How many people arrived in the United States between 1840 and 1920?

3. For how many years was the Chinese Exclusion Act in force?

4. During which ten-year period did the greatest number of people enter the United States?

5. What effect did immigration laws and quotas have on the number of people entering the United States?

6. List three areas from which immigrants to the United States have come in recent years.

## Thinking and Writing

1. Why do you think the gateway to America is called a "golden door"?

2. Why was Ellis Island sometimes called the "Island of Tears"?

3. In your own words, tell how Mary Antin must have felt as she sailed into New York harbor.

4. Compare problems immigrants of the 1800s faced with problems that today's immigrants face.

# Chapter 16:

# An Age of Reform

| 1869 | | 1920 |
|---|---|---|
| | era of social and political change | |

**Ida Tarbell**

## Chapter Learning Objectives

- Tell who the reformers, progressives, and the muckrakers were.
- Describe how progressives tried to make America more democratic.
- Describe the early movement for women's suffrage.

# Words to Know

**bribes**   money given to get someone to do something against the law

**conservation**   the protection of natural resources

**consumers**   those who buy goods

**income tax**   tax on the money people earn

**investigation**   a search for facts

**natural resources**   things we need that are produced by nature; they include forests, minerals, water, and soil

**primary**   an election in which people choose a political party's candidates

**slums**   crowded, run-down parts of town where poor people live

**suffrage**   the right to vote

---

The early 1900s were an exciting time in America. There was a feeling that honest citizens could make changes for the better. People like Ida Tarbell were writing and speaking about the problems they saw around them. Those who worked for change, who wanted to make America a better place, were known as reformers or progressives. In this chapter you will read about the period in which they lived.

## Muckrakers Stir Up America

As industry expanded, some people became very wealthy. The homes of the rich could be seen in any city. Yet close by were the most terrible **slums**. People there lived in poverty.

Many Americans worried that democracy was in danger. They worried that wealthy people and big business would soon run the country. Things had gotten out of hand, some said. Some companies had become giants. You have already read about trusts and monopolies. The country had never been against anyone's making money by working hard. But the trusts seemed to be going too far.

Those who wrote about corruption and greed and the problems of the poor were called "muckrakers." The word *muck* is used to describe dirt, filth, rotting leaves. A "muckraker" is one who "rakes up muck." The muckrakers made America aware of the need for reform.

## Upton Sinclair

> Mary had a little lamb,
> And when she saw it sicken,
> She shipped it off to Packingtown,
> And now it's labeled chicken.

Packingtown was the name given to the stockyards of Chicago. Cattle from throughout the West were taken there to be killed. The meat was then packed, and sent to cities all over the country.

The writer Upton Sinclair had heard the rhyme about Packingtown. But he didn't think it was very funny. He had an idea that some very strange things were going on there. He went into the stockyards to report on them to the public.

**Upton Sinclair**

Sinclair saw sick animals being killed beside healthy ones. He found meat scraps lying on damp dirty floors. Workers spat on the floors when they felt the need to. Rotting meat was scooped up with the remains of dead rats and pieces of rope and wood.

This was made into sausage and canned ham. Government health inspectors were taking **bribes** to overlook the filthy conditions.

When Sinclair finished his **investigatio**n, he felt he would never again eat meat. He decided to write a book that would tell people just what they were eating. He wanted people to know about working conditions in the plants. His novel *The Jungle* was published in 1906.

Sinclair was a muckraker. His writings shocked the country into action. President Theodore Roosevelt and the Congress passed the Pure Food and Drug Act and the Federal Meat Inspection Act. These acts meant a turning point in the protection of **consumers**. *The Jungle* didn't improve the lot of the stockyard workers. But it did make a difference in the quality of the food Americans ate.

"I aimed at the public's heart and by accident I hit it in the stomach," said Sinclair.

## Words from the Past

"It was a nasty job killing these sick cows, for when you plunged your knife into them they would burst and splash foul-smelling stuff into your face . . . . It was enough to make anybody sick, to think people had to eat such stuff as this. But they must be eating it—for the canners were going on preparing it, year after year."

Upton Sinclair, *The Jungle*

## Ida Tarbell

Another of the muckrakers was Ida Tarbell. She was one of the leading writers of her day. Since she wrote histories, her main interest was in the past. But she also had reason to be interested in the present. Her father had once run a small oil company. Then he had been forced out of business by Standard Oil. Ida Tarbell spent five years investigating John D. Rockefeller's company. In 1902, she began writing about it.

Standard Oil was the largest oil refining company in the world. Ida Tarbell's study, *History of the Standard Oil Company* (1904), showed how it got that way. She discovered, for instance, that secret deals had been made between the oil company and the railroads. Standard had forced the railroads to give back some of the money they'd been paid to ship the oil. The rail companies then had to charge other oil companies more for service. Rockefeller was able to sell his oil at a cheaper rate. The smaller companies lost their customers. They were forced to sell their businesses to Standard Oil.

The owner of one refinery said, "There was only one buyer on the market, and we had to sell at their terms."

To most Americans, what had happened was wrong. When they read Ida Tarbell's reports, they began demanding controls on unfair business practices. This resulted in the anti-trust laws you read about in Chapter 14.

## Jacob Riis

As a police reporter for a New York City newspaper, Jacob Riis saw life at its hardest. In 1890, his book *How the Other Half Lives* described some of the problems the cities were facing. In it he wrote about an ordinary slum building.

**Jacob Riis**

Jacob Riis started movements to build parks and playgrounds in New York City. He was determined to improve the city's crowded slums. President Theodore Roosevelt once called Riis "America's most useful citizen."

## Words from the Past

"Be careful! The hall is dark and you might fall over the children pitching pennies there. Not that it would hurt them. They get kicks and slaps every day. They don't have much else. That woman you just bumped into was filling her buckets from the outside hydrants. The people who live here have their sinks in the halls, not their apartments. Everyone on the floor uses one sink. In summer, the terrible smells from the sinks poison everyone."

Jacob Riis, *How the Other Half Lives*

## Jane Addams

Jane Addams grew up in a wealthy part of Chicago. As a young girl, she was given almost anything she wanted. She had no idea how bad things were just a few miles from her home. Then she saw her first slum. Other rich young people had seen the slums and had chosen to turn their backs on them.

At the age of 29, Addams shocked her family by moving into one of Chicago's slums. "There are people there who need help, and I want to help them."

She founded a **settlement house** called Hull House. Here there were nursery schools, gyms, and a playground. There were college-level courses and classes in reading and writing and child care. There were doctors and nurses. There were theater programs, music groups, and social clubs. Hull House even had a summer camp in the country. At Hull House immigrants learned to live and work in America. People came from around the world to study how Hull House was helping the people of Chicago.

Jane Addams worked for better child labor laws, women's right to vote, and world peace. In 1931, she was awarded the Nobel Peace Prize.

When people praised Jane Addams, she'd look at them in a funny way. "Think what I have gained! Think how I have grown!" she'd say. If joy and understanding were the gifts she gave, they were also the gifts she received.

Once Jane Addams caught a burglar breaking into Hull House. Instead of having the man arrested, she found him a job.

## Progressives Call for Change

These people who led the reform in America were called progressives. They were mostly middle class people who saw that things were going wrong. The work of the progressives brought about many needed changes in American government.

## Civil Service Act

In 1883, progressives encouraged the federal government to pass the Civil Service Act. Until then, government jobs were often given to friends and political supporters. This practice was a "spoils system." The Civil Service Act changed this. Now people were hired on the basis of their ability to do the work. Tests were given. Those with the highest scores got the jobs.

Do you know anyone who has taken a civil service test in order to work for the government?

## Secret Ballot

The progressives worked for new voting laws. Voting had been taking place in open polls. Each party had ballots of different colors. Anyone could see which party people were voting for by the colors of their ballots. Progressives demanded secret ballots cast in closed polling booths.

## Direct Primary

Most candidates for office had been chosen by party leaders. The progressives wanted the people to have a voice in choosing the candidates. The direct primary system was begun. Voters of each party would hold an election called a **primary**. In it, the voters themselves would choose the party candidates.

## Progressives Pass New Amendments

In 1913, progressives worked for the passage of the 16th Amendment. It set up a federal **income tax**. People would pay taxes according to how much money they made. The rich paid a larger share of taxes than the poor.

In 1913, the 17th Amendment was also added to the Constitution. This amendment called for U.S. senators to be elected directly by the people of the states. Until 1913, the senators had been chosen by small groups of people in each state. Often these people did not represent the majority. The Progressives wanted the voices of all citizens heard in government.

### History Practice

Answer these questions on a separate sheet of paper.

1. Who were the muckrakers and what did they try to do?

2. What industry did Upton Sinclair attack in *The Jungle*?

3. What is another name for the reformers?

# Women's Rights

In 1870, the 15th Amendment said that all men had the right to vote. But democracy was not complete. As time went on, more people insisted that women, too, had that right.

On July 19, 1848, a meeting had been held in Seneca Falls, New York. More than 300 people were present. They came to talk about how women in America were refused their rights. Women could not vote. A married woman could not own property. If a marriage ended in divorce, women had no legal right to their children. Women had to pay taxes, but they had little in the way of rights and protection.

Elizabeth Cady Stanton and Lucretia Mott were two leaders at the meeting in Seneca Falls. Together with Susan B. Anthony, they led a long fight for women's **suffrage**, the right to vote. Their first victories came in the West. Wyoming gave women the right to vote even before it became a state. This was in 1869.

In 1872, Susan B. Anthony broke the law. On election day, November 5, she went to the polls with 15 other women. They were going to vote! Susan led the group into the polling place. She was the first American woman to vote in a national election. She was arrested for her crime.

These early leaders of the women's suffrage movement—Stanton, Mott, and Anthony—would not live to see the end of the battle. New leaders, like Carrie Chapman Catt, worked to win the vote. There were marches and hunger strikes. The battle was finally won. The 19th Amendment, added in 1920, granted women suffrage.

**Why do you think some people were against women's right to vote?**

## Great Names in History: Ernestine Rose

She was often called the "Queen of the Platform." She fought for the rights of women with fiery speeches and endless energy.

Ernestine Rose was born in Poland. Her father arranged for her marriage to an older man. Ernestine did not want to marry the man. She convinced her father and a Polish court that the marriage contract should be broken.

Ernestine later chose her own husband, an Englishman. They immigrated to America. Ernestine ran a successful business and made use of her great speaking ability. She became an abolitionist and worked to end slavery. In time, she turned her attention to women's rights. Women, she could see, had no legal rights at all. Until they were married, their earnings were controlled by their fathers. Then their husbands took control. Ernestine Rose felt that women were only a little better off than slaves.

She worked side-by-side with Elizabeth Cady Stanton, Lucretia Mott, and Susan B. Anthony. In 1860, her speech-making paid off. New York State gave women new rights. Women could inherit property. They could sign contracts. They received equal control over their children. But they still could not vote. Ernestine Rose continued to make speeches. She stood on platforms before angry groups of men. "Freedom, my friends, does not bloom in one night . . . All who love liberty have to labor for it."

Ernestine Rose died in 1892. This was 28 years before the 19th Amendment granted American women the vote.

# The Conservation Movement

When the first white settlers came to America, they found a land rich in natural resources. There were forests, rivers, and good soil. But during the push westward, little thought was given to the proper use of those resources. Miners took ore from the ground as if it would never run out. There seemed to be plenty of oil, coal, timber, and clean water. Farmers turned cattle and sheep loose on the plains to eat the grass. Buffalo were hunted by the thousands.

During the Age of Reform, people started to see that the nation's resources were limited. President Theodore Roosevelt urged the government to begin conservation programs. "The forest and water problems are perhaps the most vital . . . problems of the United States," he said.

Roosevelt set aside almost 150 million acres of government timberland as national forests. He called a national conservation meeting in 1908. He made Americans aware that they could not waste their natural resources.

## History Practice

Answer these questions on a separate sheet of paper.

1. Where were women first able to exercise the right to vote?

2. Name three leaders in the fight for women's suffrage.

3. Which amendment to the Constitution gave women in the United States the right to vote? When did it become law?

# Chapter Review

## Summary

<table>
<tr><th colspan="2">CHRONOLOGY OF MAJOR EVENTS</th></tr>
<tr><td>1869</td><td>Women's suffrage law passes in Wyoming Territory</td></tr>
<tr><td>1883</td><td>Civil Service Act</td></tr>
<tr><td>1890</td><td>Jacob Riis publishes How the Other Half Lives</td></tr>
<tr><td>1904</td><td>Ida Tarbell publishes History of Standard Oil</td></tr>
<tr><td>1906</td><td>Upton Sinclair publishes The Jungle</td></tr>
<tr><td>1906</td><td>Pure Food and Drug Act passes</td></tr>
<tr><td>1906</td><td>Meat Inspection Act passes</td></tr>
<tr><td>1908</td><td>President Roosevelt calls national conservation conference</td></tr>
<tr><td>1913</td><td>16th Amendment sets up federal income tax</td></tr>
<tr><td>1913</td><td>17th Amendment calls for direct election of U.S. senators</td></tr>
<tr><td>1917</td><td>18th Amendment prohibits making or selling alcoholic drinks</td></tr>
<tr><td>1920</td><td>19th Amendment gives women the vote</td></tr>
</table>

- Reformers were concerned that America remain a true democracy.

- Muckrakers wrote about greedy businessmen and the problems of the poor.

- Progressives helped bring about the Civil Service Act, secret balloting, and direct primaries. They also worked for passage of the 16th and 17th Amendments.

- Elizabeth Cady Stanton, Lucretia Mott, and Susan B. Anthony were leaders of the women's suffrage movement.

- The 19th Amendment granted women suffrage in 1920.

- The nation began to see the need for conservation.

## Chapter Quiz

1. Who did Roosevelt call "America's most useful citizen"?

2. Why might settlement houses be important to immigrants?

3. What must workers do to get Civil Service jobs?

4. How did the direct primary system affect the way political candidates were chosen?

5. How did senators enter Congress before the 17th Amendment was passed?

6. The 15th Amendment gave men the right to vote. The 19th Amendment gave women the right to vote. How many years were there between the passage of these two laws?

## Thinking and Writing

1. Compare the muckrakers with consumer rights groups of today.

2. Some people were against President Roosevelt's conservation programs. Why do you think this was so?

3. What efforts are made today to conserve natural resources?

# Unit Five Review

Use the information in chapters 13 through 16 to answer the questions on this page.

## A. Who did it?

1. He led his army into a Sioux ambush at Little Big Horn.
2. He was chief of all Sioux and did not want to live on a reservation.
3. People called him silly when he arranged for the purchase of Alaska.
4. He lit up America with his invention of the electric light.
5. He was the "father of the assembly line."
6. He was the first president of the American Federation of Labor.
7. He was a corrupt businessman who cheated the city of New York.
8. He stirred up trouble for the meat packing industry.
9. She gave up a life of luxury to run a Chicago settlement house.
10. She was the first woman to cast a vote in a national election.

## B. Think about what you have learned, then answer the following questions.

1. Explain why buffalo were important to the Native Americans. Describe what happened to the buffalo herds.
2. Rapid industrial growth caused problems in American cities. Give three examples of such problems.
3. Compare Andrew Carnegie and John D. Rockefeller. In what ways were they alike?
4. Give three reasons why immigrants came to the United States.
5. Define "muckraker." Tell about one famous muckraker.

# Unit Six

# Power, Prosperity, and Progress

# Chapter 17

# A World Power

| 1898 | 1914 |
|------|------|
| Spanish-American War | Panama Canal is completed |

**Destruction of the battleship *Maine***

## Chapter Learning Objectives

- Tell why the United States went to war with Spain.
- Describe what happened to the Philippines, Puerto Rico, Guam, and Cuba after the war.
- Explain U.S. relations with Latin America.
- Describe the building of the Panama Canal.

## Words to Know

**annex** to obtain; to include
**crisis** a time of great danger or trouble
**expand** to become larger
**imperialism** the practice of setting up an empire by forming colonies in other lands or controlling the wealth or politics of weaker nations
**interfere** to get in the way of
**isolation** separation
**Latin America** the Western Hemisphere south of the United States

By the turn of the century, the western part of the United States had been settled. Americans were now becoming interested in foreign countries. There had been an industrial boom. Better farming methods had been developed. More products were being sold. Businesses were looking for new markets. **Expansion**, however, could lead to certain problems. In this chapter, you will read about some of those problems.

## Americans Look to Foreign Lands

Some Americans did not want to become involved with foreign countries. "It is wrong to want power over others, to try to control other lands," they said. "Let other countries take care of themselves. We should mind our own business!" People who thought this way were called **isolationists**. They wanted to isolate, or separate, America from foreign matters.

Others thought that the United States had a duty to spread the American way of life. They believed we would be spreading democracy.

In 1898, America jumped into world affairs by getting involved in a **crisis** in Cuba. Before long, America's powers would be tested in a war with Spain.

What facts of geography isolated the United States from other world powers?

## Explosion on the *Maine*

On the evening of February 15, 1898, the American battleship *Maine* was harbored at Havana, Cuba. Many sailors on the *Maine* were getting ready for sleep. On deck, only a few lights were burning. The night was warm and quiet.

Spain controlled Cuba. It had been treating the Cubans very badly. Cuba was fighting to be free of Spain. Many Americans supported the Cubans. Spain, therefore, wasn't happy to have the *Maine* in Havana. The ship had been there for a month, its big guns showing off American power.

Suddenly, at 9:40 P.M., there was a loud noise. The *Maine* rocked a bit and caught fire. Then a larger blast ripped apart the front of the ship. The air was full of fire. Pieces of the *Maine* rained down.

The blast killed 266 sailors. Spanish and American ships pulled those still living out of the water. The *Maine* settled into the mud, still burning.

No cause could be found for the explosions. But American newspapers thought they knew the answer. They printed it in big headlines. The papers said that the Spanish had blown up the *Maine*. They said we had to go to war. Three months later, we did.

## The Spanish-American War

No one knows who or what really blew up the *Maine*. Now, nearly 100 years later, many experts think it was an accident that happened on the ship itself. The Spanish had no real reason to set the explosion. They wanted to stay out of war with the United States. They knew that the United States was a stronger country. Most Americans didn't want a war, either. How, then, did it start?

In 1896, William McKinley became president of the United States. He was against going to war because he feared it would hurt business. But he was not a strong president. Three things were pushing him to declare war.

First, thousands of Cubans were being held against their will in Spain. Many were dying. Americans were angry about this and other crimes. Cuba, they said, was struggling to be free, just as America had struggled to be free of England. Many Americans wanted the United States to lend the Cubans a hand.

Second, some Americans believed the United States had a right to **expand** into other parts of the world. They wanted to gain new markets for the many goods the country was producing. And they saw war with Spain as a way to get more land and to make the United States a world power. As things in Cuba got worse, the call for expansion grew louder and stronger.

Third, the newspapers were yelling for war. It had started with two New York papers, the *Journal* and the *World*.

To attract readers, each printed the bloodiest stories of Spanish crimes in Cuba that it could. In many cases, the stories weren't even true, but they sold papers.

In 1897, McKinley urged Spain to make changes in Cuba. When Spain began to do so, it looked as if everything might be settled peacefully. But on February 9, 1898, the *New York Journal* printed a stolen letter. In the letter a Spanish official insulted the United States president.

Then, on February 15, the *Maine* blew up.

**"Remember the Maine" became a battlecry for war.**

**Can you think of a recent time when newspapers shaped public feeling? Find a news article that you think would cause people to become angry.**

The call for war grew louder. McKinley told Spain to end the problems in Cuba right away. Spain waited too long to agree. On April 19, Congress declared that Cuba was free from Spain. Spain then declared war on the United States. In return, on April 25, 1898, the United States declared war on Spain.

**President William McKinley**

# The Shortest War

Trouble in Cuba set off the war, but the first battle took place halfway around the world. Spain had ruled the Philippine Islands for many years. Part of the Spanish navy was stationed there at Manila Bay.

Early on May 1, 1898, six American ships under Commodore George Dewey entered the bay. There they faced ten Spanish ships. The Spanish leader knew he couldn't win. His ships were old and unfit to fight. He moved nearer to shore to give his men a chance to save themselves. Dewey's ships opened fire at 5:40 A.M. By 7:35, the Spanish fleet at Manila was destroyed.

The Filipinos had been fighting against Spain for the same reasons the Cubans had. The Spaniards were harsh rulers. In the belief that the United States would help them win their freedom, the Filipinos now fought even harder. When American soldiers reached Manila in August, Dewey took the city.

In Cuba, Spain had 200,000 soldiers ready to fight. Seventeen thousand American soldiers landed near Santiago. But at the time, Spain could move only 13,000 troops to meet them. In a battle on July 1 and 2, the American army fought its way up San Juan Hill overlooking Santiago.

On July 3, the Spanish navy was trapped at Santiago. It tried to escape. The American navy was waiting. It sank all the Spanish ships. That left Spain's army completely cut off. On July 16, the Spanish in Santiago gave up.

The Spanish government took steps toward peace. By the time Manila fell on August 13, the war was over. It had lasted less than four months.

**Commodore Dewey was known as the "Hero of Manila."**

## The Price of War

Secretary of State John Hay called it "a splendid little war." Many Americans agreed. It had been quickly and easily won. America was now a world power. And the nation had become "richer"—President McKinley and Congress decided to keep the Philippines under American control. Spain sold the Philippine Islands to the United States for $20,000,000. The United States also took Puerto Rico in the Caribbean Sea and Guam in the Pacific rather than set them free. Spain no longer held any colonies in the Americas.

### Then and Now

**Then:** In 1898 the Spanish-American War gave the United States the opportunity to control **The Philippines, Puerto Rico,** and **Guam.** A small group of Americans argued against taking control of other nations. They did not believe in **imperialism.** They called themselves the Anti-Imperialist League. Their group included some of the people you have read about. Jane Addams, Samuel Gompers, and Andrew Carnegie were all anti-imperialists. So was the famous writer Mark Twain. They believed that imperialism went against the basic ideals of the United States.

**Now: The Philippines** is an independent republic. Filipinos gained their independence on July 4, 1946.

**Guam** is a self-governing U.S. territory. The people of Guam elect their own governor.

**Puerto Rico** is a self-governing part of the United States called a commonwealth.

Not everyone thought the war had gone well. The United States had lost only 379 men in battle. But another 5,083 soldiers had died.

A sickness called yellow fever, spread by mosquitoes, had killed some of the soldiers. Rotten beef sold to the army by American meat packers had killed many others.

The American navy had done well. Yet it would have had no chance against England or another of the great powers.

And the American army had been badly run. It had won because the Spanish army was in even worse shape.

Finally, many people were upset by our keeping the Philippine Islands. They said that by taking a colony we seemed to be forgetting the American Revolution.

During that war, we had broken a foreign power's control over the United States. Now we were the ones who had become the foreign power. We were the ones who were exercising control over another country.

The Filipinos wanted to run their own country. It took the United States more than two years to defeat them and gain control.

By then, the American army was holding many Filipinos as prisoners. And tens of thousands of Americans and Filipinos were dead.

But most people in the United States thought the battles had been worth it. To them, the war had shown that America was a nation on the rise. It was worthy of respect.

In 1900, Dr. Walter Reed discovered that yellow fever was spread by mosquitoes. This made the disease easier to control. It could be checked by destroying the mosquitoes' breeding places.

## Great Names in History: Teddy Roosevelt and the Rough Riders

The Spanish-American War produced a new hero for America. He was Theodore Roosevelt, a man who would later become president.

During the war, Roosevelt led an army outfit known as the Rough Riders. The Rough Riders were an interesting band. They included cowboys, hunters, polo players, gamblers, and police officers. The Rough Riders were known as "good shots and good riders."

Their day of greatest glory came on July 1, 1898. This was during the Battle of San Juan. Teddy Roosevelt led his men up "Kettle Hill." More than 1500 Rough Riders were wounded or killed in that battle. But those who made it home were called heroes.

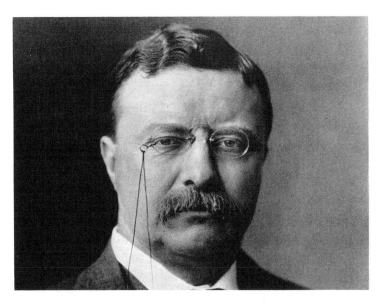

**Vice-president Teddy Roosevelt became the youngest U.S. president when President William McKinley was assassinated in 1901.**

## History Practice

Answer these questions on a separate sheet of paper.

1. List three things that had been pushing President McKinley toward war.

2. What happened to Spain's colonies in the Americas after the Spanish-American War?

3. Name three places the United States gained from the war with Spain.

# The Panama Canal

In 1903, Theodore Roosevelt was president. He knew the United States had a problem. Its navy had to patrol both the Atlantic and Pacific oceans. To get from one to the other, a ship had to sail around South America. The trip took much too long.

Roosevelt had a plan. He wanted to cut a giant canal through Panama. That way ships could move quickly between the oceans. A French company had tried this and failed. But Roosevelt believed that the United States could do it. And the Americans believed Roosevelt.

Our nation did not own Panama, however. The South American country of Colombia did. The United States offered Colombia a certain amount of money for the rights to build the canal. Colombia felt the amount was too small. It turned down the offer.

The United States then took advantage of fighting between Panama and Colombia. The United States supported a revolution in which Panama won independence from Colombia. Panama became a separate country. It received the money that would have gone to Colombia.

In 1907, the digging began. Over 40,000 people worked on the canal. Mostly they used picks and shovels. There were also 100 steam shovels. Each lifted eight tons of dirt. And there were 115 trains to carry the dirt away.

Men dug the canal through jungle lands. It was not an easy place to work. Mosquitoes spread yellow fever and malaria. Many workers fell sick. The diseases were often deadly.

President Roosevelt came to Panama to watch. He told the workers, "You are doing the biggest thing of

**The building of the Panama Canal**

its kind that has ever been done." They dug through the swamps, the jungles, and the mountains. They moved over 350 million tons of earth. They cut a ditch 300 feet wide and 40 miles long. In January of 1914, the first ship passed through the completed canal.

In 1978, the United States and Panama signed treaties. The Panama Canal would gradually return to Panama's control. By the year 2000, Panama is to have complete control of the canal.

## Relations with Latin America

Construction of the Panama Canal caused some hard feelings between the United States and **Latin America**. Many Latin Americans felt this country should have kept out of conflicts between Panama and Colombia.

Colombia felt cheated. Panama did not like the U.S. presence in that country. In 1921, the United States paid Colombia $25 million to make up for its loss of Panama. The United States also increased its yearly rent to Panama for the canal zone.

The United States has often concerned itself with what happens throughout the Americas. The control, presence, or influence of foreign countries in Latin America has been considered a threat to the United States. According to the Monroe Doctrine, European nations would not be allowed to hold power in the Americas.

Roosevelt used the slogan "speak softly but carry a big stick" in his dealings with foreign countries. What do you think that phrase means?

Throughout the years, America has sent troops to such Latin American countries as Cuba, Haiti, the Dominican Republic, and Nicaragua. The U.S. forces were not always welcomed. Many Latin Americans did not want the United States' hand in their affairs. There have been many arguments over the difference between "**interfering**" and "helping out."

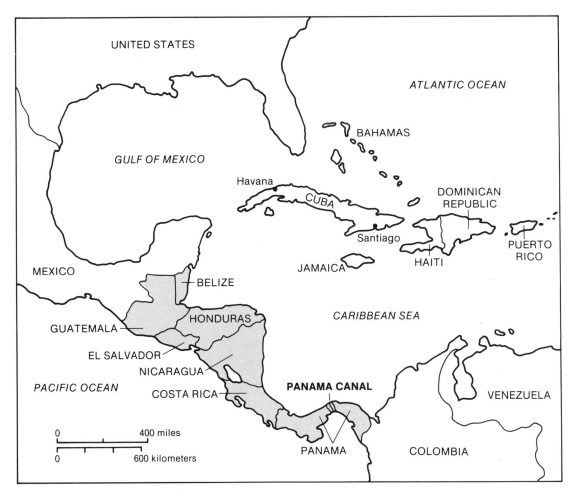

**Central America**

**Map Study**

Study the map. Then answer the questions on a separate sheet of paper

1. Which two oceans are linked by the Panama Canal?
2. According to this map, how many countries make up Central America?
3. Name two Central American countries that border Mexico.

# The Pan American Union

In 1890, an effort was made to improve relations between all American nations. Twenty-one republics of North, Central, and South America formed a group called the Pan American Union. The Union aimed to promote friendship and understanding between the people of the Americas. In 1910, Andrew Carnegie gave the Union its beautiful headquarters building in Washington, D.C.

## History Practice

Answer these questions on a separate sheet of paper.

1. Why was the Panama Canal built?

2. How did the United States gain the land needed to build the canal?

3. What was the purpose of the Pan American Union?

# The United States Gains Hawaii

In 1898, the United States **annexed** the Hawaiian Islands. Americans had shown an interest in Hawaii for a long time. New England trading and whaling ships stopped at the islands in the early 1800s. Missionaries traveled there in 1820. They taught the natives to read and write English and told them about American life. Americans put money into Hawaiian pineapple and sugar plantations. In 1887, Hawaiians gave the United States rights to use Pearl Harbor as a naval base.

Then, in 1893, Americans led a revolution in Hawaii. Queen Liliuokalani, the ruler of the islands, was forced from her throne. The Republic of Hawaii was created. Five years later the United States annexed the Hawaiian Islands. The Territory of Hawaii was set up in 1900. In 1959, Hawaii became the 50th state in the Union.

# Trade with the Far East

Do we import many items from the Far East today? Name some of those items.

The United States began trading with China in the 1800s. Many nations recognized China's wealth. Some threatened to take over Chinese territory. China, fearing for the safety of its own lands, threatened to cut off all trade. In 1899, the United States initiated an "Open Door Policy." Its purpose was to keep China open to trade. Secretary of State John Hay was behind the Open Door Policy. He promised the United States would help keep other powers from taking over China's territory.

America's Commodore Matthew Perry opened trade between the United States and Japan in 1854. Japan had been an isolated nation. It had cut itself off from the rest of the world. Perry approached the Japanese emperor with a show of strength. He also brought gifts of modern inventions, such as the steam engine. He convinced the emperor that trade with the United States would be good for Japan.

New trading partners made the United States a wealthier, stronger nation.

**Commodore Perry arriving in Japan, 1854**

# The Years Ahead

In 1913, many Americans felt we were on top of the world. The nation had won the Spanish-American War. It led the world in business and industry. It was a major trading power. The future looked bright.

But the great European powers were building up their armies. These included England, France, Germany, Austria-Hungary, Italy, and Russia. They were taking colonies and controlling trade routes around the world.

The different countries had chosen sides. Germany and Austria-Hungary had promised to defend each other if there was a war. England, France, and Russia had done the same. War between any two countries on opposite sides would draw in the others.

Still, most Americans weren't concerned about this. The United States was cut off from the rest of the world and its problems by two oceans. Americans had always gone their own way. What was there to worry about?

## History Practice

Answer these questions on a separate sheet of paper.

1. How was Hawaii added to the United States?

2. Which nation did the "Open Door Policy" keep open to world trade?

3. Why did Commodore Matthew Perry go to Japan?

4. In 1913, how did most Americans feel about conflicts brewing in Europe?

# Chapter Review

## Summary

<table>
<tr><td colspan="2" align="center">CHRONOLOGY OF MAJOR EVENTS</td></tr>
<tr><td>1854</td><td>Matthew Perry opens U.S. trade with Japan</td></tr>
<tr><td>1890</td><td>Pan American Union formed</td></tr>
<tr><td>1898</td><td>United States annexes Hawaii</td></tr>
<tr><td>1898</td><td>Spanish-American War</td></tr>
<tr><td>1899</td><td>Secretary of State Hay introduces Open Door Policy in China</td></tr>
<tr><td>1914</td><td>Panama Canal opens</td></tr>
</table>

- American interest in foreign lands increased around the turn of the century.

- An explosion on the American battleship *Maine* encouraged Americans to call for war with Spain. President McKinley did not want war, but public opinion pushed toward it.

- In April, 1898, the Spanish-American War began. By August, the United States had won the war.

- The Spanish-American War gave the United States control of the Philippines, Puerto Rico, and Guam. It also gave the United States more power and respect in the world.

- The Panama Canal was built in ten years. It linked the Atlantic and Pacific oceans.

- The canal created some hard feelings between Latin America and the United States.

- The United States annexed Hawaii. It became a territory in 1900.

- The United States found valuable trading partners in Japan and China.

- European powers were building empires and armies.

## Chapter Quiz

1. Which country ruled Cuba before 1898?

2. How long did the Spanish-American War last?

3. Tell what kind of government there is today in the Philippines, in Guam, and in Puerto Rico.

4. What event led to Theodore Roosevelt's becoming the youngest U.S. president?

5. In the late 1800s, why did China threaten to cut off trade with other countries?

6. What led to Hawaii's becoming a republic?

## Thinking and Writing

1. How did the Spanish-American War give the United States the image of being a world power?

2. Why do you think the Panama Canal was called a "marvel of the age"?

3. In what way did the building of the Panama Canal cause bad feelings in Latin America?

4. Do you think one country has the right to get involved in another country's affairs? Explain.

**Chapter 18**

# The World at War

**Assassination of
Ferdinand**

## Chapter Learning Objectives

- Explain the purpose of an alliance.
- Tell which alliances held power in Europe in 1914.
- Explain the incident that sparked World War I.
- Describe the events that led the United States to war.
- Describe the terms of peace at the end of World War I.

# Words to Know

**alliance**   a joining together for some purpose; an agreement by treaty

**civilians**   people not belonging to the armed forces

**dictatorship**   a government in which power is held by a few people or by one person

**heir**   a person who receives property or position when the person holding it dies

**slogan**   a saying

**spies**   people sent by a government to learn military secrets

**submarines**   boats that travel underwater

---

The year 1914 was a good one for most Americans. Industries like steel, coal, and iron were making large profits. The United States was selling goods around the world.

Automobiles were replacing the horse and buggy. Henry Ford had produced a car most Americans could afford. The country was growing quickly. It was becoming stronger every year. The times were changing, and the changes were exciting. But one of the biggest, saddest, and bloodiest changes the world had ever seen was about to happen. In this chapter you will read about World War I.

In the early 1900s, European nations started to build up their armed forces. Britain had always had the strongest navy. When Germany started building up its navy, Britain began to worry.

## Overseas

Things were different in Europe. It was on the brink of war. Nations had taken sides. They were struggling for power. They had formed **alliances**. Each alliance pledged to protect and stand by its member nations. On one side was the alliance called the Central Powers. In 1914, the Central Powers were Germany, Austria-Hungary, and Italy.

On the other side were the Allies. These were England, France, and Russia. (Italy soon changed sides and joined the Allies.)

Members of each alliance had promised to defend each other. A conflict between any of them would draw the others into war.

## One Event Brings War

Few Americans had ever heard of Sarajevo or Serbia. But on June 28, 1914, a driver made a wrong turn in the town of Sarajevo. One month later, the world went to war. Over 8 million people would die in the fighting. Another 20 million would die of disease and hunger.

Archduke Franz Ferdinand was **heir** to the throne of Austria-Hungary. He was in Sarajevo to look over his troops. June 28 was a holiday. Crowds of people lined the route along which the archduke and his wife would pass. Also in Sarajevo were seven Serbians who planned to kill the archduke. They thought this would help free the Serbs living in the area under Austro-Hungarian rule. With bombs and guns, the Serbians joined the crowd. They spaced themselves along the route.

When the archduke's driver made a wrong turn, a general riding with him yelled to stop. The driver did stop—five feet away from one of the Serbians. The assassin, Gavrilo Princip, fired twice. Franz Ferdinand and his wife were killed.

The murder did not cause a great deal of alarm in the United States. But soon the world fell apart.

One month after the archduke's murder, Austria-Hungary declared war on Serbia. Russia moved its army to defend Serbia. The Serbians were Slavic, as the Russians were. Germany had a treaty with Austria-Hungary. It declared war on Russia and France. And Britain declared war on Germany.

The assassination at Sarajevo was not really the *cause* of World War I. The tensions between powerful nations were already there. The archduke's murder was an *excuse* to begin the fighting. Most countries involved hoped to gain more land and more power.

World War I was also known as the "Great War."

## History Practice

Answer these questions on a separate sheet of paper.

1. Which countries belonged to the Central Powers? Who were the Allies?

2. What country changed its alliance?

3. What major country was Archduke Franz Ferdinand in line to rule?

4. How was Germany drawn into the war?

## America Stays Neutral

Americans were shocked by the war. But President Woodrow Wilson believed it wouldn't touch the United States. So did most of the public. On August 4, Wilson declared the United States a neutral country. He hoped this would help settle things between the warring countries.

Most Americans wanted the United States to be neutral. Some felt the United States could talk the other countries out of fighting. Some believed we shouldn't get involved because both sides were to blame for the war. And many felt that any war in Europe was no business of ours. These feelings were very strong. Wilson was elected president again in 1916. The **slogan** used in his campaign was "He kept us out of war."

## Why America Entered World War I

By late 1916, the fighting in Europe had been going on for two years. There was no end in sight. The United States still wanted to stay out of it. But people were no longer neutral. For several reasons, most Americans wanted victory for the Allies.

Americans had strong feelings for the British and the French. America's speech, laws, and many of its early settlers had come from England. France had helped us during the Revolutionary War. And America did a lot of business with the Allied countries.

Many people also had strong negative feelings toward Germany. Belgium was a neutral country. Germany had attacked it. Also, German **spies** in the United States had tried to stir up trouble among American workers. They'd even planted bombs in factories.

Germany had decided to end British control of the oceans. It wanted to stop arms shipments to the Allies. Germany had posted notices in American newspapers. They warned travelers that it was not safe to sail on British ships. One notice read, "Travelers sailing in the war zone on ships of Great Britain or her allies do so at their own risk." German **submarines** began sinking British ships. In May of 1915, a German sub sank the passenger liner *Lusitania*. Nearly 1,200 people, including 128 American **civilians**, were killed. The United States began to think of war.

The German submarines of World War I were the first ever used in war. Do navies use submarines today?

## Democracy vs. Dictatorship

In addition to the deaths of American civilians in the sinking of the *Lusitania*, Americans were concerned about other issues as well. Many believed this was a war between **dictatorship** and democracy.

The Central Powers were dictatorships. All the power was held by a few rulers. One of the Allies, Russia, was also a dictatorship. But the other two, Britain and France, were democracies, as the United States was. Many Americans thought it was important that the Allies win. Still, America remained neutral. But in the early months of 1917, a number of events helped bring us into the war.

At the beginning of 1917, there was a revolution in Russia. The old dictatorship was thrown out. For a short while, it looked as if the new government would be a democracy. In the end, another dictatorship took over. But for a few months, Americans were very excited by the revolution. At the time, many felt it right to fight with the Allies. The Allies stood for democracy against dictatorship.

## The Zimmerman Letter

Arthur Zimmerman was an official of the German government. On January 17, 1917, he sent a secret message to another German official in Mexico. Zimmerman knew that Mexico and the United States were not getting along well. He wanted Mexico to agree to a treaty with Germany. If the United States were to enter the war, Mexico would then side with Germany. Zimmerman promised Mexico land in Texas, Arizona, and New Mexico. British spies uncovered Zimmerman's message. They gave it to President Wilson. Many Americans were so angry they wanted to go to war right away.

Why do you think Zimmerman's letter made Americans so angry?

## America Takes a Stand

Finally, there was the shipping problem. Germany had agreed in 1916 to stop sinking merchant ships without warning. In March of 1917, this changed.

Germany said that its submarines would sink all ships sailing to Allied countries. On March 12, a German sub sank the *Algonquin*. This was an unarmed American ship. On March 18, three more American ships were sunk.

Most Americans now believed Germany was a threat to the world's safety and peace. President Wilson decided there was only one thing to do. On April 2, he called a meeting of Congress. We must join in a war "to make the world safe for democracy." On April 6, 1917, Congress agreed. We went to war.

## History Practice

Answer these questions on a separate sheet of paper.

1. How did President Wilson feel, at first, about the United States and World War I?

2. Give three reasons why most people wanted this country to remain neutral.

3. Give three reasons why the United States entered World War I.

## Blood and Darkness

The war the United States entered was not like any the world had known before. The American army fought mainly in France. Month after month, thousands and thousands of men died to gain a few hundred yards of ground. Then they'd lose it again. New weapons were used. For the first time, warfare included poison gas, tanks, and airplanes. World War I was the most brutal war ever.

The United States had not been ready for war. Industry had to switch to making ships, tanks, and guns. But it soon turned them out in record numbers. This helped the course of the war.

American military ships sharply cut the number of merchant ships sunk by German submarines.

The American army hadn't been prepared, either. It took time to get men signed up and trained. And it took time to move them to Europe. When General Pershing got to France in June of 1917, he had only 14,500 soldiers. But the number grew quickly. By November, 1918, Pershing had over 2 million troops.

American soldiers in World War I were sometimes called "doughboys." The marching soldiers pounded the mud to "dough" beneath their boots.

## Then and Now: War in the Air

**Then:** Airplanes were used in battle for the first time in World War I. At first they were used to find enemy troops and to take pictures of war zones. In 1914, the best plane could only fly 90 miles per hour. It carried just two people.

Planes changed rapidly. Soon fighter pilots battled in planes that flew at 175 miles per hour. They carried heavy machine guns and bombs. Air battles became a regular part of the war. When two pilots fought each other in the air, it was called a "dogfight." Pilots who shot down more than five enemy planes were called "aces." Germany's top ace pilot was Baron von Richthofen. He was also known as the "Red Baron." Eddie Rickenbacker was once a race car driver. He became America's most famous flying ace.

**Now:** Jet powered planes fly well over 1,000 miles per hour. A single plane can cost up to $30 million to build. A modern-day spy plane called the Blackbird flies on the edge of outer space. Nations pump money and research into a race for the best planes. They spend millions on defense systems to protect against these warriors in the sky.

**Machine gun crew**

## Learn More About It: The War Effort at Home

Americans at home joined the war effort. Herbert Hoover was head of the Food Administration. He encouraged Americans to conserve food. It was needed for soldiers overseas. Americans were asked to give up wheat on Mondays and Wednesdays. They were asked to give up meat on Tuesdays and pork on Wednesdays and Saturdays. People planted "victory gardens" and grew their own vegetables.

The lives of many American women changed because of World War I. More women left home to work in factories during the war. When the war ended, many continued to work.

---

In 1918, American power poured into the war. The Allies began to get the upper hand. They stopped several heavy German attacks. Then they went on the attack themselves. But the fighting was still slow and bloody. The Allies fought along a 200-mile-long battle line. World War I soldiers used a new style of fighting. They dug long trenches along battle fronts. Soldiers spent days and nights in those muddy holes. Finally, the Allies drove the German army out of France.

As the Allies pushed toward Germany, the Central Powers fell apart. Bulgaria gave up on September 30. Turkey gave up on October 30, and Austria-Hungary on November 4. Germany, the last holdout, gave up seven days later. On November 11, 1918, World War I ended.

## Conditions of Peace

A meeting was held in Versailles, France. The Treaty of Versailles was completed in early 1919. Among the things it said was that:

- Germany had started the war and must pay large amounts of money to the Allies.
- Germany must not build up its army or navy again.
- Germany must give up its colonies in Asia and Africa.

The German government had to sign the peace treaty. But the German people did not like taking total responsibility for the war. The conditions of the treaty hurt their economy terribly.

As part of the peace, President Wilson planned a League of Nations. In it, countries would meet to work out their problems. The League would also act as a sort of court of world law. Wilson hoped it would keep the world safe from wars like the one just ended.

Other countries agreed to Wilson's idea. But to everyone's surprise, the United States did not join the League.

Two-thirds of the Senate had to approve the plan. It came before Congress several times. Each time it fell just short of passing. Many Republican senators felt that the League of Nations could draw the United States into foreign wars. Too many Americans still did not want to become involved in the affairs of other nations. The League of Nations was never very strong. This was mainly because the United States wouldn't join it. Wilson's cause was lost. And so was his hope for a way to stop world wars.

## History Practice

Answer these questions on a separate sheet of paper.

1. What were three things used in war for the first time in World War I?

2. What were three conditions of the Treaty of Versailles?

3. What was the purpose behind the League of Nations?

4. Why did the United States refuse to join the League of Nations?

# Chapter Review

## Summary

| CHRONOLOGY OF MAJOR EVENTS | |
|---|---|
| 1914 | Archduke Franz Ferdinand assassinated in Sarajevo |
| 1914 | War declared in Europe |
| 1915 | German sub sinks British luxury liner *Lusitania* |
| 1915 | Italy enters war on Allied side |
| 1916 | Americans reelect President Wilson |
| 1917 | Russian revolution |
| 1917 | America discovers Zimmerman letter |
| 1917 | German sub sinks American ship *Algonquin* |
| 1917 | America declares war |
| 1918 | Allies win World War I |
| 1919 | Treaty of Versailles, League of Nations |

- European nations formed alliances. They pledged to protect each other.

- One alliance was the Central Powers: Germany, Austria-Hungary, and for a time, Italy. The other was the Allies: England, France, and Russia.

- The assassination of Archduke Franz Ferdinand of Austria-Hungary sparked WWI.

- President Woodrow Wilson encouraged America to remain neutral.

- Several things led America into the war. They included: German submarine activity, the idea of dictatorship vs. democracy, the Zimmerman letter.

- New methods of warfare were used in WWI: poison gas, airplanes, tanks, trench warfare.

- American forces helped turn the war in favor of the Allies.

- The war ended with Allied victory on November 11, 1918.

- A peace treaty was drawn up in Versailles, France. It set up the League of Nations.

## Chapter Quiz

1. How many people died as a result of World War I?

2. Which countries had a treaty with Archduke Franz Ferdinand's country?

3. Which countries were U.S. allies in World War I?

4. In which country did most U.S. troops fight? What were some of the new methods of war used then?

5. How long did World War I last? For how long was the United States involved in it?

6. Why didn't the United States join the League of Nations?

## Thinking and Writing

1. Explain how the assassination of Archduke Ferdinand could force all of Europe into a war.

2. How could the use of fighter planes and bombers change the way a war would affect civilians?

# Chapter 19

# The Boom Years

| 1920 | 1928 |
|------|------|
| 19th Amendment gives women the vote | Herbert Hoover elected president |

**Calvin Coolidge**

## Chapter Learning Objectives

- Tell which political party led the government during the 1920s.
- Explain what happened to labor unions in the twenties.
- Describe three ways life changed for women during the twenties.
- Tell why the twenties were a time of prosperity.

# Words to Know

**economy**   the way goods, wealth, and services are produced and used; the total amount of these and how they are divided among people

**intolerance**   an unwillingness to accept people of different races or backgrounds or with different ideas

**persecute**   to treat badly; to harm

**plot**   secret plan

**prosperity**   wealth; well-being

**racism**   the belief that differences make one race better than another

**radicals**   people who favor big changes

**rumors**   stories spread from person to person that may or may not be true

**scandal**   something shameful that shocks people

---

After World War I, America was tired and worn out. President Wilson had talked about world peace, but his dream of a League of Nations had fallen apart. Americans became less interested in international problems. They worried more about things at home than about peace treaties. Americans became isolationists. They wanted a good **economy** and booming businesses.

## Labor Unions Weaken

Businesses had been facing hard times. In 1919, over 4 million employees took part in nearly 4,000 strikes. A police strike in September left Boston without protection from crime. In November, a coal strike sent United Mine Workers off their jobs. Three hundred thousand steel workers went on strike from September, 1919, until January, 1920.

By the early 1920s, however, the labor unions grew weaker. America was exporting more goods. There were plenty of jobs. The strikes of 1919 had not been very successful. Workers began to lose interest in the unions.

Presidents Roosevelt, Taft (1909–1913), and Wilson had tried to control big business. They'd tried to improve conditions for workers. But now the government usually sided with industry. Workers who tried to fight for change lost out. The government even began to strip the power from earlier laws. These included child labor laws.

## The Red Scare

A "Red scare" also turned many Americans against the unions. Some people believed that communists, or "Reds," were in some way responsible for labor strikes. Americans had become very concerned about communist threats in the United States. During World War I, a group called the Bolsheviks had taken power in Russia. The Bolsheviks were communists. **Rumors** of communist **plots** spread across America. Bombs sent through the U.S. mail were blamed on communist **radicals**. In New York City a bomb did explode on Wall Street. It killed 38 people.

Americans were frightened. People with radical ideas of any kind were suddenly accused of being communists. Many were arrested.

In 1920, two Italians, Nicola Sacco and Bartolomeo Vanzetti, were arrested for murder. They were charged with killing a payroll master and his guard in Braintree, Massachusetts. Sacco and Vanzetti had both dodged the draft in World War I. They both had handed out leaflets criticizing the U.S. government. They both owned guns. But neither man had ever been in trouble before. Vanzetti was a peaceful fish peddler and Sacco worked in a shoe factory.

Many witnesses to the crime said that neither Sacco nor Vanzetti were the killers. One witness placed Vanzetti at the murder scene. Both Sacco and Vanzetti insisted they were innocent. But they were convicted and sentenced to death. Many people said

The early twenties were years of fear . . . fear of anything or anyone different. Many Americans distrusted people of a different color, religion, or nationality.

**Nicola Sacco (right) and Bartolomeo Vanzetti**

they did not receive a fair trial because they were immigrants and had some radical ideas about the government. However, after a six-year battle to save their lives, both men were executed.

For more than 50 years the case of Sacco and Vanzetti remained a subject of controversy. Finally, in 1977, the governor of Massachusetts issued a proclamation. While it did not state that the men were innocent, it did say that they had been "improperly tried."

Can you think of other times in history when people were denied a fair trial because they were members of a minority?

## Americans Elect Harding

In the 1920s people wanted to forget the problems of the world. They wanted to make money and enjoy the new things around them. The United States elected a new president. He was quite different from Woodrow Wilson. Republican Warren G. Harding was a good-natured but weak man. Harding's main idea was to let business run itself. He didn't want the government to watch over it.

Harding appointed new men to government offices. Some of them turned out to be very corrupt. One was found guilty of selling government supplies worth $250 million. Harding's secretary of the interior, Albert Fall, took bribes from oil companies in Teapot Dome, Wyoming. When the Teapot Dome **scandal** was uncovered, Fall went to prison.

President Harding did not discover all the scandals during his term. But he did learn of some. It is thought he fell sick from the strain. Harding died on August 2, 1923, while still in office.

## President Coolidge

When Harding died, Calvin Coolidge was serving as vice-president. Coolidge took over as president. He finished Harding's term. Coolidge, like Harding, felt the most important thing for America was strong business. Government should encourage business, not regulate it, the Republicans believed. "The business of America," Calvin Coolidge said, "is business."

Coolidge won the election of 1924. Business did prosper. "Keep Cool with Coolidge" became America's slogan.

## President Herbert Hoover

Coolidge decided not to run for a second term of office. In 1928, another Republican, Herbert Hoover, was elected president. Hoover ran against Democrat Al Smith. Smith was a Roman Catholic. In an age of **intolerance**, this made him unpopular. Hoover won by a landslide.

Hoover had been a successful businessman and public official. He promised good times. There would be "two chickens in every pot and a car in every garage."

How might such a slogan read today?

## Taking Off

Business took off in the 1920s. Industry made more money and put out more goods than ever before. The buying power of skilled workers rose, too. People bought whatever could be produced. They purchased cars, radios, washing machines, and furniture. They were hungry for anything that looked as if it might make life better. As the boom went on, many thought it would never end. They felt that the age of prosperity had arrived.

### History Practice

Answer these questions on a separate sheet of paper.

1. What happened to labor unions in the 1920s?

2. What crimes were Sacco and Vanzetti accused of?

3. How did the Republican administrations of the 1920s feel about government's role in big business?

4. What were some of the problems that arose in Harding's administration?

## Americans Behind the Wheel

Henry Ford's Model T wasn't a beautiful car. It stood seven feet tall, came with no extras, and was painted black. It was called a "flivver."

A flivver's engine had no electric starter. The driver had to walk to the front of the car to start it with a hand crank. On good days, the engine would explode into life after a few hard turns. The driver had to race back to the controls to keep the engine from dying. If the hand brake hadn't been set hard enough, the flivver could start moving by itself.

On June 4, 1924, the 10-millionth Model T rolled off the assembly line.

The Model T had three speeds, two forward and one reverse. There was no fuel pump; the gas simply drained out of the tank into the engine. On steep hills, the gas could stop flowing. Smart drivers turned their cars around and went up the hills backward.

By 1924, there were over 15 million cars on the road. More than half of them were Model Ts. People once traveled only as far as they could walk or ride a horse in a day. Now, they could drive for miles and miles in a short afternoon. America took to the road and never looked back. Henry Ford had put the country on wheels. They were the tall spoked wheels of his Model T.

## A Time of Contrasts

Life was changing quickly in the 1920s. It was a time of contrasts. The differences between city and country life and between the new ways and the old were becoming greater.

Conditions improved for many skilled workers. Their pay went up. Often the number of hours they worked went down. But for farmers and miners, things got worse. They were making less money than they had in years. Wages in general had risen. But there were still a great many people living in poverty.

In some places, mainly cities, new freedoms came with the new ways of life. Women and others who'd long been kept "in their places" moved forward.

But **racism** grew throughout the nation. The Ku Klux Klan hated all African Americans, Jews,

Catholics, and foreigners. They wore white robes and hoods. They spread fear. They murdered people. In some places, the Klan ran whole towns. In 1924, its membership rose to 4.5 million.

The 1920s also saw the passage of the 18th Amendment. Prohibition, as it was called, was meant to stop the production and sale of alcoholic drinks. From the beginning, it seemed more people were breaking the law than were obeying it. Every city had its secret bars. They were called "speakeasies," "blind pigs," and "beer flats." When the government closed one, another would open. Groups of criminals

Once the Ku Klux Klan was only in the South. After World War I, groups sprang up in other parts of the United States.

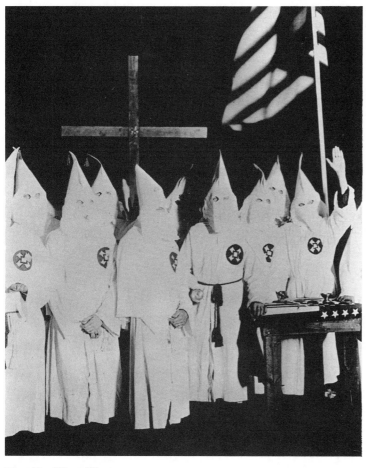

**The Ku Klux Klan**

took over the business and got rich. Al Capone ran the largest gang; it was based in Chicago. He had 700 men under him and took in $60 million a year.

People who favored Prohibition were called "Drys." People against Prohibition were called "Wets." Can you think of some arguments the Drys might have given? What might the Wets have said?

Today the sale of liquor is still regulated by government laws. What are some state or local regulations in your area?

---

### Great Names in History: Carrie Nation

Carrie Nation protested the use of liquor of any kind. She fought for the passage of the Prohibition Amendment. Carrie had been married to a doctor who drank very heavily. Her bad experiences led her to form a branch of the Women's Christian Temperance Union. This was a group that fought against the sale of liquor. Carrie did not stop with speeches and sign-carrying. She broke into saloons and smashed bars, tables, and chairs with hatchets. Carrie Nation was arrested many times. She was unpopular with many people. But her strong protests helped bring about Prohibition.

---

The government had trouble making people follow the 18th Amendment. Speakeasies and bootleggers kept liquor flowing. In 1933, the 21st Amendment ended Prohibition.

## Women in the 1920s

For almost 150 years, women had no voice in American government. Many women, like Susan B. Anthony, Carrie Chapman Catt, and others, had struggled long and hard to change that. In August of 1920, they won. The 19th Amendment gave all women the right to vote in presidential elections.

Life changed quickly for women after World War I. While men had been off to war, women had done many of their jobs. Now that peace had come, these women didn't all go back to the lives they had known. Women now worked in record numbers. And they didn't do only "women's work," such as teaching and nursing. They also did "men's work," such as selling land and running businesses.

Modern young women were called "flappers." The flappers helped to break down the rules that made some things all right for men but not for women. They spoke their minds. They danced the Charleston and the Black Bottom. They drank and smoked. They stood at speakeasy bars with men and traveled about without males to "protect" them. Flappers had short hair and wore short dresses and bright lipstick. They reminded the world that what had been was not what would always be.

## New Life in Harlem

African Americans made little progress during these years. They were **persecuted** by the Ku Klux Klan and others. Their pay did not rise along with that of other workers. Often they were kept from exercising their right to vote.

But in New York City's Harlem, there was a flowering of new black city life. A strong group of black writers lived and worked there. Among them were Langston Hughes, James Weldon Johnson, and Countee Cullen. Their stories, novels, plays, and poems gave many black people a sense of their own beauty and worth.

And Harlem had jazz. People came from all over to hear the best of this hot new music. They listened to Fletcher Henderson, Duke Ellington, Louis Armstrong, and Bessie Smith. The music was so popular that the 1920s became known as "The Jazz Age."

Crowds came to hear black musicians play at Harlem's most popular jazz spot, the Cotton Club. However, African Americans were not allowed to sit in the audience.

## American Heroes

It was a time for heroes. Americans of the 1920s cheered famous people from all walks of life. By the twenties, motion pictures had become big business. Movie fans had new stars. Sports events drew big crowds, and sports figures became heroes too. There was baseball hero, Babe Ruth; boxing champ, Jack Dempsey; football's Red Grange; and tennis star, Helen Wills.

One of the most famous heroes was Charles Lindbergh. In May, 1927, Lindbergh made the first solo flight across the Atlantic. He flew the *Spirit of St. Louis* from Garden City, New York, to Paris, France. Fans called Lindbergh the "Lone Eagle" and "Lucky Lindy."

Five years later, America would have a heroine of the air. Amelia Earhart became the first woman to fly across the Atlantic alone.

## "I Have No Fears for the Future . . ."

**Some people were living very high while others were living very low. People were buying things on credit that they couldn't pay for. What do you think was in store for America?**

When Hoover became president in 1928, he said, "I have no fears for the future of our country. It is bright with hope." People believed the boom would go on forever. But the economy wasn't just hot, it was overheated. Businesses were depending on people to keep buying new things. Many people, however, were buying things on time. They were paying part of the cost each month, instead of paying it all at once. And many farmers, miners, immigrants, and minorities still had a hard time earning a living at all. Yet in early 1929, many Americans believed they'd found the key to everlasting wealth and progress.

## History Practice

Answer these questions on a separate sheet of paper.

1. How did America treat African Americans, Jews, Catholics, immigrants, and other minorities during the twenties?

2. What did the 18th Amendment prohibit?

3. How did life change for American women in the twenties?

# Chapter Review

## Summary

| CHRONOLOGY OF MAJOR EVENTS |
| --- |

| | |
| --- | --- |
| 1919 | 18th Amendment |
| 1920 | 19th Amendment |
| 1920 | Sacco and Vanzetti trial |
| 1920 | Warren G. Harding elected 29th president |
| 1920 | First regular radio broadcast in America |
| 1923 | Harding dies in office; Coolidge takes over |
| 1924 | Calvin Coolidge elected 30th president |
| 1927 | Charles Lindbergh makes solo flight across Atlantic |
| 1927 | Babe Ruth sets new home run record |
| 1928 | Herbert Hoover elected 31st president |

- Isolationist Americans wanted to tend to business at home.
- The twenties brought weakened labor unions.
- A "Red scare" caused many people to be accused of being communists.
- Many Americans distrusted immigrants and members of minority groups. Racism spread.
- Presidents Coolidge and Hoover pledged to keep business booming.

- Until 1933, the 18th Amendment prohibited the sale of liquor.

- The 19th Amendment gave women the vote. More women worked outside their homes.

- Americans of the twenties liked glitter and glamour. They had many heroes.

- The glitter and glory of the twenties would fade. Some people were living very high. Others were not earning livings at all.

## Chapter Quiz

1. What was the Teapot Dome Scandal?

2. What belief did presidents Coolidge and Harding both have?

3. List three ways the automobile changed America.

4. How long did Prohibition last?

5. What did Langston Hughes, James Weldon Johnson, and Countee Cullen have in common?

6. Which groups did not benefit from the prosperity of the twenties?

## Thinking and Writing

1. The 1920s are sometimes called the "Roaring Twenties." In what ways do you think the twenties were "roaring" years?

2. In what ways did American life get better in the twenties? What things were going wrong?

3. The "Wets" were against Prohibition. The "Drys" were for it. Why do you think the 18th Amendment was later repealed?

# Chapter 20

# The Great Depression

| 1929 | 1938 |
|---|---|
| Stock Market Crash | War Clouds in Europe |

**Leaving home to look for work**

## Chapter Learning Objectives

- Explain some of the causes of the Great Depression.
- Tell how life changed for people who lived in the Dust Bowl.
- Describe American life during the Great Depression.
- Tell how the New Deal helped the American people.

# Words to Know

**decade**   ten years
**dictator**   a ruler with complete power
**drought**   a long period of dry weather
**migrant**   a worker who moves from one place to another as seasons change and crops ripen

**panic**   a sudden great fear
**recovery**   a return to health
**repeal**   to take back or do away with

During the 1920s, many Americans had discovered a new sport. They played the stock market. For $20, $50, or $100, anyone could buy a share of stock and own a small piece of some company. They could even own a piece of U.S. Steel. If the price of the stock went up, a person could sell it and make money. In the 1930s, this changed dramatically. In this chapter, you will read about the Great Depression.

## The Crash

In the 1920s, everyone from bus drivers to bankers bought stock. And why not? Business was good, and stock values were rising. With so many people buying, prices doubled and even tripled. They kept climbing until September 3, 1929. At this point, more than 3 million people were playing the market.

On the next day, prices slipped a bit. More people wanted to sell than to buy. No one worried. It had happened before. But the prices kept on slipping.

On Monday, October 21, the **panic** began. People were losing lots of money. They wanted to sell. On Monday, 6 million shares were sold. On Tuesday, another 6 million. On Wednesday, 8 million. Prices dropped $20 or more each day.

Do you know anyone who "plays the stock market"? Newspapers give a stock market report each day. Look in the business section. See which stocks are going up and which ones are falling.

Black Thursday came on October 24, 1929. The New York Stock Exchange, where the buying and selling took place, went crazy. It was a madhouse full of screaming dealers. They were waving handfuls of paper and selling at any price. Out on the street, crowds watched their money disappear. RCA fell from $68 to $56 to $44 a share. General Electric went from $315 to $298 to $283. Almost 13 million shares were sold.

For the next few days, the market held steady. Bankers were buying stock to keep the prices up. Then on Tuesday, October 29, the market crashed again. Now even the bankers rushed to sell. Over 16 million shares were dumped. The market had lost $8 billion in a week. It had lost $32 billion in a month. Many people had bought stocks "on margin." That meant they had to put up only 10% of the stocks' value in cash. They could pay the rest later. But the margin payments became due when the market began to drop. To get money, many people had to sell their stocks—no matter how little the stock was worth. Many people lost everything they had. They were wiped out. America woke up from the dream of prosperity to find itself in the Great Depression.

## What Had Happened?

A depression is the opposite of prosperity. When many people are unemployed, they can't buy goods. When there are more products than people can buy, businesses and factories close. Then more people are out of work. A depression feeds on itself.

The stock market crash wasn't the only cause of the Great Depression. Business was very sick. In the 1920s, it had produced more goods each year. By the end of the **decade**, it was putting out more than people could buy. When the goods didn't sell, prices went down. Companies made less money. They cut working hours, lowered salaries, and fired workers. When workers made less money—or lost their jobs—they purchased even less. Between 1929 and 1932, 100,000 businesses closed their doors for good.

The United States had cut off trade with foreign markets. Tariffs were put on goods from other nations. Americans could not sell their goods abroad to help the economy.

The jobless rate among black people was often six times higher than it was among white people.

Banks began to fail. The stock they owned had become worthless. And the banks had made loans to businesses and workers that no one could pay back. They hadn't kept enough of their customers' money. In the panic, more and more people tried to withdraw their cash. The weaker banks failed as they ran out of cash. In 1931, almost 200 banks a month were failing. Many people who had put money in those banks never got it back.

## Breadlines and Dust Bowls

The Great Depression fell hardest on workers. In 1932, the unemployed and their families numbered over one-third of all the people in the United States.

President Hoover said that local groups should take care of those in need. But the groups had no way to care for so many people who had no money, food, or hope. In city after city, they lined up for handouts of bread and soup.

A teacher asked a student, "What's wrong?"
"I'm hungry."
"Why don't you go home and eat?"
"I can't. Today is my sister's turn to eat."

Many of the unemployed were forced to beg for money just to survive. "Brother, Can You Spare a Dime?" was the name of a popular song in the 1930s.

Farmers made only half as much money in 1932 as they had in 1930. When they couldn't pay off their loans, the banks took their property. And in 1932, the midwestern states were hit by **drought**. Bad farming practices and 18 months of little rain had dried out the soil. The winds came up and made giant dust storms that blocked the light of the sun. The storms ruined crops. As much as 300 million tons of soil blew away in a day. The area became known as the Dust Bowl.

## Then and Now: People Without Homes

**Then:** During the Great Depression many people had nowhere to live. They'd lost their jobs, money, and homes. Some built dwellings with cardboard, scrap lumber, tin, and tar paper. Whole villages of these shacks grew up in many American cities. They were called shantytowns. Sometimes they were called Hoovervilles because many people blamed President Hoover for their troubles.

There were a lot of Hoovervilles in the West. Rumors of jobs brought the unemployed. When they arrived, they found things bad in the West too. They had come as far as they could, so they settled into shacks.

**Now:** Today there are people who cannot afford housing. Many men, women, and children live on America's streets. Are there homeless people in your city? What is being done to help them?

Farmers were already poor from years of falling prices. For many, this was the end. Their lands and crops were ruined. Their houses were buried in dust. They packed their families into old cars and headed west to make a new start. In four years, 300,000 people drove to California. Most were told, "Go back. There's no work for you here." Farm families traveled from place to place, trying to find work. They became **migrants**. But most often, there was no work to be found.

## History Practice

Answer these questions on a separate sheet of paper.

1. Why did prosperity turn to depression between 1929 and 1932?

2. How was the nation affected when many people were unemployed?

3. Name two causes for the Dust Bowl.

# What Did Hoover Do?

President Hoover and his administration believed that government should not interfere with business. At first the Hoover administration did little to help. Hoover believed citizens would grow stronger if they helped themselves.

Hoover finally saw that Americans did need some help. The Federal Farm Board gave some support to farmers. Public works projects were set up. The government helped build dams, roads, buildings, and airports. Boulder Dam in Colorado was a public works project. It was later renamed Hoover Dam. These projects gave jobs to many Americans.

The Reconstruction Finance Corporation loaned money to businesses, banks, railroads, and farmers.

Many people escaped their troubles by going to the movies. The "talkies" made movies come alive. Walt Disney created Mickey Mouse to make people laugh.

## Roosevelt's New Deal

Hoover's programs weren't enough. In 1932, between 13 and 16 million people were out of work. The value of stocks on the New York Stock Exchange had fallen 75 percent. Fear was widespread. It was an election year. The voters wanted action. They elected a newcomer, Franklin Delano Roosevelt, president. With Roosevelt, also known as FDR, action was what they got.

Roosevelt took office on March 4, 1933. Most banks had already closed to keep from being wiped out. On March 5, Roosevelt closed *all* the banks. He also ordered Congress into a special meeting. The banking system was reworked. Laws were pushed through to make it safer. On March 16, three-quarters of the major banks reopened.

Roosevelt also held "fireside chats" over the radio. "The only thing we have to fear is fear itself," said FDR. Roosevelt also said that one-third of the nation's people were "ill-fed, ill-clothed, and ill-housed." He said the government should change that.

Roosevelt approached the farm problem with programs to raise crop prices. He also worked to change the farming practices that had started the Dust Bowl.

Hearing directly from their president and seeing his quick action, people regained hope. At last, someone was doing something.

People showed their trust by putting money back in the banks.

The next election year was 1936. Eight million people still needed jobs. The depression wasn't over. But industry was growing. The banks were safe, and unemployment was dropping. Prohibition, which was unpopular, had been **repealed**. This happened, in part,

FDR was the first president to appoint a woman to his cabinet. Frances Perkins was secretary of labor. Perkins was a social worker who battled to improve conditions for working people.

**A "fireside chat" with FDR**

so that more people could have jobs making and selling alcohol.

The National Industrial **Recovery** Act was passed. Companies worked together to set rules for hours, pay, prices, and how much could be produced. Other programs gave people jobs putting up buildings and fighting fires and floods.

Roosevelt's many plans and programs were called the New Deal. It had won people over. The president was reelected by the largest vote ever.

The New Deal put millions of people back to work.

But The New Deal also cost billions of dollars. Taxes went up. The government borrowed money.

| | NEW DEAL PROGRAMS | |
|---|---|---|
| AAA | Agricultural Adjustment Administration | paid farmers to grow fewer crops so prices could rise |
| CCC | Civilian Conservation Corps | gave jobs planting trees and building dams |
| FDIC | Federal Deposit Insurance Corporation | insured savings in banks |
| FERA | Federal Emergency Relief Administration | gave states money to help the needy |
| NRA | National Recovery Administration | set minimum wages and maximum work hours |
| PWA | Public Works Administration | created jobs building schools, bridges, dams, and courthouses |
| SEC | Securities and Exchange Commission | regulated stocks and provided stock information |
| TVA | Tennessee Valley Authority | created jobs building dams to control flooding in the Tennessee River Valley |
| WPA | Works Projects Administration | created jobs building roads, parks, bridges, and public buildings |

Some people felt it was costing too much. Others felt the government had to help people no matter what the cost.

How can you find out if there are any buildings, dams, or parks in your area that the WPA, PWA, TVA, or CCC built?

## Learn More About It: Social Security

In 1935, the Social Security Act was passed. People paid money to Social Security during their working years. When they retired or were too sick to work, the money was paid back to them in monthly payments.

We still have a Social Security System today.

## Roosevelt and the Supreme Court

In 1936, the Supreme Court ruled against the AAA. It said the government had to stop paying farmers to grow fewer crops. The Court ruled the NRA unconstitutional, too. It said the president couldn't set minimum wages and maximum work hours. Roosevelt began to worry. It looked as though the Supreme Court might upset his New Deal.

In 1937, Roosevelt called for seven changes in the Court system. Six were accepted. The seventh caused huge debate. It said that when a Supreme Court justice reached 70, a younger man should help him. Some people said Roosevelt was trying to "pack" the Court with justices who favored the New Deal. Roosevelt's proposal failed.

But soon there were retirements and deaths among the justices. By 1944, all but two had been appointed by Roosevelt. The New Deal programs were safe.

Some people called Eleanor Roosevelt the "eyes and ears" of President Franklin Roosevelt. As the president's wife, she traveled the country visiting areas hardest hit by the Depression. She saw the soup kitchens and the shanty towns. Then she called for programs that would provide job training and better medical care. Some people criticized Eleanor Roosevelt. They said the first lady should stay out of politics. But Eleanor didn't listen to the critics. She worked to improve the quality of life and to guarantee human rights for all Americans. She became known as the most active first lady in American history.

## Social Unrest

The 1930s were a time of much social unrest. After the market crashed, people looked to the government for help. But President Hoover seemed to ignore what people were going through. Big business had also failed to solve any of the country's problems.

In 1933, some dairy farmers dumped the milk their cows had produced. They hoped to lower the supply and force up prices.

Angry citizens began to turn their anger into action. In 1932, men who'd fought in World War I marched on Washington asking for help. They were driven off by the army. Farmers tried to use force to stop the sale of their neighbors' lands. They burned their own crops to drive up prices. Factory workers staged strikes.

When Roosevelt came in, the government took a larger role. It used money to help people. It took more control over business. These actions shocked the wealthy. But many people wanted the help. They felt that a government that taxed them *should* be helping them.

Labor unions grew during the depression. The Wagner Act stopped employers from firing workers who joined unions. As unions became stronger, there were long and sometimes bloody strikes. The unions demanded better conditions and pay from the steel, auto, and other industries. In 1936, a strike shut down shipping ports on the West Coast for three months. Companies often used the police or hired thugs to attack the strikers and drive them off. But the unions slowly made gains in more and more companies.

## More Trouble Ahead

America pulled through the worst of the depression within a few years. But it became harder to move forward. In 1938, 8 million job seekers were still out of work.

Europe had also been hit by the depression. People there were suffering. Their governments were very weak. Adolf Hitler in Germany and Benito Mussolini in Italy used these troubles to become **dictators**. They built up their armies and took over weaker countries. Japan, too, had enlarged its army. It was a threat to peace in the Far East.

The United States was worried by all this. But it had its own problems to solve. And it remembered that the First World War had not made the world "safe for democracy."

### History Practice

Answer these questions on a separate sheet of paper.

1. Name three things President Roosevelt did to try to end the depression.

2. Why were many Americans happy with the New Deal?

3. What happened to labor unions during the 1930s?

# Chapter Review

## Summary

| CHRONOLOGY OF MAJOR EVENTS |
| --- |

| 1929 | Herbert Hoover becomes 31st president |
| --- | --- |
| 1929 | Stock market crash |
| 1932 | Midwest becomes Dust Bowl |
| 1932 | Franklin D. Roosevelt elected 32nd president |
| 1933 | Tennessee Valley Authority created |
| 1935 | Social Security Act |
| 1936 | Roosevelt reelected |
| 1937 | Roosevelt asks for changes in Supreme Court |

- In the stock market crash of 1929, many people lost money.

- The depression was also caused because more goods were being produced than people could buy.

- During the depression many banks and businesses failed.

- In 1932, the unemployed and their families made up one-third of the population.

- A drought in the Midwest and bad farming practices caused dust storms that destroyed farms.

- Franklin Roosevelt reworked the banking system and set up programs to help unemployed Americans. Roosevelt's plans were called the New Deal.

- Slowly, America began pulling out of the depression. But a depression had hit Europe, too. Powerful dictators took advantage of the poor economy. They gained power in Germany and Italy. Japan built up its army.

## Chapter Quiz

1. During the 1930s, what role did the movies play in American life?

2. How did the government try to help farmers? How did it try to help bankers?

3. What did the PWA and the WPA do?

4. What was the CCC?

5. Why were some Americans worried about Roosevelt's New Deal programs?

6. As the depression came to an end in the United States, what was happening in Europe?

## Thinking and Writing

1. What would your life have been like during the Great Depression?

2. Why do you think FDR was a popular president?

3. How much say do you think government should have in business?

# Unit Six Review

Use the information in Chapters 17 through 20 to answer the questions on this page. Write your answers on a separate sheet of paper.

## A. Who was it?

1. He led the Rough Riders in the Spanish-American War.
2. She ruled Hawaii until a revolution forced her from the throne.
3. He opened trade between the United States and Japan.
4. His assassination sparked World War I.
5. "Two chickens in every pot," promised this president in 1928.
6. He ran a Chicago gang during Prohibition, making a fortune from illegal alcohol.
7. He was an American hero who first flew solo across the Atlantic Ocean.

## B. Explain . . .

1. . . . how the United States gained rights to build a canal in Panama.
2. . . . why the United States did not join the League of Nations.
3. . . . what happened in America during the "Red scare."
4. . . . how the New Deal helped bring America out of a depression.

## C. Think about what you have learned, then answer the following questions on a separate sheet of paper.

1. Define *isolationist*. Give examples of times when America acted like an isolationist nation.
2. What did the explosion on the battleship *Maine* and the assassination of Archduke Franz Ferdinand have in common?
3. Give three reasons why the United States entered World War I?

# The Second World War and Postwar America

# Chapter 21

# World War II

| 1939 | 1945 |
| --- | --- |
| Hitler's invasion of Poland | Japanese surrender; end of war |

**The attack on Pearl Harbor**

## Chapter Learning Objectives

- Tell what Hitler did when he gained power in Germany.
- Describe the fighting in World War II.
- Describe the event that caused the United States to declare war on Japan.
- Tell how World War II ended.

# Words to Know

**concentration camp**    a prison camp for people feared by a government

**Holocaust**    the killing of millions of Jews by Nazi Germany; the word *holocaust* means great destruction of life by fire

**internment**    the keeping of people in a place, such as a prison, usually during wartime

**pacifist**    a person who believes problems between nations should be settled peacefully, never by war

**patriotic**    showing love and loyalty toward one's country

**ration**    to limit the amount of something given out

**relocate**    to move to a new place

**war bonds**    certificates sold by the government as a way to raise money to support a war

---

Ask those old enough to remember just where they were on December 7, 1941. They will probably be able to answer you right away. On that date the United States was plunged once again into a world war. In this chapter, you will read about World War II and the events leading up to it.

## World War II Begins

In the late 1930s, most Americans had no desire for war. But around the world, things were taking a bad turn. Italy had invaded and crushed Ethiopia in 1936. In the Far East, Japan was looking for more natural resources. It was taking land from weaker countries.

World War I left much of Europe in a depression. The economy of Germany had collapsed. People could not find jobs. Many people were ready to accept a dictatorship as a way to solve their problems.

Under the cruel dictatorships that came into existence in Germany and Italy, individual people had no rights. What they wanted was considered of no importance. The only thing that mattered was what the state wanted.

## The Dictators

Benito Mussolini was the dictator who had held power in Italy since 1927. His political party was the Fascist party. Anyone who did not support the Fascists was considered a criminal. Mussolini was a cruel leader. Those who opposed him were thrown in jail or murdered.

Adolf Hitler was dictator of Germany. He had turned the country into a war machine that was grabbing land from other countries. Hitler ended democracy in Germany. He arrested those who spoke out against him and had them thrown into jail or **concentration camps**. Hitler and the Nazi party wanted control of everyone.

At the end of World War I, Germany had promised it would not rebuild its military. Now Hitler pledged to make Germany strong again. He stirred the Germans' spirit of nationalism. He built up the army. He set factories to making guns and tanks and submarines. No one stopped him.

Hitler spread a terrible hatred throughout Germany, the hatred of Jews. He planned, in fact, to wipe out the entire Jewish population. He built his

When Hitler was named Chancellor of Germany in 1933, he claimed the Nazi party was for "...peace, work, bread, honor, and justice."

plot against the Jews on lies. He blamed the Jews for Germany's defeat in World War I. He said the Jews were traitors and were the cause of all of Germany's problems. Many Germans, hard hit by the depression, were ready to blame their troubles on anyone.

Nazis arrested Jews throughout Germany and in all lands that Germany conquered. People were dragged from their homes and sent to concentration camps. There, most died from starvation or disease or were murdered in gas chambers. Hitler and the Nazis were bent on destroying an entire race.

The German treatment of the Jews was too horrible for the world to believe. Political prisoners, prisoners of war, and gypsies were also killed in the Nazi concentration camps. It was not until the end of the war, when the camps were freed, that the whole story was known. The Nazis had murdered 6 million Jews. This horror became known as the **Holocaust**.

Millions of Russians, Poles, Gypsies, and Slavs had also been killed.

Hitler's dream of power was a nightmare for the German Jews.

## Hitler Takes New Lands

Hitler invaded one region after another—the Rhineland, the Sudetenland, Czechoslovakia. Each time this happened, he told the world he would stop. But he never did. In May of 1939, Hitler made a military agreement with Italy.

Germany and Italy became known as the Axis. They agreed to help each other as each took lands from other countries. During the war there were five other Axis countries. They were Japan, Hungary, Finland, Bulgaria, and Romania.

**Germany invaded Poland September 1. The next day Europe was at war.**

In September of 1939, Hitler invaded Poland. Poland had treaties with England and France. These two countries then went to war with Germany and Italy. Those fighting the Axis nations were called the Allies. Europe was now the scene of a second world war.

**Jewish prisoners in Hitler's Germany**

## In the United States

In 1939, more than half the people in the United States believed we shouldn't take sides. There were groups like the America First Committee. They blamed the English and Jewish people for trying to drag America into the fighting. Isolationists said America had no reason to become involved in war. They said the Pacific and Atlantic Oceans would protect this country from the dictators abroad. A **pacifist** movement was very strong in the United States in the 1930s. Pacifists believed that any war was wrong and that the Untied States must stay out of armed conflicts.

In 1937, Congress passed a series of Neutrality Acts. These laws made isolationists happy. They were meant to keep Americans from becoming involved with warring nations. They said that U.S. citizens could not sell weapons to warring countries. Also, citizens could not travel on ships belonging to those countries. The Acts were meant to prevent Americans from becoming involved in something like the World War I sinking of the *Lusitania*. In 1939, President Roosevelt would see the Neutrality Acts

Hitler's sweep through
Europe was known as
a "Blitzkrieg," or
"lightning war." In
World War I, soldiers
fought in the trenches.
In World War II, the
German army kept
moving.

amended. "I regret that Congress passed the Acts," he would say.

Early in 1940, Hitler's army smashed through Norway, Denmark, Belgium, Luxembourg, and Holland. Then Germany and Italy took control of France. Only England remained free. In August, Hitler's airplanes started bombing it over and over. In one night, the bombing caused 1,500 fires in London alone. One month later, Germany and Italy formed the Axis Pact with Japan.

American opinion changed quickly. Now, more than half the country wanted to help England. Roosevelt had been elected president for a third time. He made sure it did get help. For a year, war goods poured into England. Roosevelt vowed to give Britain all help "short of war."

## Pearl Harbor

It was December of 1941. The brutal war raged throughout Europe.

On the other side of the Pacific Ocean, Japan was at war with China. It was pushing into Southeast Asia.

The American government opposed Japan's invasions. It had increasingly bad relations with that country. Still, the United States remained neutral as the war continued.

The morning of December 7 was a quiet one in Hawaii. Most of the American navy's Pacific fleet was at rest in Pearl Harbor. The sailors had just finished breakfast. At Wheeler and Hickham fields, the army's airplanes were lined up in neat rows.

At 7:02 A.M., a soldier saw something on his radar screen. It looked like a large flight of airplanes. It seemed to be headed for Pearl Harbor from 130 miles away. "It's not important," the soldier was told. "Turn off your screen and go to breakfast."

The attack on Pearl
Harbor shocked a
nation into war.

# World War II in Europe

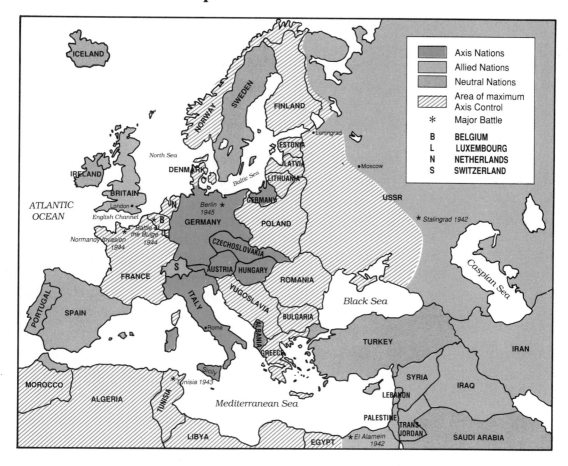

## Map Study

Study the map. Then answer the questions on a separate sheet of paper.
1. Which European nations were the Axis Powers?
2. Which countries were allies of the Axis Powers?
3. Which countries made up the Allied Powers?
4. Which countries remained neutral during all or most of World War II?

At 7:55 A.M., a low-flying plane appeared. It streaked across the water toward eight American battleships. It dropped a single bomb and then roared away. The flag of Japan flashed on its wings as it turned. Suddenly, wave after wave of Japanese planes filled the air.

In two hours, 18 American ships were put out of action. At Wheeler and Hickham, 188 planes were destroyed and 159 damaged. Over 2,400 Americans and Hawaiians were killed. There were 1,200 more hurt. The Japanese lost 5 submarines, 29 planes, and 100 men.

On December 8, President Roosevelt went before Congress and asked for a declaration of war. He got it easily. The United States went to war with Japan on December 11, 1941. As members of the Axis, Germany and Italy declared war on the United States that same day.

The attack on Pearl Harbor had blasted America's Pacific fleet into near ruin. And it had also blasted the United States right into the thick of World War II.

## History Practice

Answer these questions on a separate sheet of paper.

1. Which dictators were in charge in Germany and Italy?

2. Why were the people of these countries ready to accept a dictatorship?

3. What event made it easy for President Roosevelt to get a declaration of war from Congress?

# The War at Home

The American navy had been badly hurt at Pearl Harbor. The U.S. Army was rated only 17th in the world. It was not as strong as Poland's army, which Hitler had destroyed in less than a month.

Industry went back to making ships, tanks, guns, and planes. Companies that had made sewing machines turned to making weapons of war. Factories stayed open around the clock. Millions of Americans moved from rural areas to work in the factories of the cities. The need for workers meant new jobs for women and minorities. Workers agreed not to go on strike. They turned out more than anyone had thought they could. It was called a "miracle of production."

Shipyards raised their output by 20 times. One put together a complete ship in less than five days. The Allies were able to out-produce the Axis nations. That meant more ships, more guns, more airplanes, and more tanks.

Americans had to pay for World War II. Income taxes went up. Special taxes were put on alcohol, jewelry, and movie tickets. People loaned the government money to run the war by buying **war bonds**.

Americans gave up some things during World War II. Products that were needed overseas were sometimes scarce at home. Certain foods were **rationed**. Tires and gasoline and shoes were rationed, too. Other items, such as soap, chocolate, toilet paper, and bubble gum were in short supply.

The government encouraged people to grow their own vegetables in backyard "victory gardens." Americans took pride in "making do" with what they had, to help the war effort.

Women working in shipyards and aircraft plants were often nicknamed "Rosie the Riveter."

Has a shortage of any product ever affected your life? What was the product? How did you cope with the shortage?

## Minority Groups in Wartime

For the most part, Americans worked together. But there was still prejudice. Black soldiers were often put in special all-black troops. When blacks gave blood to the Red Cross, it was kept apart from other blood. Black workers left the South by the thousands. They moved to the industrial cities of the North, where factory jobs were waiting. But the jobs they found were usually the lowest paying.

The Japanese Americans were treated very badly, too. In 1942, the government forced Japanese Americans on the West Coast into **internment** camps. Families were **relocated** to one of several camps in the western United States. They hadn't done anything to deserve this. Two-thirds of them were native-born citizens. No Japanese Americans were ever found to be spies or to be hurting the war effort. They fought willingly and bravely for the United States. They were quite **patriotic**. In fact, they won more combat medals than any other group. Still, they lost their homes, their jobs, and their businesses.

Many Mexicans came to the United States as farm workers. They helped raise the food necessary to support the soldiers overseas. But the Mexicans were met with prejudice in jobs and in housing.

No German-Americans or Italian-Americans were taken to special camps. Why do you think people of Japanese descent were interned and not German- or Italian-Americans?

Learn More About It: The Fighting 442nd

An army unit called the 442nd was formed entirely of Japanese Americans. The "Fighting 442nd" battled bravely in Europe. Many of its soldiers were killed or wounded. Daniel Inouye, who later became a U.S. Senator from Hawaii, was one of the 442nd's many heroes. While these soldiers fought, most of their relatives were confined in internment camps.

## The War in Europe

The United States had to fight in both Europe and the Pacific. English and American leaders decided that Europe was the more important area of combat. However, it was almost a year before the United States was ready to join the fight in Europe. It took that long for the Allies to decide on a plan of action.

In the meantime, Germany suffered a major defeat in Russia. Russia had helped Germany in the early part of the war. But it switched sides when Hitler invaded Russia in mid-1940. The Russian army stopped the Germans at Stalingrad. It started pushing them back out of Russian territory.

Finally, the Allies decided to drive German and Italian troops out of North Africa before invading Europe. In October, 1942, the British attacked the Germans in North Africa. The British were led by General Montgomery. The general in command of German troops in Africa was Erwin Rommel. American troops arrived in North Africa in late 1942, led by General Dwight D. Eisenhower. The battle turned against the Germans when the Americans arrived. By May, 1943, most of the fighting in Africa had ended.

General Rommel was often called "The Desert Fox."

In July, English and American troops left North Africa by sea and invaded the Italian island of Sicily. After winning quickly in Sicily, they landed on the Italian mainland. They swept north. Near the middle of the country, they were met and bogged down for months by Germany's forces. Italy surrendered to the Allies in September, though the German army continued to fight there.

May 8, 1945, was called "V-E Day." Around the world people cheered victory in Europe (V-E).

The Allies struck their main blow by invading Hitler's Europe on June 6, 1944, D-Day. Allied soldiers stormed the beaches at Normandy in northern France. They pushed through the French countryside and freed Paris on August 25. By November, they had driven the Germans out.

In December, Hitler launched one last attack near the northwestern border of Germany. The Americans were pushed back. But by late January of 1945, the Germans were stopped. Soon after, the Americans advanced toward the German capital of Berlin. The Russians were marching on Berlin from the east. The two armies met on April 25, 1945. On April 30, with his country in ruins and his army in pieces, Hitler killed himself. On May 7, the last of the German army gave up. The war in Europe was over.

**The ruined German city of Ulm**

# The War in the Pacific

Less than ten hours after Pearl Harbor, the Japanese had attacked again. An attack in the Philippines destroyed most of what remained of America's Pacific air force. General Douglas MacArthur was in command of the American troops in the Philippines. He escaped to Australia. The Japanese took island after island. In five months, they almost reached Australia.

As the United States rebuilt its army and navy, the tide began to turn. Battles between the American and Japanese navies were fought mainly with planes carried on aircraft carriers. In 1942, at the battles of the Coral Sea and Midway, American planes sank many Japanese ships. The Battle of the Coral Sea saved Australia from Japanese attack. The Battle of Midway became known as the turning point in the Pacific struggle. MacArthur and the Americans gained control of the Pacific.

Japan lost four carrier ships and many pilots in the Battle of Midway.

The American navy began winning back places the Japanese had taken. These included New Guinea, Guadalcanal, and Tarawa. The Americans needed the islands for air bases. From them they could launch an attack on Japan. The Americans planned to capture island after island until they reached the Japanese mainland. The death toll in the island battles was very high. Each island was the scene of a bloody fight that led to another battle on the next island.

In late October, 1944, the Japanese put the rest of their navy into a battle near the Philippines. The American forces almost completely destroyed the Japanese fleet and retook those islands. Early in 1945, U.S. marines landed on Okinawa and Iwo Jima, islands not far from Japan. The marines took the islands in battles that cost thousands of lives.

**Iwo Jima**

## The Road to the End

American airplanes then bombed Japan. They destroyed Yokohama, Osaka, and other cities. In Tokyo, two days of firebombing killed 84,000 people.

America was winning the war in the Pacific. In Europe, Germany and Italy had already been defeated. But many Americans felt the Japanese might be ready to fight to the death. Some were saying that only further invasion of Japan would end the war. And that might mean the death of over a million American soldiers.

## Science Steps In

Since 1940, scientists in the United States had been working on a new weapon. It would prove to be more powerful than any the world had known. On July 16, 1945, the weapon was tested in the New Mexico desert. It worked. Its power to destroy was so great that some who saw the test thought it should never be used.

The final decision rested with the president. Franklin D. Roosevelt had died in April during his fourth term in office. The new president, Harry S. Truman, would decide. Was the new weapon too horrible to use? Would an invasion really cost a million American lives? Truman decided America would drop the atom bomb.

Robert J. Oppenheimer, an American physicist, directed the building and testing of the atom bomb. After the war, Oppenheimer worked to pass laws controlling the use of atomic energy.

## The End of World War II

America warned Japan it must surrender or face terrible destruction. Japan would not give up.

At 2:45 A.M., on August 6, 1945, an American bomber, the *Enola Gay*, left the ground. It took off from the western Pacific island of Tinian on its way to Hiroshima, Japan. It carried a single, fat, odd-looking bomb called "The Thin Man." The bomb weighed 9,000 pounds.

At 8:05 A.M., the *Enola Gay* was ten minutes from Hiroshima. No Japanese fighter planes came up to meet it. Hiroshima had never been bombed. It was normal for planes headed elsewhere to fly over.

At 8:15 A.M., "The Thin Man" was dropped. Hiroshima was going about its morning business. People were going to work, making breakfast, walking over the Aioi bridge. Then there was a flash that was brighter than the sun. A fireball consumed the Aioi bridge and everything around it. Over a mile away, steel doors and stone walls glowed red-hot. A mushroom-shaped cloud rose from a base of flames. The superheated air started fires all over the city. Over 80,000 people were killed. Those near the blast simply disappeared. More than 62,000 buildings were destroyed.

Hiroshima, a city of 320,000 people, was in ruins.

The first atom bomb had been dropped. Three days later, a second bomb was dropped on the city of Nagasaki. Japan gave up on August 15.

World War II had ended. And the atomic age had begun.

Japan's formal surrender took place on September 2, 1945, aboard the battleship *Missouri*. General MacArthur signed the treaty for the Americans.

More than 18 million died fighting in World War II. More Russian soldiers died than soldiers of all other nations combined.

### History Practice

Answer these questions on a separate sheet of paper.

1. Describe how the American government treated Japanese Americans during World War II.

2. Name three countries in which American troops fought during World War II.

3. What happened on D-Day?

4. What forced Japan's final surrender?

# Chapter Review

## Summary

| CHRONOLOGY OF MAJOR EVENTS |
| --- |

| | |
| --- | --- |
| 1927 | Benito Mussolini takes power in Italy |
| 1933 | Hitler takes control of Germany |
| 1933 | Franklin Roosevelt becomes 32nd U.S. president |
| 1937 | Congress passes Neutrality Acts |
| 1939 | Germans invade Poland; England and France declare war on Germany and Italy |
| 1939 | Neutrality Acts amended |
| 1941 | Japanese attack Pearl Harbor; United States enters World War II |
| 1942 | Japanese Americans relocated to internment camps |
| 1942 | American troops arrive in North Africa |
| 1942 | Battles of Coral Sea and Midway in Pacific |
| 1944 | Allied invasion of Normandy (6/6) |
| 1944 | Allies free Paris (8/25) |
| 1945 | Harry Truman becomes 33rd president |
| 1945 | Berlin falls; Germany surrenders |
| 1945 | Atom bomb dropped on Hiroshima (8/6) |
| 1945 | Atom bomb dropped on Nagasaki (8/9) |
| 1945 | Japan surrenders (8/15) |

# Chapter Review

- Dictators took advantage of Europe's depression to gain power. Hitler led the Nazis in Germany. Mussolini led the Fascists in Italy.

- Japan, like the European dictatorships, wanted new lands and a larger empire. In Germany, Hitler ended elections, arrested anyone who opposed him, and persecuted and imprisoned Jews.

- The Nazi attempt to kill all Jews became known as the Holocaust.

- Hitler sent a rebuilt German army to conquer nations. At first, no one tried to stop him. France and England declared war when he took Poland.

- Germany, Japan, and Italy joined together to form the Axis Powers. Those who opposed the Axis Powers, including France and England, were called the Allies.

- At first, America remained neutral. America declared war when Japan bombed Pearl Harbor.

- At home Americans helped the war effort by producing huge amounts of war goods. Women stepped in to take over jobs that had traditionally been men's.

- American troops joined the British to defeat the Germans in North Africa.

- American and British troops invaded Italy.

- On D-Day the Allies landed on the beaches of Normandy, France. They freed Paris and drove the Germans out of France.

- When the Allies took Berlin, Germany surrendered.

- In the Pacific, the Americans took island after island, moving closer to Japan.

- Japan surrendered when the atom bomb was dropped on Hiroshima and Nagasaki.

## Chapter Quiz

1. List three Axis countries and three Allied countries.

2. What event caused England and France to go to war with Germany and Italy?

3. What was the Holocaust?

4. What was V-E Day?

5. What did Generals Montgomery and Rommel have in common?

6. Which battle turned the tide of the war in the Pacific?

## Thinking and Writing

1. Italy and Germany turned to dictators to solve the problems of the depression. America faced a depression, too. Why do you think the United States did not become a dictatorship?

2. Describe three changes in the lives of Americans at home during World War II.

3. Do you think the United States should have used the atom bomb? Explain the reasons for your choice.

# Chapter 22

# The Postwar Years

**1945**
End of World War II

**1950**
Cold War continues

**People jammed Times Square in New York City to celebrate the end of World War II.**

## Chapter Learning Objectives

- Describe the problems America faced after World War II.
- Tell why the United Nations was founded.
- Describe the cold war.
- Explain what happened to Germany and Japan after World War II.
- Tell how America helped rebuild war-torn Europe.

# Words to Know

**cooperate**   to work together toward a common goal

**crisis**   a time of difficulty or danger

**divine**   godlike

**fascism**   a system of government under which each citizen's purpose is to serve the state

**figurehead**   a person who holds a high position but has no real power

**overthrow**   to violently replace one government with another

**retire**   to stop working, usually because of age

**satellite**   a country that is controlled by a stronger, more powerful one

**scourge**   something that causes great pain and suffering

**veterans**   those who have served in the armed forces

**zones**   sections marked off and divided

---

Millions of people were killed in the Second World War. The Americans who survived came home in 1945 and 1946. They looked forward to taking off their uniforms and getting on with their normal lives. What did they find when they got back? In this chapter you will read about conditions in the United States in the late 1940s.

## Home Again

Many soldiers came home hoping to find everything just as they'd left it. But prices had risen sharply. Housing was in short supply. For some, it was hard to get work. A number of industries were slow in changing over to peacetime production.

Black **veterans** hoped that things had changed while they were away. They'd fought with strength and courage to defend their country. They came home wanting to enjoy an equal share of the risks and rewards of life in America.

Often they found they couldn't ride in the front of a bus or sit at a lunch counter. They met the same racism that had been present since before they were born.

Why do you think veterans may have studied harder than younger college students?

## Learn More About It: The GI Bill

A new law had been passed in 1944. The GI Bill of Rights set aside money for returning soldiers. The government would pay for these veterans' education and job training. The government helped veterans get loans for homes, farms, and businesses. Do you know anyone who has made use of the GI Bill?

## Postwar Labor Unions

Business had been saved from the depression by the demand for war goods. Now factories had to stop making tanks and guns and start making cars and lawn mowers. Workers had new demands. The unions had been mostly quiet during the war. Problems on the job were seen as part of the war's hardships. When the war was over, the unions spoke out again for their members.

Rising prices meant a demand for higher wages. In 1946 there were labor strikes throughout the country. The federal government stepped in to end a railroad strike and a coal miners' strike.

In 1947, the Taft-Hartley Labor Act was passed. It was meant to control striking labor unions. President Truman said the act was a "threat to democracy." He vetoed the act. Congress passed the Taft-Hartley Act over his veto. The act limited the power of the unions. Among other things, it said that workers could not be required to join a union before they could be hired.

Despite the Taft-Hartley Act, the postwar years brought gains for the labor unions. Wages went up. New contracts for workers often included health insurance and **retirement** funds.

## Learn More About It: Baby Boomers

There was a baby boom in the years following World War II. For many Americans the war had meant an uncertain future. Peace brought thoughts of security, a home, and a family. It was a time to have babies.

As the children born in the late 1940s grew up, their large numbers affected daily life in America. Between 1950 and 1960 the population of the United States soared from 151 million to 179 million. What do you think happened to schools in the 1950s? What do you think happened to the job market in the late 1960s and early 1970s?

## After the Bomb Fell

In at least one way, the war had changed everyone's life. The atom bomb had arrived. The United States, Canada, and England held the secret of making atomic weapons. They shared it with no one. President Truman said it would be too dangerous to do so. But by 1949, the Soviet Union also had the secret. Others, including France and China, would follow.

The power of the new weapons was almost too much to imagine. Firebombs had destroyed European cities. Atom bombs could wipe out whole countries. American land hadn't been touched by war in nearly 100 years. Before long, it would be possible to lay it to waste in less than an hour. Later, we would learn that whole continents, perhaps the whole world, could be destroyed.

## The United Nations

Although 1945 saw the atom bomb, it also saw the birth of a new hope. In April of that year, the representatives of 50 nations met in San Francisco. They came together to form the United Nations. The group was much like the League of Nations that Woodrow Wilson had planned. The United Nations would encourage worldwide **cooperation**. The United States had not joined the League of Nations when it was formed after World War I. But both America and the world had changed since then. Less than seven weeks after the bombing of Hiroshima, all the major powers agreed to the United Nations.

The United Nations (U.N.) set up headquarters in New York City. Its purpose was clear: "To save succeeding generations from the **scourge** of war." The U.N. seeks to keep world peace.

The United States, the Soviet Union, Great Britain, China, and France are known as the Big Five of the United Nations. *The General Assembly* is made up of representatives from all member nations. Most nations have one vote in the General Assembly. *The Security Council* works to keep world peace. *The Economic and Social Council* works to improve living conditions throughout the world. *The International Court of Justice* helps settle arguments between nations.

Since 1945 the U.N. has often been called on to keep peace in different parts of the world. U.N. members also try to solve world problems. They have helped poor nations battle hunger, and improve their education and medical care. The U.N. has provided relief after natural disasters like floods and earthquakes.

**U.N. Headquarters in New York**

## History Practice

Answer these questions on a separate sheet of paper.

1. How did the government control labor unions after World War II?

2. By 1949, which four countries knew how to make an atom bomb?

3. What is the purpose of the United Nations?

## The Beginning of the Cold War

The Soviet Union and the United States had fought together to defeat Germany. They were also both founding members of the United Nations. But since the war, they'd become quite **hostile** to one another. Each felt the need to protect itself. Each worried about the other's strength. Perhaps it was fear of the bomb that kept them from starting a shooting war. Instead, a new kind of conflict developed. Every move in the "cold war" hinted at destruction and death on a very large scale.

Oddly enough, it was because the Allies had won the war that many of the problems arose. The countries of Europe were in great disorder. Their governments were weak and helpless. Getting these countries back on their feet became the task of the Soviet Union and the United States.

Was World War II a "cold war" or a "hot war"?

## A Divided Germany

During World War II, the Allied leaders held meetings. They planned what would happen to Germany after its defeat. They held one important meeting in Yalta in the Soviet Union. They held another in Potsdam, Germany. They decided that after the war Germany would be divided into **zones**.

The Allies divided Germany into four parts. The Soviet Union had fought against Germany from the east. Eastern Germany came under Soviet rule. The United States, Great Britain, and France were in charge of the larger western part. The nations placed armed troops in their zones.

The Soviet Union also oversaw government activities in such places as Poland, Romania, and Hungary. Most Americans believed the Second World War had been fought to end **fascism**. Now

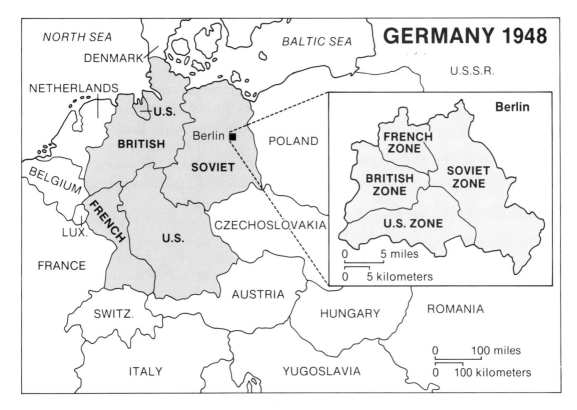

GERMANY 1948

NORTH SEA
DENMARK
NETHERLANDS
BALTIC SEA
U.S.S.R.
U.S.
Berlin
BRITISH
POLAND
SOVIET
BELGIUM
FRENCH
LUX.
FRANCE
U.S.
CZECHOSLOVAKIA
SWITZ.
AUSTRIA
HUNGARY
ROMANIA
ITALY
YUGOSLAVIA

Berlin
FRENCH ZONE
BRITISH ZONE
SOVIET ZONE
U.S. ZONE
0    5 miles
0    5 kilometers

0    100 miles
0    100 kilometers

**Map Study**

Study the map. Then answer the questions on a separate
sheet of paper.

1. Which four nations controlled Germany after World War II?
2. Which four nations controlled the city of Berlin after World
   War II?
3. Which nation controlled the zone in which Berlin was
   located?

it seemed that in Eastern Europe one form of
dictatorship was being replaced with another.
The United States feared that Soviet control would
reach into other parts of the world. Our government
decided it wouldn't let this happen. The gap between
the world's two strongest nations grew larger.

## The Truman Doctrine

The United States wanted to stop communism from spreading to other countries. Truman knew that nations weakened by the war would be perfect targets for takeovers. In 1947, Truman announced a plan to give aid to such nations. America would send money to Turkey and Greece. The Truman Doctrine's purpose was to keep the Soviet Union from gaining control around the Mediterranean.

The Soviet Union and the United States had been allies in World War II. But after the war they became enemies.

## The Marshall Plan

Secretary of State George C. Marshall had a plan too. It was based on the same idea as the Truman Doctrine. But it was to work on a larger scale. Again, the idea was that starving, depressed people were more open to communism. Marshall wanted to help rebuild Europe after World War II. The Marshall Plan called on America to help European countries build farms, factories, and railroads. By lending money and sending supplies, we would help Europe get on its feet again.

The Marshall Plan was offered to countries throughout Europe, including the Soviet Union and its **satellite** nations. The Soviet Union and its satellites refused. But 16 European nations accepted the aid. Some Americans felt the Marshall Plan cost too much money. Most felt it was worthwhile. They felt it would keep nations from turning to communism.

## Truman Wins Second Term

The year 1948 was an election year. Truman wanted to continue as president. He ran a hard-fought campaign against Republican Thomas E. Dewey.

## Learn More About It: The Iron Curtain

Winston Churchill had said the Russians were putting an "iron curtain" of communism and secrecy around Eastern Europe. He said it shut off Eastern Europe from the West.

Have you ever heard the expression "behind the iron curtain"? Why do you think Churchill described the curtain of secrecy as made of "iron"?

All polls showed that Dewey would win. On election night, with the early votes counted, the *Chicago Tribune* printed the headline: DEWEY DEFEATS TRUMAN.

When the final results were in, however, Truman had won the election. His victory was called the greatest upset in U.S. history.

**Harry Truman's victory**

## Then and Now: Postwar Japan

**Then:** United States troops occupied Japan after World War II. General Douglas MacArthur was put in charge. He was to change Japan into a democratic nation. Japan had to get rid of its armed forces. The emperor, Hirohito, was allowed to remain as a **figurehead** only. He could no longer claim to be all-powerful or **divine**. The United States helped Japan rebuild its factories, businesses, and schools.

**Now:** Japan became one of the greatest economic powers in the world. It put all its efforts into building its industries. Today Japan has trading partners around the world. It is a leader in the manufacture of electronic equipment, automobiles, and machinery. Japan has a strong educational system and 99 percent of its people are able to read and write. Japan has few natural resources. And it produces few raw materials of its own. But by concentrating on industry, it has become an economic giant.

## Crisis in Berlin

The first big **crisis** of the cold war took place in Europe in 1948. The capital of Germany, Berlin, was in the Soviet Union's zone. However, it too had been divided four ways. America, Britain, and France were going to make their parts of Berlin and Germany a single unit. So the Soviet Union cut off roads and rail lines into Berlin. By this blockade, they hoped to force the Western powers out of the capital.

Neither side was ready to go to war. But it was a very tense time. When supplies in Berlin ran low, the Western countries, led by America, took action. They began the Berlin airlift. Large amounts of food, clothing, and other goods were flown in. At one point, a plane was landing in Berlin every three minutes. After 324 days, the Soviets gave in. The roads were reopened. But Berlin remained a divided city. The cold war was nowhere near over.

# NATO

In 1948, Soviet communists went into Czechoslovakia. They **overthrew** that country's democratic government. Czechoslovakia became another Soviet satellite.

The Berlin blockade and the takeover of Czechoslovakia increased fear of the spread of communism. In 1949, the United States, Canada, and ten Western European nations met and signed an agreement. They joined together in the North Atlantic Treaty Organization (NATO). An attack against any one of them would be considered an attack against all.

NATO set up an armed force to defend the treaty. General Dwight Eisenhower was named first commander of the NATO forces. NATO allowed the free countries to present a strong front against communism. But the Soviet Union would also grow stronger in the coming years.

## History Practice

Answer these questions on a separate sheet of paper.

1. Why was the United States eager to aid Europe?

2. What was the Marshall Plan?

3. Why did nations join together to form NATO?

# Chapter Review

## Summary

| CHRONOLOGY OF MAJOR EVENTS | |
|---|---|
| 1945 | Allied leaders hold Yalta Conference |
| 1945 | U.S. drops atom bomb on Japan; WWII ends |
| 1945 | United Nations founded |
| 1947 | Taft-Hartley Act sets controls on labor unions |
| 1947–48 | Truman Doctrine and Marshall Plan provide aid to Europe |
| 1948 | Berlin air lift |
| 1948 | Communists take over Czechoslovakia |
| 1948 | Truman reelected U.S. president |
| 1949 | NATO set up |
| 1949 | Soviet Union tests atom bomb |

- Postwar America saw rising prices, housing shortages, and continued racial prejudice.

- Workers demanded higher wages to meet rising costs; labor unions grew stronger.

- The atom bomb forced the world to face the possibility of worldwide destruction.

- Fifty nations sought to keep world peace by forming the United Nations.

- The Allies divided postwar Germany into zones. Berlin became a divided city.

- The Soviet Union controlled satellite nations in Eastern Europe.

- The United States feared that communism would spread throughout Europe.

- The Truman Doctrine and the Marshall Plan provided aid to war-torn Europe.

- The United States helped Japan rebuild its economy.

- NATO was formed to present a front against communism.

## Chapter Quiz

1. What did the GI Bill of Rights do?

2. Who belongs to the U.N.'s General Assembly?

3. Who are the Big Five?

4. What did the Allies do with Germany after World War II?

5. Name two countries that received American aid under the Truman Doctrine.

6. Why did the Soviet Union blockade Berlin?

## Thinking and Writing

1. What is the difference between a hot war and a cold war? Explain how the development of the atom bomb might make one more likely than the other.

2. Is an organization like the United Nations necessary? Why or why not?

**Chapter 23**

# The Fifties

| 1949 | 1960 |
|---|---|
| First Soviet atom bomb tests | "Eisenhower prosperity" |

**Ethel and Julius Rosenberg**

## Chapter Learning Objectives

- Name three events that increased Americans' fear of communism between 1949 and 1950.
- Tell why U.N. troops went to Korea.
- Describe the actions of Senator Joseph McCarthy during the cold war.
- Describe two cold war crises during President Eisenhower's terms.
- Describe the American economy in the 1950s.

## Words to Know

**accusations**   charges that someone has done something wrong

**decay**   rot or decline

**decency**   proper behavior; goodness; kindness

**freedom of association**   the freedom to spend time with those one chooses

**migrate**   to move from one place to another

**pollute**   to make dirty

**stalemate**   the halting of a struggle when neither side will give in

**suburbs**   areas where people live near large cities

---

The years after World War II were marked with anger and fear. The hot war had ended, but the cold war had begun. Russia became the enemy Germany had been. Communism replaced fascism as the system that seemed the most threatening to our own. In this chapter you will read about the postwar years and the decade of the 1950s.

## Stolen Secrets

The world was shocked in September of 1949 when Russia exploded its first atom bomb. No country was more surprised than the United States. We were aware that the Russians had been trying to build a bomb. But nobody believed they'd be able to do so before the late 1950s. What had happened?

On February 3, 1950, England arrested Klaus Fuchs, a British scientist. Fuchs had worked on the bomb in the United States. He had given information about it to Americans who were spying for Russia.

Across the country headlines read, "U.S. Gave Russia Atom Secret." By August 18, five Americans were arrested. They were Harry Gold, David Greenglass, Julius Rosenberg, Ethel Greenglass Rosenberg, and Morton Sobell.

Julius and Ethel Rosenberg went on trial in March of 1951. Gold and Greenglass confessed to spying and spoke against the Rosenbergs in court. The Rosenbergs said over and over that they were innocent. But the court found them guilty. They were sentenced to death.

Many people thought that justice had been served. But others believed the trial had been unfair. They felt that Gold and Greenglass couldn't be trusted. The evidence against the Rosenbergs was weak, they said. The stolen secrets weren't that important. Whoever had given them to Russia should not have to be killed.

After two years, the case finally reached the Supreme Court. At noon on June 19, 1953, the court voted six to three against the Rosenbergs. At 8 P.M., they were to die. A special phone line was kept open to their jail. They were told their lives might be spared if they confessed their guilt. Right up to the end, they both said they were innocent.

Julius and Ethel Rosenberg died in the electric chair. They were the only Americans ever to be sentenced to death for spying in peacetime.

Before World War II, communism had a different reputation than it did after the war.

# A Time of Bad Feelings

In late 1949, China became a communist country. Civil War had been raging in China since 1920. The Chinese communists were led by Mao Tse-tung. The Nationalist Chinese, led by Chang Kai-shek, fought the communists for control of China. The United States supported Chang Kai-shek and the Nationalists.

In 1949, the communists took control. The Nationalist Chinese fled to the island of Formosa, which is now called Taiwan. There they set up a small republic. Mainland China became the People's Republic of China.

Only a few weeks after China went communist, Russia tested the bomb. Fear of communism brought on a "Red Scare" that swept the nation. Public hearings meant to flush out hidden communists found few spies. But they did hurt many innocent people.

American citizens were questioned about their beliefs, their friends, and the organizations they belonged to. Knowing a member of a group that someone said had communists in it could cost a person his job. People became very careful about what they said and whom they were seen with. It didn't matter how good anyone's record was. The Red Scare became a bigger threat to freedom of speech and **freedom of association** than communism itself.

Taiwan is about one-fourth the size of Illinois. But, it has almost twice as many people as Illinois—almost 20 million. The population of mainland China is over 1 billion.

There was also the fear that if the cold war turned hot, the atom bomb might be used. To most, that didn't seem a very smart way to solve problems. But some were upset with the idea of fighting endlessly to hold back communism. They wanted a war that could be finished and won.

Great Names in History:
Robert Oppenheimer

Robert Oppenheimer was an American scientist. He had headed up the project that built and tested the first atom bomb. In 1954, Oppenheimer was accused of being a communist spy. His brother had once been a member of the Communist Party, and Oppenheimer had known other communists. Oppenheimer was called before a government committee for a hearing. The committee decided he was innocent and had never been a communist or a spy. Still, the **accusations** ended Robert Oppenheimer's scientific work for the government. Many Americans were angry. They thought it was wrong that false accusations should hurt the career of a brilliant scientist.

## War in Korea

On June 25, 1950, communist North Korea invaded South Korea. The two countries had been threatening each other for some time. On June 6, the United Nations ordered North Korea to withdraw. The North Korean government refused. A U.N. force, made up mostly of U.S. soldiers quickly formed. It set out to help South Korea defend its territory. The U.N. troops were led by General Douglas MacArthur.

At first, the Korean War was popular with Americans. It was seen as a way to fight communism. But the American soldiers were quickly pushed back by the North Koreans. Then the Americans forced the North Koreans up to the northern part of their country, near China.

**U.S. soldiers in Korea**

The Chinese attacked with an army of over 300,000. The Americans and South Koreans were badly beaten. They were driven back to the line between North and South Korea, the 38th parallel. There the war remained. Neither side gained much ground. Both lost many lives. It was 1951, and the war in Korea had come to a **stalemate**.

At that point General MacArthur and President Truman began to disagree on battle plans. MacArthur wanted to bomb bases in China and end the war quickly. "There is no substitute for victory," MacArthur said. Truman disagreed. He felt that bombs dropped on China could lead to a third world war, an atomic war. President Truman said MacArthur could not bomb China. MacArthur would not give up his idea. He tried to take his plans to Congress for approval. Truman said that, as president, he had to keep control of the armed forces. He took away MacArthur's command. General Matthew Ridgway replaced MacArthur as commander of the U.N. troops in Korea.

Some Americans were not pleased with Truman's decision. MacArthur had been a hero in the Pacific during World War II. They felt a hero should not be fired. Others agreed with Truman's unwillingness to risk a worldwide war.

The Korean War lasted from June of 1950 until July of 1953. Many people were killed. More than a million Korean men, women, and children died in the war. Although the United States never declared war on Korea, United Nations troops were mostly made up of American soldiers. More than 33,000 of those soldiers were killed and more than 100,000 were wounded. By the end of the war, neither side had gained any ground. It was a war that no one won.

In his farewell speech to Congress, General MacArthur said "Old soldiers never die...they just fade away."

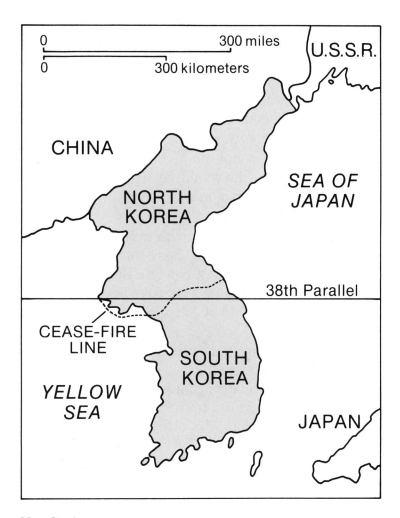

**Map Study**

Study the map above. Then answer the questions on a separate sheet of paper.

1. Which two countries border Korea to the north?
2. What two areas were divided by the 38th Parallel?
3. What country lies across the ocean southeast of Korea?

## McCarthyism

The Red Scare grew worse with the rise of Joseph McCarthy. He was a U.S. Senator from Wisconsin. Before February 11, 1950, Senator McCarthy was almost unknown. On that day, he began making speeches about communists. He said he had a list of communists who were working for the government.

The number of people on McCarthy's list kept changing. One day, he would say he had 205 names; on another day, 57; and on another, 81. No one was shown McCarthy's list.

Some people thought McCarthy was a hero. Many thought he was a liar who was just looking for power.

McCarthy couldn't back up his accusations with proof. He threw out so many lies at once that people couldn't disprove them fast enough. But his stories were so wild they became front-page news. When his charges were shown to be false, he made up new ones.

McCarthy's accusations ruined many people's lives. He had a fake photograph made to show his enemy, Senator Millard Tydings, talking to a communist. Tydings lost his next election. Two people who worked for McCarthy accused an innocent man who worked for Voice of America radio. Believing his life was ruined, the man killed himself. McCarthy even said Protestant church leaders were controlled by communists.

The country listened because it was hungry for an easy answer. McCarthy had one: communists were handing the country over to the Russians.

Things came to a head when David Schine, one of McCarthy's helpers, was drafted. Soon after, McCarthy was charged with trying to blackmail the army into favoring Schine. McCarthy said the army was just trying to stop him from checking up on it.

On April 22, 1954, the Army-McCarthy hearings began. They were shown on television. For 36 days, people all over the country watched McCarthy in action. He was shouting and bullying people. He listened to no one. He attacked without reason. Joseph Welch, the army's lawyer, stood up to him. In one powerful speech, Welch asked, "Have you no sense of **decency**?"

Enough people finally saw McCarthy for what he was. The Senate passed a strong statement against him. He lost his power in Congress. His attacks had not found one communist in an important job. Nor had they brought about one useful law.

Do you remember reading about the Red Scare of the early 1920s in Chapter 19? How was the McCarthy era like those years?

## History Practice

Answer these questions on a separate sheet of paper.

1. Name two events of 1949 that made Americans worry more about communism.

2. Which Western country provided most of the soldiers for the U.N. troops fighting in Korea?

3. Who won the Korean War?

# Old Enemies Become New Friends

Remember that the United States occupied and controlled Japan after World War II. In 1952, the Japanese got control of their own government. They let the United States keep troops and military bases in their country. Japan and the United States formed friendly trade relations.

# Eisenhower: A New President

In 1952, Dwight David Eisenhower was the Republican candidate for president. If Eisenhower were elected, Richard M. Nixon would be his vice-president. President Truman chose not to run for reelection. The Democrats nominated Governor Adlai Stevenson from Illinios.

The war was going on in Korea. Perhaps Americans thought a president with a military background could end that war quickly. On election day they chose World War II hero Dwight D. Eisenhower. Eisenhower was the first career military man to become president since Ulysses S. Grant. And this was the first time in 20 years a Republican had won the presidency.

President Eisenhower was faced with the cold war. He spoke to the world about peace. The Soviet leader Joseph Stalin died in 1953. It seemed then that some sort of peace might be possible. In 1959, the Soviet leader Nikita Khrushchev visited the United States. He met with Eisenhower. The two nations were talking. Tensions seemed to be lessening.

In 1956, Eisenhower ran for reelection, again against Democrat Adlai Stevenson. Eisenhower won his second term. But he would be working with a Congress made up largely of Democrats.

The United States continued to be involved in international crises during Eisenhower's second term. In 1956 tensions mounted over Egypt's Suez Canal. Though it ran entirely through Egyptian territory, the canal was operated by an international company. It was open to ships of all nations.

In October, Israeli troops advanced toward the Suez Canal. The Israeli government said it had learned that Egypt was planning an attack on Israel. France and Great Britain were concerned about the safety of the canal and the free flow of oil from the Middle East. They demanded that they be allowed to

**Ask people who could vote in the fifties if they remember Eisenhower's campaign slogan, "I Like Ike!"**

occupy areas in the canal zone to ensure its safety. When Egypt refused, the British and French bombed Egyptian airfields and moved their troops into the canal zone.

The Soviet Union supported Egypt. The Soviets threatened to use force if foreign troops did not leave the canal zone. The United Nations called for an immediate withdrawal of French, British, and Israeli troops. The Eisenhower administration voted against its allies and in favor of the U.N. resolution. Great Britain, France, and Israel withdrew, and a cease-fire was put into effect. A possible war was avoided.

In May of 1960, Soviet Premier Khrushchev invited President Eisenhower to visit the Soviet Union. Then an American spy plane was shot down over the Soviet Union. The Soviets captured the plane's pilot, Francis Gary Powers. Powers admitted he was on a spy mission. An angry Khrushchev took back his invitation to Eisenhower.

## The New States of Alaska and Hawaii

The United States grew during Eisenhower's second term. In 1959, both Alaska and Hawaii were admitted as states of the Union. Alaska was number 49 and Hawaii number 50. These were the first states that did not border on other states.

Alaska, purchased in 1867 from Russia, became the largest state in the Union. Americans had once called Alaska "Seward's Folly." They said Secretary of State Seward was crazy for buying a worthless piece of land. But Alaska was rich in timber, fish, gold, and oil.

Hawaii lies about 2,400 miles southwest of California. American planters built sugar and pineapple plantations there in the late 1800s. They gained economic control of the islands. The 50th state gave America agricultural products, a site for military bases, and beautiful recreation areas.

## New Homes in the Suburbs

Do you live in a city, a suburb, or rural area?

In the 1950s, many people bought automobiles. Roads, highways, and super-highways linked cities across the nation. The automobile freed people from living near their workplaces. Many who could afford to do so chose to leave the crowded cities. They **migrated** to the **suburbs** that sprang up where once there had been farmlands. Whole new communities were born. Banks and other businesses opened branches in the suburbs. Schools and shopping centers were built. Most people living in the suburbs went into the cities only to work.

Huge housing developments sprang up outside the cities. Many developers built rows and rows of identical houses. Mass production allowed these homes to be sold at low prices. Acres and acres of farmland were replaced by housing developments. Much of rural America was disappearing. What problems could be caused by the loss of farmland?

And what happened in the cities? The poor still lived there. Industry still **polluted** the air. With new building focused on the suburbs, cities began to **decay**. Some inner-city areas became run-down. Stores stood empty. In the 1950s many American cities were in danger of dying.

## A Time of Good Feelings

In many ways the 1950s were difficult years. There was the cold war, the atom bomb, the Korean War, the Red Scare, and McCarthyism. But those years and the years after were also good years for many people.

By 1959, the stock market had reached record highs. Business was soaring.

The demands of the Korean War had meant a boom for industry. Businesses grew larger and larger. People bought on credit even more than they had in the 1920s.

## Learn More About It: War and Economics

War and threats of war often generate a business boom. Many companies get rich making weapons, planes, and other military supplies.

President Eisenhower worried that industry was becoming too dependent on military build-up. Too many people were counting on jobs in war-related industries. What would happen to all those jobs in peacetime?

It was a time of odd contrasts. The number of people holding jobs rose. But so did the number of people who couldn't find work. Salaries went up. But so did the cost of living. Many industries did very well. But farms, railroads, and coal mines did poorly.

Still, many Americans lived in greater comfort than at any time in the last 25 years. After World War II and the Korean War, they felt they had earned it. They wanted steady jobs, quiet lives, and homes of their own. And all these things seemed, at least to middle-class whites, to be within reach.

The cost of living is the amount of money paid for food, clothing, and housing.

## History Practice

Answer these questions on a separate sheet of paper.

1. Who was the American war hero who became president in the 1950s?

2. Who was the Soviet leader who visited America in the 1950s?

3. Which two states were added to the union in 1959?

4. Where in America was building booming in the 1950s? What areas of America were in trouble?

# Chapter Review

## Summary

| CHRONOLOGY OF MAJOR EVENTS | |
| --- | --- |
| 1949 | Soviets test atom bomb |
| 1949 | China becomes a communist country |
| 1950–53 | Korean War |
| 1952 | Eisenhower elected 34th president |
| 1953 | Julius and Ethel Rosenberg executed |
| 1954 | Army-McCarthy hearings |
| 1956 | Eisenhower elected to second term |
| 1959 | Statehood for Alaska and Hawaii |
| 1960 | U.S. spy plane shot down over Soviet Union |

- In 1949, the Soviet Union tested the atom bomb and China went communist. In 1950, five Americans were arrested for giving atomic secrets to the Russians. These events made Americans more fearful of the spread of communism.

- North Korean troops moved into South Korea. The United Nations sent troops to stop them. The Korean War ended in a stalemate.

- Senator Joseph McCarthy stirred up the Red Scare.

- The cold war was in danger of becoming hot when a U.S. spy plane was shot down over the Soviet Union.

- Alaska and Hawaii became states.
- Large numbers of Americans began moving from cities to suburbs.

## Chapter Quiz

1. What did Julius and Ethel Rosenberg and Robert Oppenheimer have in common?

2. What did Mao Tse-tung and Chang Kai-shek have in common?

3. What event resulted in Senator Joseph McCarthy's loss of power?

4. What was the Suez Canal crisis about?

5. How many years ago were the 49th and 50th states admitted to the Union?

6. What does the cost of living include?

## Thinking and Writing

1. Why would the Communist Party takeover of China be a great worry to the United States?

2. The president is the Commander-in-Chief of the American armed forces. He can give orders to generals. How did this fact affect the course of the Korean War? Do you think the president should have this power? Explain why or why not.

# Unit Seven Review

Use the information in Chapters 21 through 23 to answer the questions on this page. Write your answers on a separate sheet of paper.

**A. Which came first?**
  1. VE-day or D-day?
  2. the bombing of Hiroshima or Japanese surrender?
  3. the League of Nations or the United Nations?
  4. the cold war or World War II?
  5. the Soviet Union's first test of the atom bomb or the U.S.'s first test of the atom bomb?

**B. Decide if you agree or disagree with each of the following statements. If you disagree, rewrite the statement so that you can agree with it.**
  1. The Holocaust was the Nazi murder of 6 million Jews.
  2. Hitler was never able to take Paris, France.
  3. The Soviet Union and the United States were founding members of the United Nations.
  4. The Truman Doctrine and the Marshall Plan both gave aid to Europe.
  5. President Eisenhower fired General MacArthur during the Korean War.
  6. McCarthy proved that many Americans were communists.
  7. When Japan took back control of its own government, it kept friendly relations with the United States.
  8. American cities were booming during the 1950s.

# Unit Eight

# The Road to Tomorrow

# Chapter 24

# A New Day

**1951**
Live television broadcast

**1962**
John Glenn orbits earth

**Jonas Salk, right, and associates**

## Chapter Learning Objectives

- Describe the events that marked the beginning of the space age.
- Tell how technology changed American life after World War II.
- Tell how nuclear energy was put to peacetime use.

# Words to Know

**antibiotics** chemicals produced to kill or stop the growth of germs

**astronaut** a person trained to travel in outer space

**atmosphere** all the air around the Earth

**cosmonaut** a Soviet space explorer (like American "astronaut")

**epidemic** the rapid spread of a disease to a large part of a population

**immunity** protection against disease

**nuclear** having to do with the nucleus, or center, of the atom

**satellite** an object that circles the earth, another planet, or a moon

**technology** science put to practical use

American **technology** advanced in the fifties and early sixties. Television sets brought entertainment and information into American living rooms. Medicines killed germs and fought disease. Rocket engines carried people into outer space. These are examples of science put to work to benefit people. When World War II ended, scientists paid more attention to peacetime advances.

## The Early Space Age

During World War II jet planes were developed. These planes could fly faster than the old propeller planes. First they replaced the propeller engines in fighter planes. Then they replaced them in passenger planes.

But the jet engine could not fly into outer space. It needed air to work. And there is no air in outer space. American scientist Robert Goddard had experimented with rocket engines in 1926. Goddard died in 1945. But the U.S. Army used his ideas. Rockets would let man explore the space beyond the earth's **atmosphere.**

The word *Sputnik*
means "traveler."

The Soviet Union made the first journey into space. On October 5, 1957, the Soviet Union sent up a **satellite**. *Sputnik I* orbited the earth. This Soviet launch marked the beginning of the space age. Both the Soviets and the Americans thought that the nation with the best space technology would have an advantage in the cold war. The space age became a time to see who could conquer space first.

In January, 1958, America sent up its first satellite, the *Explorer I*. Since then both nations have placed many satellites in orbit around the earth. The satellites carry different equipment. Some collect information about weather. Others are used to send television signals. Some satellites are used in spying. They take pictures and send reports on activities around the world.

## Early Journeys in Space

Humans first entered space in 1961. Soviet **cosmonaut** Yuri Gagarin was the first man in space. He orbited the earth once and safely returned. Three weeks after Yuri Gagarin went into space, the United States sent up an **astronaut**. Alan Shepard traveled 116 miles into space. In 1962, the United States sent astronaut John Glenn up to make three successful orbits around the earth. In 1963, cosmonaut Valentina V. Tereshkova became the first woman space traveler.

Astronaut Alan
Shepard's craft was
called *Mercury*. John
Glenn's was named
*Friendship 7*. What do
you think would be
some good names for
spaceships?

The day would come when the United States and the Soviet Union would meet in space. In 1975 crews of the Soviet *Soyuz 19* and the American *Apollo 18* linked in space. They shared a meal and held a joint news conference. The world watched this gesture of peace.

**Alan Shepard**

## History Practice

Answer these questions on a separate sheet of paper.

1. What event began the space age?

2. What does it mean to orbit the earth?

3. What jobs do satellites do?

## Pictures from Space

Unmanned space probes traveled millions of miles into space with cameras aboard. The probes photographed the surface of planets like Mars and Venus. An unmanned craft went to the moon and sent back televised pictures of the surface. These pictures led the way to actual travel to the moon. In Chapter 28 of this book, you will read about America's further journeys into space.

## New Medicines Save Lives

It is hard to imagine a world without **antibiotics**. We take these life-saving drugs for granted today. But once, simple infections turned into killers. Antibiotics are often called "wonder drugs" or "miracle drugs." They have the ability to kill disease germs. Penicillin was the first antibiotic to be discovered. This was done by the British scientist Alexander Fleming in 1928. At first antibiotics could only be produced in small amounts. Over the years, scientists learned to produce them in large quantities.

Vaccines save lives by preventing disease. Vaccines are made up of dead or weakened disease germs. The body takes in a small, harmless amount of the germ. This encourages it to fight the disease and develop an **immunity** to it.

In 1954, Americans lined up to get polio vaccine. The terrible, crippling disease had been attacking people, especially children. There was an **epidemic**. American scientist Jonas Salk discovered a vaccine that would protect against polio. A few years later, scientist Alfred Sabin came up with a polio vaccine that could be given by mouth. Today vaccines protect Americans against measles, mumps, the flu, and other diseases that once killed thousands.

## Atomic Power in Peacetime

After World War II scientists could work on peaceful uses for the energy that came from splitting an atom. In 1954, the first atomic-powered submarine was launched. The *Nautilus* left Groton, Connecticut, on January 21.

Think of medical problems today that are quickly cured by antibiotics. Imagine how serious those illnesses could become without the "wonder drugs."

Smallpox, a disease that once killed Americans, was wiped out once a vaccine was developed. What other diseases have been wiped out by vaccine?

In the late 1950s and early 1960s the United States began using **nuclear** energy to produce electrical power. America's first nuclear-powered plant began generating electricity in 1957. It was located near Pittsburgh, Pennsylvania. By 1973, 39 nuclear plants were producing 4.5 percent of U.S. electricity. Ten years later, more than 80 plants were operating.

## Television Changes American Life

After World War II, something new and exciting came into Americans' lives. Television sets were for sale! At first, not many people bought the sets. They were expensive. The screens were tiny and the pictures were greenish and not very clear.

But television sets improved quickly. The screens got larger. The pictures became clearer. The price went down. By 1953, 20 million TV sets had been sold in America.

Then life changed for many people. Americans stayed home in the evenings and watched their new TVs. The movie business dropped and so did the restaurant business. Fewer Americans went to libraries and bookstores.

Comedy, drama, talk shows, and quiz shows were very popular. Many radio shows simply carried over into television. Comedians like Jack Benny, Red Skelton, George Burns, and Gracie Allen all moved from radio to TV. Perhaps the most successful show of the decade was "I Love Lucy," starring Lucille Ball.

Television changed the sports world, too. Before television there were only a few professional football teams. Interest soared when television started broadcasting the games.

Rock and Roll music's first big star was Elvis Presley. When he appeared live on "The Ed Sullivan Show," teenage audiences screamed with delight. Elvis became a national hero.

Have you seen any TV programs rerun from the 1950s? How are today's programs different?

Television made the world seem smaller. People could see for themselves what was going on across America and the world. In 1952, television played its part in the presidential election. Republican candidate Dwight Eisenhower made 50 campaign ads for television. The Democratic candidate, Adlai Stevenson, scheduled only a few. But one of Stevensons speeches replaced an "I Love Lucy" broadcast. Angry Lucy fans sent Stevenson letters reading "I Love Lucy; I like Ike."

## Then and Now: Television in America

**Then:** During the 1950s television broadcasts came into American homes over the airwaves. At first, television stations broadcast in black and white only a few hours each day. Programming began around 2:00 or 3:00 in the afternoon and stations went off the air by 11:00. By 1960, just over 45 million American households had television sets.

**Now:** By 1990 93.1 million households had television sets. During the 1980s cable television became available. The system delivered programs to homes by cable instead of broadcasting them over the airwaves. Cable TV improved reception and offered more program choices. Many specialty cable stations operated around the clock. By 1988 cable systems brought television entertainment to around 42 million American homes.

# The First Computers

Computers were developed after World War II. The early ones were slow and as large as big rooms. They cost hundreds of thousands of dollars. Even by 1960, there were only about 5,000 computers in use in the United States. The industry had begun to grow, but the real computer age was yet to come.

Change became a way of life in the 1950s. Americans quickly took for granted television, jet planes, wonder drugs, even spaceships. And they were all things that had not even existed just a short time before.

## History Practice

Answer these questions on a separate sheet of paper.

1. Name two medical discoveries that helped Americans live longer lives.

2. How was atomic power used after the war?

3. What were three changes television made in American life?

4. Name two differences between early computers and computers today.

# Chapter Review

## Summary

| CHRONOLOGY OF MAJOR EVENTS | |
| --- | --- |
| 1951 | First live television broadcast |
| 1952 | Dwight Eisenhower elected president |
| 1953 | Jonas Salk develops polio vaccine |
| 1954 | First atomic-powered submarine launched |
| 1957 | Soviets launch *Sputnik I* satellite |
| 1957 | First American atomic power plant |
| 1958 | Commercial jet planes begin service |
| 1962 | Astronaut John Glenn orbits the earth |

- The space age began when the Soviets launched the *Sputnik I* satellite in 1957.

- Soviet cosmonaut Yuri Gagarin was the first man in space. He was followed by American astronaut John Glenn.

- Vaccines developed after World War II saved many lives. The polio vaccine that Jonas Salk developed stopped an epidemic.

- Atomic power was developed.

- Television became popular in the 1950s.

- Electronic computers were developed after WW II.

## Chapter Quiz

1. When were jet planes developed?

2. What was *Explorer I*?

3. Who was the first person to journey into space? the first American? the first woman?

4. What did Jonas Salk and Alfred Sabin have in common?

5. How long ago did the first nuclear power plant begin generating electricity?

6. Give three reasons television was not immediately popular.

## Thinking and Writing

1. How are the space travelers of today like Christopher Columbus and other early explorers? How are they like the American pioneers who traveled west?

2. Some people say too much tax money goes to the space program. Do you think America should be putting billions of dollars into the space program? Give reasons for your answer.

3. Some people say that the invention of television improved the quality of life in America. Others say television has had a bad effect. What do you think? Explain your answer.

4. Compare the role television played in the 1952 Eisenhower-Stevenson presidential campaign with the role television plays in political campaigns today.

# Chapter 25

# Civil Rights

| 1955 | 1963 |
|---|---|
| Montgomery bus boycott | Civil rights march on Washington |

**Rosa Parks**

## Chapter Learning Objectives

- Explain Martin Luther King's method for social change.
- Describe the Supreme Court rulings on segregation.
- Explain the goals of the black civil rights movement.
- Describe the struggles of other minority groups to protect their civil rights.

# Words to Know

**bail**   money left with the court as a guarantee that an arrested person will show up for trial

**boycott**   to join together in refusing to buy goods or services

**civil rights**   the rights of a citizen

**inspire**   to encourage

**integrate**   to bring together

**overcome**   to triumph over; to rise above

**resist**   to withstand; to oppose

**typical**   usual

In the last century, Congress had added the 13th, 14th, and 15th amendments to the Constitution. These laws made black Americans free citizens. That should have brought them all the rights enjoyed by other Americans. But this equality didn't come about. In most places, blacks were refused jobs, housing, education, and protection under law. What was there for whites wasn't there for blacks. In this chapter you will read about the **civil rights** movement in the 1950s and 1960s.

## Rosa Parks Says No

It was Thursday, December 1, 1955. In Montgomery, Alabama, Rosa Parks, a 42-year-old black woman, was waiting for her bus. She was tired from a long day's work. When the bus came, she got on it and sat down. In a short while, a white man got on the bus. He decided he wanted her seat and told her to move. Rosa Parks said no. The white driver reminded her that blacks had to ride in the back of the bus. He said he'd call the police. Rosa Parks kept her seat. At the next stop, she was arrested.

This wasn't unusual. Black Americans dealt with prejudice every day. But at that point, Rosa Parks's arrest was too much for blacks in Montgomery. Fifty people showed up at the police station.

They came to pay Rosa's $100 **bail**. She went home to wait for her trial on Monday. The black people of Montgomery spent the weekend setting up a **boycott**. They asked blacks to stay off the city buses.

On Monday, Rosa Parks was found guilty of breaking the law. She was fined $14. Her lawyer decided to take the case to the Supreme Court if necessary.

Also on Monday, the boycott began. Blacks walked, drove in car pools, or got to work any way they could. Except by bus. The boycott went on for 381 days. The city lost more and more money as the buses stayed empty.

One of the organizers of the boycott was Dr. Martin Luther King, Jr. King was a minister and black leader who preached "victory over your enemies through love."

Montgomery's blacks kept up the boycott against all odds. Their leaders were arrested. Four black churches were bombed. King's home was blown up. In spite of the attacks, black people remained peaceful. King had said, "Let nobody pull you so low as to hate them."

On November 13, 1956, the United States Supreme Court ruled that Montgomery's law was against the Constitution. The city dropped its law. More importantly, people saw they could change things when they worked together. And it had all started when Rosa Parks said no.

## Martin Luther King Calls for Nonviolent Protest

Martin Luther King, Jr. was the son of a minister. His family was well respected. Throughout his childhood in Atlanta, Georgia, Martin Luther King did not know poverty. But he did know racial discrimination. King lived in a segregated world. He recognized that segregation was wrong and, as a young man, decided to fight it.

King studied to be a minister. He became well known as a civil rights leader during the Montgomery bus boycott. Martin Luther King said that the battle against segregation must be fought in a nonviolent way. "We must meet hate with love. We must meet violence with nonviolence." King spoke of love and forgiveness.

Dr. King was arrested and jailed many times, but he insisted that the fight against racism be a peaceful one. Even when he met hatred, ugliness, and destruction, he insisted nonviolence was the way to equality. Dr. King has been compared to Mohandas Ghandi, who led India's fight for independence. Like Ghandi, King never changed his ideas about peaceful **resistance**.

In 1963, 100 years after the Emancipation Proclamation, Martin Luther King led a march on Washington. On a hot summer's day, 250,000 people went to the nation's capital. They demanded that African Americans receive their civil rights. Americans watched on television as blacks and whites marched side by side. They listened to King tell America: "I have a dream that my four little children will one day live in a nation where they will not be judged by the color of their skin but by the content of their character. . . . "

On April 4, 1968 Martin Luther King was assassinated by a man named James Earl Ray. News of his death angered many black Americans. Riots exploded in cities across the country. But the murderer's bullet did not end Dr. King's dream. Those who fight for **equality** are still inspired by his words and deeds.

**Martin Luther King, Jr.**

## Words from the Past

This song was sung by civil rights workers. It was sung by blacks who were tired of segregation, and by people everywhere who were sick of injustice and inequality:

"We shall **overcome**,
We shall overcome,
We shall overcome some day.
Oh, deep in my heart, I do believe,
We shall overcome some day."

# The Supreme Court Speaks

In 1896, the Supreme Court had handed down the Plessy vs. Ferguson "separate but equal" ruling. In this ruling the Supreme Court had declared it was legal to segregate blacks and whites in public places. This was permitted if equal services were provided for each group. Those who wanted to keep blacks down made much use of this.

Cities and towns built separate schools and separate eating places for blacks and whites. There were separate hotels, parks, libraries, theaters, rest rooms, drinking fountains, and much else. Though they were separate, these places and things were not of equal worth. Whites got the best and blacks the worst. In 1940, for example, Southern states spent three times as much money on white students as on black students.

In 1952, the National Association for the Advancement of Colored People (NAACP) went to the Supreme Court in the case of *Brown vs. the Board of Education of Topeka, Kansas.* A black girl named Linda Brown was not allowed into a whites-only school near her home. Linda Brown's father knew this was wrong. He took their case to court. The NAACP stepped in to help the Browns. The NAACP said the law of the land was being broken. The schools were *not* equal. Black children were not getting the education they deserved. Other groups said the states had the right to segregate.

The court listened to both sides and held the case for almost two years. Then in 1954, it ruled against the idea of "separate but equal." Separate schools for

**Thurgood Marshall led the team of lawyers who presented the Brown case for the NAACP. In 1967, Thurgood Marshall became the first black man to serve as a Supreme Court judge.**

blacks and whites, the court stated, would never be equal. All states were ordered to **integrate** their public schools.

It was a great moment in the struggle for equality. The Supreme Court had said the Constitution clearly did not allow public segregation.

## A Showdown at Little Rock

Some states quietly began to integrate their public schools. But the deep south fought bitterly against having to do so. Three years after the Brown decision, its schools were still completely segregated. People began to wonder if the federal government would make these states follow the Constitution. The answer came from Little Rock, Arkansas.

Governor Faubus claimed that he sent in the National Guard "to preserve order."

In September of 1957, Little Rock's public schools were under a court order to integrate. Nine black students planned to attend Central High School along with the 2,000 white students there. On the night before classes were to start, Governor Orval Faubus sent the Arkansas National Guard to Central High. He ordered them to keep the black students out. Faubus said he was just trying to stop violence by angry whites. But Mayor Woodrow Wilson Mann said it was Faubus who had stirred people up by calling out the guard. Before that there had been no hint of violence.

President Eisenhower met with Faubus in Washington. There, Faubus agreed to remove the guard. Back in Little Rock, however, he did not. Another court order was handed down. This time, Faubus did recall the guard. But by then, things were out of control. Crowds of whites tried to attack the black students when they got to school. The students were taken away for their own safety.

**Army troops in Little Rock, Arkansas**

Finally, Eisenhower sent in the army and took control of the state's national guard. On the morning of September 25, soldiers ringed Central High. At 9:25, the nine students were led into the building.

The government had shown it would use its power to integrate the schools. But the fact that soldiers had been needed was a bitter blow to America's pride.

And the battle at Little Rock wasn't over. The black students faced much violence from white students. In September of 1958, the Little Rock schools asked the Supreme Court to put off integrating for several more years. The NAACP's response came from Thurgood Marshall. He said, "There can be no equality or

The 1950s and 1960s were sometimes called a "Second Reconstruction." What does this name mean?

justice for our people if the law steps aside, even for a moment, at the command of force and violence." The Supreme Court agreed and ruled against the schools.

## Direct Action

Black people remembered the success of the bus boycott. They took direct action against prejudice. Following the example set by Martin Luther King, Jr., they used nonviolent protests.

One means of protest was the sit-in. On February 1, 1960, four black college students in Greensboro, North Carolina, sat down at a whites-only lunch counter. When they were told to leave, they said they would remain where they were until they were served. They stayed until the store closed.

They returned the next day and were joined by five friends. In a week, more than 100 blacks were sitting in at the city lunch counters. From there, the protests spread across the South. Protesters were kicked and threatened, but they went on with their sit-ins. Within a year, Greensboro's lunch counters and theaters were integrated.

Blacks also took action through "freedom rides." On May 4, 1961, a group of black and white protesters left Washington, D.C., by bus. They planned to protest segregated travel by riding buses throughout the Southern states. At Anniston, Alabama, one of the buses was firebombed. In Birmingham, Alabama, freedom riders were beaten by a crowd. The riders were arrested at stops all along the way. They were attacked with fists, clubs, and tire chains. But with each attack, more people came from all over the country to join them. By the end of the year, buses, trains, and stations throughout the South had been forced to integrate.

# The High Price of Freedom

In 1964, three civil rights workers were murdered in Mississippi. They were Northerners who'd gone south to encourage African Americans to register to vote. Many African Americans weren't using this right. Some were afraid of what white people would do if they tried to go to the polls. In some states, a poll tax was used to keep people from voting. In 1964 the 24th Amendment outlawed the use of a poll tax in federal elections.

The Civil Rights movement of the 1950s and the 1960s broke down some barriers to equality. The federal government passed laws insuring voting rights for all African Americans. The Civil Rights Act of 1964 protected African Americans against segregation in employment and education. It also guaranteed equal rights in the use of public places. No longer could parks, buses, or any public facilities be labeled "off-limits" to people of any race. And the Civil Rights Act of 1968 outlawed racial prejudice in housing rentals or sales.

## History Practice

Answer these questions on a separate sheet of paper.

1. What did the Montgomery bus boycott accomplish?

2. How did the case of *Brown vs. the Board of Education* affect the "separate but equal" rulings?

3. Why did the federal government send the army to Little Rock, Arkansas, in 1958?

4. What was the purpose of a poll tax?

## America's Hispanic Population

It wasn't only blacks who had a hard time getting a fair chance in America. Other minority groups also faced prejudice and discrimination.

Spanish-speaking Americans, Hispanics, make up a large part of the U.S. population. The largest number of Hispanics are Mexican Americans, or Chicanos.

Many Mexican Americans became farm workers in America's Southwest. Whole families of migrant workers moved from place to place following the harvest seasons.

Like Martin Luther King, Cesar Chavez called for nonviolent protest. He encouraged acts of civil disobedience including strikes and boycotts. Once Chavez fasted for 25 days to provide an example of courage and determination for all Mexican Americans.

Farmers often took advantage of the migrant workers. The workers were often underpaid, poorly housed, and poorly fed. Their children received little or no education. Eventually, the farm workers began to organize. In the 1960s, Cesar Chavez started a labor union called the United Farm Workers. Chavez and the union worked to win rights for Mexican Americans.

In 1965, the UFW and Cesar Chavez called for a grape strike. The strike against grape growers was called "La Causa" (the Cause). People around the nation helped by boycotting grapes.

Mexicans came to the United States hoping to find more jobs and a better life. In the early 1950s, large numbers of Puerto Ricans began to come to the United States for the same reasons. While most of the Mexican immigrants had settled in the Southwest, the Puerto Ricans came largely to the cities of the East. Since most had little money, they settled in poorer neighborhoods. They faced all the problems **typical** for new immigrants: a new culture, a strange language, prejudice and discrimination from white America. Still, many Puerto Ricans overcame the odds. They opened businesses and got educations.

**Cesar Chavez**

## Native Americans

One minority group has remained, to a large degree, outside American society. Native Americans are today the poorest group in the country. Their children receive the least education. They have the hardest time finding jobs.

Native Americans were once forced to live on reservations. They were not granted the rights of citizenship until 1924. In the 1930s, the federal government encouraged Native American groups to set up reservation governments and develop their lands. The government also encouraged the Native Americans to move to the cities, to join urban society. The government promised them jobs and job training. Most of those promises were not kept. Since World War II, the Native American population has grown rapidly. Native Americans now choose whether or not to live on reservations. About one-half of America's one million Native Americans live in the nation's cities.

Native Americans have protested their lack of civil rights. In 1969, a group took over Alcatraz, an empty federal prison on an island in San Francisco Bay. They kept up their demonstrations there for two months and received nation-wide attention.

In 1973, Native Americans took over a village in South Dakota called Wounded Knee. In 1978, 1,000 Native Americans marched to Washington D.C. This often forgotten minority group held these demonstrations to make people aware of their problems.

## The End of the 1950s

America's minority groups have helped make America what it is today. They have lent their talents to this nation. And each group has faced prejudice and discrimination. Each has had to struggle for its civil rights. Minority Americans have had to work harder to share in the nation's prosperity. They have faced greater odds. The United States is a land of great wealth. That so many have known only poverty is, perhaps, America's greatest failure.

The 1950s ended in a struggle that continued into the 1960s. Although minorities had progressed, they still had a long way to go. But many people began the 1960s with great hope. In part, this was because they had a new president. John Fitzgerald Kennedy was elected in 1960. He was younger than any president before him and had captured the hearts of many. The nation seemed ready to solve its problems. It seemed ready, in fact, to step into a whole new age.

## History Practice

Answer these questions on a separate sheet of paper.

1. In what ways are problems faced by African Americans, Hispanic Americans, and Native Americans similar?

2. What did the 24th Amendment do?

3. Of what recent historic importance is the island of Alcatraz?

# Chapter Review

## Summary

| CHRONOLOGY OF MAJOR EVENTS | |
|---|---|
| 1954 | Racial segregation in schools ruled unconstitutional |
| 1955 | Montgomery bus boycott |
| 1957 | National Guard called to Little Rock to enforce school integration |
| 1960 | John F. Kennedy elected 35th president |
| 1960 | Lunch counter sit-ins in Greensboro, N.C. |
| 1961 | "Freedom rides" |
| 1963 | Martin Luther King leads march on Washington |
| 1965 | United Farm Workers grape strike |
| 1968 | Martin Luther King assassinated |
| 1969 | Alcatraz Island taken over by Native Americans |

- The Constitution said blacks were free citizens. But they were not treated as such. In the 1950s they began demanding their civil rights.

- Martin Luther King was leader of the civil rights movement. He insisted on peaceful demonstration and resistance.

- In the case of *Brown vs. the Board of Education* the Supreme Court ruled against the separate but equal law. However, integration did not come easily.

- The late fifties and early sixties saw nonviolent protests against segregation. There were sit-ins, marches, and freedom rides. They were often met with violence and sometimes death.

- Hispanics, Native Americans, and other minority groups have also had to struggle for their civil rights.

- As the nation moved into the sixties, minorities still struggled for their rights and privileges as Americans.

## Chapter Quiz

1. What did Rosa Parks and Martin Luther King have in common?

2. What is nonviolent resistance?

3. Who is Thurgood Marshall?

4. What did Orval Faubus and Woodrow Wilson Mann have in common?

5. What do the letters UFW stand for? Who is the head of this union?

6. Which ethnic group could be said to stand at the bottom of the economic ladder?

## Thinking and Writing

1. How would you have felt if you had lived in Little Rock, Arkansas, when the schools were being integrated?

2. Describe the way Martin Luther King fought for civil rights and justice.

# Chapter 26

# The Troubled Sixties

| **1960** | **1975** |
|---|---|
| John F. Kennedy elected president | Vietnam War ends |

**John F. Kennedy**

## Chapter Learning Objectives

- Tell what made Kennedy a popular president.
- Describe the Bay of Pigs invasion.
- Describe the Cuban missile crisis.
- Describe American involvement in the Vietnam War.

# Words to Know

**bodyguard**   a person who provides physical protection for another

**cease fire**   halt to fighting for an agreed upon time period

**escalate**   to raise the level of conflict

**generation**   the people born at about the same time

**missile**   an object shot or thrown through the air at a target

**truce**   an agreement to stop fighting

**underdeveloped**   having little or no industry

John Kennedy was a well-liked president. People felt he understood them. He was just 43 years old when he took office. Kennedy was handsome and athletic. He was the first Catholic to become president. Minority group members often felt he was on their side. At his inauguration, he had said, "Ask not what your country can do for you. Ask what you can do for your country." Kennedy inspired millions. And the decade that began with his election contained some of the most dramatic changes the world had seen.

**"The torch has passed to a new generation," Kennedy said.**

## Crisis in Berlin

President Kennedy's term was only seven months old when he was faced with a showdown with the Soviet Union. In August, 1961, the Soviets built a wall through the city of Berlin. The Berlin Wall was put up to stop East Berliners from crossing to freedom in West Berlin. Just before the wall was built, Soviet leader Nikita Khrushchev demanded that the Western Powers get out of Berlin. He said there should only be one Berlin and the Soviets should control it. Some feared that Khrushchev meant to go

**During the winter of 1989–90 the Berlin Wall came down.**

to war over the issue. Kennedy was firm. The Western Powers would not leave Berlin. The Soviets did not attack.

## The Bay of Pigs

Like all presidents, John F. Kennedy knew failure as well as success. One such failure came for Kennedy in April of 1961, in an invasion at the Bay of Pigs in Cuba.

Cuba, 90 miles off the U.S. coast, had been a communist nation with strong ties to the Soviet Union since 1959. Until then, the dictator of Cuba had been Fulgencio Batista. Batista had been on friendly terms with the United States. Communists overthrew Batista and replaced him with a new leader, Fidel Castro. Castro became friends with the Soviet Union.

President Eisenhower had made plans to help Cuban rebels fight Castro. A Cuban force, trained in the United States, was ready to attack Cuba. Kennedy continued Eisenhower's plans.

In April of 1961, that force of about 1,500 invaded Cuba. They expected help from other rebels within Cuba. They expected help from the U.S. Air Force. The invaders landed on the beaches of the Bay of Pigs. There were no Cuban rebels there to join them. Kennedy did not send military help. Most of the invading rebels were killed or captured. Kennedy accepted the blame for the Bay of Pigs invasion.

## The Cuban Missile Crisis

Still, Kennedy was very popular. He won the respect of much of the world during the Cuban **Missile** Crisis. In October of 1962, American spy planes brought home some upsetting pictures. There were Soviet missiles set up at bases in Cuba. These missiles could reach into the heart of the United States. There were Soviet soldiers and jet bombers there, too.

President Kennedy asked the Soviet Union to remove their troops and weapons from Cuba. He added strength to his demand by setting up a naval blockade around the island. American ships would not allow Soviet ships to bring any arms or supplies to Cuba. Kennedy said that any ships trying to break the blockade would be sunk. And at the time, there were some Soviet ships headed for Cuba.

Soviet leader Nikita Khrushchev threatened that Kennedy's blockade might lead to war. A nervous America anxiously watched and waited for news. Schools held air raid drills and prepared for the worst. In the end, Khrushchev did not want a nuclear war. He sent President Kennedy a letter. The Soviet Union would take back its missiles if the United States promised not to invade Cuba. Kennedy agreed. The Soviet ships turned back. It was a cold war victory for Kennedy and the United States. But for a time, the countries had teetered on the brink of all-out war.

The American government said it couldn't allow offensive missiles to be placed just 90 miles from the United States.

## The Nation Mourns

People turned out in large numbers to see the president whenever he appeared in public. On Friday, November 22, 1963, Kennedy was in Dallas, Texas, to meet with the state's Democratic Party leaders.

The skies were clear and sunny. Kennedy rode through the streets of the city with the bulletproof top removed from his car. Riding with the president were his wife Jacqueline, and Texas Governor John Connolly and his wife. Kennedy waved to the crowds that lined the streets. At about 12:30 P.M., the car was nearing Dealey Plaza. Mrs. Connolly turned to the

Ask people you know just where they were on Friday, November 22, 1963. Most people can easily remember.

president and said, "You sure can't say that Dallas doesn't love you, Mr. President."

A moment later, several shots rang out. Kennedy jerked backwards and then slumped forward in his seat. As his **bodyguards** scrambled to protect the president and the rest of the passengers, the car raced off to the hospital. Almost instantly, radio and television stations around the country flashed news of the shooting.

At the hospital, doctors tried desperately to save the president's life, but it was hopeless. At 1:00 P.M. President Kennedy was pronounced dead.

The government announced that a man named Lee Harvey Oswald had been arrested for Kennedy's murder. Oswald said he hadn't done it. On Sunday, TV cameras showed Oswald being led through the crowded halls of the Dallas jail. Suddenly, a man pushed forward. The man pulled a gun and fired. Oswald fell dead as police struggled with the attacker, Jack Ruby.

Kennedy was the fourth American president to be murdered. But none of these deaths, except perhaps Abraham Lincoln's caused such sadness. Many felt Kennedy's death was a sign that the coming years would be troubled and full of violence.

Listen to some of the folk music and rock music of the 1960s. Many of the ideas of the youth of the 1960s were expressed in that music.

## New Ideas of a New Generation

In the 1960s, the United States did not see itself as isolated from the rest of the world. That view was part of the past. We gave foreign aid in the form of money, goods, weapons, and soldiers. We showed our strength in many places where we thought communism might take hold. We raced with the Russians to control outer space. And we raced with them to build more and better atomic weapons.

The 1960s were also a time of youth. A great many children had been born right after World War II.

Now the "baby boom" children were reaching adulthood. They were better fed, better clothed, and better schooled than any earlier **generation**. They were to take America to new heights.

But some young people were turning away from what their parents held dear. They acted and dressed differently. After the assassination of Kennedy, some lost their faith in the government almost completely. America, they said, did not really believe in freedom. It believed in money. Rather than prepare for good jobs, they would prepare for a new and better society. They spoke of a world based on peace and love rather than on greed and war. Old clothes and long hair became symbols of a break with the past. Rather than praising what America did right, they pointed out what it did wrong. There is always a gap between age and youth. But in the 1960s, it often seemed a mile wide.

Young people of the '60s who rebelled against traditional values were called *Hippies*. Some people called them Flower-children because flowers became their symbol of peace and love. Greenwich Village in New York and Haight-Ashbury in San Francisco became urban centers for the Hippie community.

## Learn More About It: The Peace Corps

Americans of the sixties did more than just talk about peace and love. They took action. An organization called the Peace Corps was made up of American volunteers. The volunteers were mostly young. They went to nations where people needed help. The Peace Corps was run by President Kennedy's brother-in-law, Sargent Shriver. Among other things, Peace Corps volunteers set up schools in **underdeveloped** nations. They built bridges and taught new methods of farming and of health care. The very first Peace Corps volunteers were teachers in Ghana, Africa, in 1961. Today volunteers serve in over 59 different countries.

# The Great Society

Kennedy had wanted the government to take a strong role in righting the country's wrongs. So did Lyndon Johnson, who became president when Kennedy was killed. Johnson promised a "Great Society." He worked to clean the country's water and air. He launched a "war on poverty." He helped pass laws to improve housing, health care, and education.

Johnson's Medicare bill gave a health insurance plan to people 65 years old and over. An education bill provided $1.5 billion in public school aid, especially in poor areas. Lyndon Johnson was able to continue his war on poverty into a second term. He won a landslide victory over Republican candidate Barry Goldwater in the 1964 presidential election.

The most important laws passed during these years were the Civil Rights and Voting Rights Acts of 1964. They made it against the law to discriminate against people because of their race, sex, religion, or ethnic background. The government took steps to see that the states and cities obeyed these new laws. It had not always done this.

President Johnson started a "model cities" project to clean up decaying old neighborhoods.

Much of the civil rights work discussed in Chapter 25 took place in the South. But more than half of all black Americans now lived elsewhere. Many of them lived in big cities. In the cities, blacks faced high unemployment, rising crime, and poor housing. Unlike many whites, most blacks didn't have the money to move out of the cities to the suburbs. They couldn't afford to look for the "good life." Many blacks felt hopeless and angry. The assassination of Martin Luther King made some decide that peaceful protest was not the road to justice. Between 1965 and 1968, riots broke out in Los Angeles, New York,

Chicago, Newark, Detroit, and other cities. One of the worst riots was in a black area of Los Angeles called Watts. Thirty-four people were killed as police tried to control rioters. In 1967, there were riots in more than 60 urban areas. The television news showed flaming streets filled with soldiers.

Instead of integration, some blacks wanted separatism, power as a separate group. Black power, they felt, would mean there would be black-owned businesses, black-run schools, and black government leaders. A few joined armed groups like the Black Panthers.

The riots and the call for black power showed that there were important problems in America. But these things frightened and angered many white people, and the gap between the races grew wider.

## History Practice

Answer these questions on a separate sheet of paper.

1. What happened during the invasion of the Bay of Pigs?

2. How did President Kennedy handle the Cuban missile crisis?

3. How did Lyndon Johnson first become president of the United States?

4. Which U.S. president promised America a "Great Society?"

## The History of Vietnam

Before World War II, Indochina was a French colony. During World War II, the Japanese took over control of Indochina. When the Japanese lost the war, the French returned. But the people of Indochina wanted to be free of foreign control. The French tried to give the people more self-rule by dividing Indochina into three separate states. These states were Cambodia, Laos, and Vietnam. But this did not satisfy the people. They still wanted to drive out the French. Those living in North Vietnam started a revolution against the French. Their leader was Ho Chi Minh. Ho Chi Minh was a communist. The rebels of North Vietnam called themselves the Vietminh.

U.S. involvement in Vietnam started off at a very low level.

The United States helped the French fight the Vietminh by sending money and supplies. But the Vietminh defeated the French. Vietnam was then divided. North Vietnam was governed by communists led by Ho Chi Minh. South Vietnam's non-communist government was led by Ngo Dinh Diem.

Presidents Eisenhower and Kennedy both sent money and weapons to South Vietnam. Kennedy sent people to train the South Vietnamese army. The amount of aid was fairly small until the early 1960s. In the sixties, however, the United States increased its support.

## The Domino Theory

American leaders worried about something they called the "Domino Theory." If you stand up a bunch of dominoes in a line and tap one, they will all fall down, one after another. The U.S. government was concerned that if Vietnam came under Communist control, Laos, Cambodia, and other countries could follow. Vietnam could be like the first domino.

**Southeast Asia**

**Map Study**

Study the map. Then answer the questions on a separate
sheet of paper.
1.  What countries border Vietnam?
2.  What body of water lies east of North Vietnam?
3.  During the Vietnam War the capital of South Vietnam was
    Saigon. What was that city later renamed?

## The Gulf of Tonkin Resolution

By 1964, the South Vietnamese government was very shaky. It was **corrupt** and unpopular. Many of the South Vietnamese were communist supporters. The Vietcong were communist fighters from both the North and the South who lived in South Vietnam. The Vietcong wanted to take control of South Vietnam. They received support from Ho Chi Minh in the North. Lyndon Johnson had become president after Kennedy's assassination. He poured thousands of men and billions of dollars into South Vietnam.

In August, 1964, Johnson said that North Vietnamese ships had attacked American ships off the coast of North Vietnam. The ships were in an area known as the Gulf of Tonkin. Johnson ordered

**Fighting in Vietnam**

air strikes against North Vietnam. The United States Congress never declared war on Vietnam.

But Congress did give President Johnson power to escalate American involvement. This move was called the Gulf of Tonkin Resolution. By the end of 1965, there were 200,000 American troops in Vietnam. A year later, the total had risen to nearly 400,000. While the South Vietnamese army got help from the United States, the Vietcong received support from North Vietnam, the Soviet Union, and China. World powers had become involved in the civil war in Vietnam.

American military leaders thought at first that the war could be easily won. They changed their minds in February of 1968, when the Vietcong and North Vietnamese launched the "Tet Offensive." It came at the beginning of a week-long New Year's holiday called "Tet." Fighting was especially heavy in the South Vietnam capital of Saigon. The South Vietnamese and Americans did put down the attacks, but not before thousands of soldiers and civilians were killed. The Vietcong had gained control of large areas of the South.

## Hawks and Doves

At home, the Vietnam War was becoming more and more unpopular. In October of 1967, more than 50,000 people staged two days of anti-war protests in Washington, D.C.

The number of Americans fighting in Vietnam grew to 545,000 in 1969. As the war and the number of Americans killed grew, so did the protests. Several huge marches brought out hundreds of thousands of people.

American opinion was divided. The "hawks" believed America had to win in Vietnam, whatever the cost. The "doves" believed the war was wrong. The hawks said we must stop the spread of communism. The doves said that South Vietnam's leaders were dictators and that we had no business trying to run another country. They said that too many Vietnamese civilians were being killed.

Feelings against the war were strong among the young. There were protest demonstrations on many college campuses. Some men said they wouldn't serve in the armed forces. They burned their draft registration cards. This angered a good number of older Americans. They remembered World War II and were already upset that youth would not stand behind an American cause.

**Antiwar protest**

## Americans Pull Out of Vietnam

Richard Nixon was elected president in 1968. In his election speeches he promised that he would "bring an honorable end to the war."

Nixon could not send more troops to Vietnam. Americans wanted their troops to come home. Instead, he tried to end the war with heavy bombing attacks. Planes attacked North Vietnam's capital, Hanoi. In 1969, the air war spread to Cambodia. Their missions were to bomb military bases. But many civilians were killed. And North Vietnam did not give up.

In 1969, after years of growing protests, Nixon announced his "Vietnamization" plan. It would withdraw U.S. troops and turn over most of the ground combat to the South Vietnamese.

In the spring of 1970, American troops entered Cambodia. Nixon said they did so only to wipe out Vietcong bases there. American troops did leave Cambodia by June. But the attacks had set off a new wave of antiwar protests.

By the end of 1971, Nixon's gradual pull-out of troops left 140,000 Americans in Vietnam. In January, 1973, a **cease-fire** was signed by the United States, North Vietnam, South Vietnam, and the Vietcong. All U.S. troops would be withdrawn within 60 days.

But the truce did not end the war. In April of 1975, the government of South Vietnam completely collapsed. Communist forces marched into its capital city of Saigon. The two parts of the country were rejoined under communist rule as the Democratic Republic of Vietnam. Communists also took power in Laos and Cambodia. Cambodia was renamed Kampuchea.

**By the end of the 1960s, more than 40,000 Americans had died in Vietnam. And 260,000 more had been wounded, captured, or were missing in action.**

Are there any
Indochinese refugees
living in your
community? What
kinds of problems
have they faced as
new immigrants to
the United States?

## Results of the Vietnam War

Americans had suffered during the war in Vietnam. Many people felt bitter over losses there. The war cost 58,000 American lives and $140 billion. Many wondered if it had been worth the price.

Many South Vietnamese suffered under communist rule. Some fled the country. Some escaped in small boats. Often the boats were so crowded they were ready to sink. Some countries would not let the "boat people" in. Many refugees went to the United States to start new lives.

In 1982, the Vietnam Veterans' Memorial was built in Washington, D.C. It was designed by Maya Lin, an American woman whose parents were Chinese immigrants. The memorial is a huge wall that lists the names of the Americans killed or missing in the war. Many people felt this memorial was especially important. Since the war became so unpopular, many believed the veterans had never received the respect they deserved.

## Protest and Pain

Violence marked much of the 1960s. President Kennedy was assassinated. Black Muslim leader Malcolm X was assassinated. Martin Luther King was assassinated. On June 5, 1968, an assassin struck again. Senator Robert Kennedy, John Kennedy's brother, was murdered. Robert Kennedy had just won California's Democratic primary. When Robert Kennedy died, Hubert Humphrey became the most likely Democratic candidate for president.

The Democratic nominating convention was held in Chicago. Violence struck there, too, as demonstrators protested the Vietnam War. The protests ended in a riot.

Violence did not end when Republican Richard Nixon began his term as president in 1969. Nixon promised American troops would pull out of Vietnam. But many felt the pull-out was not coming fast enough. "Peace now!" many American college students demanded. Their demonstrations and strikes sometimes closed down colleges.

On May 4, 1970, tragedy struck again. During an antiwar protest at Kent State University the governor of Ohio sent in the National Guard. Four students were killed.

## History Practice

Answer these questions on a separate sheet of paper.

1. How did Presidents Eisenhower and Kennedy support the war in Vietnam?

2. In 1964, why did President Johnson increase the troops sent to Vietnam?

3. Who were Ho Chi Minh and Ngo Dinh Diem?

4. Explain the "Domino Theory."

5. Who was president of the United States when American troops pulled out of Vietnam?

# Chapter Review

## Summary

| CHRONOLOGY OF MAJOR EVENTS | |
|---|---|
| 1961 | Bay of Pigs |
| 1962 | Cuban Missile Crisis |
| 1963 | Kennedy assassinated |
| 1964 | Lyndon Johnson wins presidential election |
| 1964 | Civil Rights and Voting Rights Acts |
| 1968 | Richard Nixon elected 37th president |
| 1973 | Cease-fire in Vietnam |
| 1975 | Communist troops take Saigon |

- An American-trained troop of Cuban rebels attacked Cuba's Bay of Pigs. The invasion was a disaster.

- When Soviet missile bases were discovered in Cuba, Kennedy insisted they be removed.

- Kennedy was assassinated in 1963. Vice-president Lyndon Johnson took over the presidency.

- Johnson's "Great Society" affected poverty, racism, pollution, housing, education, and health care.

- Assassinations and riots were part of the violent 1960s.

- The Black Power movement told blacks to be strong and proud and to defend their rights.

- Indochina was once a French colony. After the French were driven out, Vietnam was divided in half. Communists governed North Vietnam. The United States supported the South Vietnamese government.

- The United States sent money, supplies, and troops to Vietnam. The number of troops grew under Johnson. Many Americans protested U.S. involvement.

- 1973 brought a short-lived cease-fire in Vietnam. In 1975, the government of South Vietnam was defeated.

## Chapter Quiz

1. Who was Fulgencio Batista?

2. Name four leaders who were assassinated in the 1960s.

3. How was the "Domino Theory" applied to Indochina?

4. By 1969, how many Americans were fighting in Vietnam?

5. Which president promised "an honorable end to the war"?

6. When was the South Vietnamese army defeated?

## Thinking and Writing

1. Why would seeing the Vietnam war on TV make Americans more eager to end it?

2. Describe three events that made the sixties "troubled" years.

# Chapter 27

# Modern Problems

**Richard Nixon as he left Washington after resigning as president in 1974.**

## Chapter Learning Objectives

- Describe the Watergate scandal.
- Describe some of the problems faced by Jimmy Carter and Ronald Reagan during their presidencies.
- Describe some of the conflicts that have arisen in the Middle East since 1948.

# Words to Know

**accord**   agreement
**bugs**   tiny microphones
**embassy**   a building where representatives from foreign nations work
**hijacking**   taking an airplane or vehicle over by force and directing it to a destination not originally intended
**hostage**   a person who is kidnapped and held until certain demands are met

**landslide**   the winning of an election by a huge number of votes
**pardon**   to forgive; to free from punishment
**recession**   a period when business is bad; less serious than a depression
**resign**   to leave a job or position

In 1974, the president of the United States, shown at left, was forced to leave office. The country struggled to regain its direction. Around the globe, the level of violence rose. The early 1970s marked the beginning of a period of great confusion.

## The Silent Majority

The early 1970s saw the rise of the "silent majority." This group was made up of working-class and middle-class whites. Many of them were unhappy with the changes of the last ten years. Some felt their jobs were threatened by the rise of minority groups. Many were against the government's programs to help the poor. They felt these programs were causing higher taxes.

Richard Nixon had been narrowly elected president in 1968. Under him, the government stopped pushing as hard as it had for integration and civil rights. It no longer cut off government money to segregated schools. It allowed slowdowns in integration. It cut the amount of money spent on social aid.

In 1972, the silent majority would help reelect Nixon by the largest number of votes ever. But the election soon fell under a dark cloud of suspicion.

## The Break-In

In June of 1972, America was preparing for the November election. Already polls showed that the Republican President would win it easily. Still, the Democrats were getting ready to choose someone to run against Nixon. The Democrat's headquarters were in a building in Washington, D.C. known as the Watergate.

After midnight on June 17, a Watergate guard was making his rounds. Near the Democratic headquarters, the guard found that the lock on a door had been taped open. Fearing a break-in, the guard called the police.

**The Watergate burglars also carried with them $5,000 in $100 bills.**

When the police arrived, they discovered five middle-aged men hiding in the building. The five had rubber gloves, cameras, radios, and telephone **bugs**.

When they were arrested, the men wouldn't answer questions. But one of them was carrying the name and phone number of Howard Hunt. Hunt sometimes worked for the White House. A trail of money, spies, and dirty tricks was soon uncovered. And it led straight to the White House.

## The Scandal

Even as the election votes were being counted, the story behind Watergate was coming out. The men caught in the Democratic headquarters had been trying to steal information. They had bugged telephones in order to find out what the Democrats were planning. These men had been paid with money from the Committee to Reelect the President (CREEP).

A special government prosecutor was appointed to investigate. America learned that people in the White House had supported these actions. Also, they had lied to cover them up.

The United States Senate also investigated the break-in and cover-up. John Dean, one of Nixon's key staff members, appeared as one of the witnesses before the special Senate committee. Dean told the committee that he'd met with former Attorney General John Mitchell and a hired spy, G. Gordon Liddy. Dean said that Liddy had planned the Watergate break-in and Mitchell had approved it. Dean said that he himself had been assigned to the cover-up. Dean also told the committee that Nixon had helped plan the cover-up from the beginning. Nixon strongly denied Dean's charges.

Then it was discovered that Nixon had bugged his own office. He had tapes of conversations that went on there. The special prosecutor investigating Watergate demanded that Nixon turn over all his tapes. The president refused. When the prosecutor went to court to sue for release of the tapes, Nixon ordered the Attorney General to fire him. The Attorney General refused and resigned in protest. His top assistant also refused and resigned. Finally, a second assistant agreed to fire the prosecutor.

The country was outraged by Nixon's actions. A new prosecutor was appointed and he took the case to the U.S. Supreme Court. The Court ruled 9–0 that Nixon had to turn over the tapes. When he did, the tapes showed that Nixon *had* known about the cover-up from early on. He had personally backed it. Parts of the tapes were missing. Scientists said they couldn't have been erased by accident.

Millions of Americans watched the televised Senate Watergate hearings that lasted throught he spring and summer of 1973.

## A President Resigns

The country was in an uproar. Nixon lost its trust. More than 20 people were tried in court and found guilty. One was the former attorney general, John Mitchell. Nine had worked for the White House. Some, including H.R. Haldeman and John Ehrlichman, were Nixon's closest aids.

On August 9, 1974, Nixon **resigned**. It was clear that Congress was about to remove him from office. Nixon became the only American president ever to be forced out before the end of his term. Vice-president Gerald Ford took over the office of president.

One month after he became president, Ford **pardoned** Richard Nixon. With that pardon, Nixon escaped any punishment for his part in the Watergate scandal. While Nixon was pardoned, many of those who helped him went to prison.

In November of 1973, Republican Senator Edward W. Brooke called for Nixon's resignation.

**Spiro Agnew**

# Vice-President Stands Accused

Nixon wasn't the only official to get into trouble. Nixon's vice-president had been Spiro Agnew. But Agnew resigned from office on October 10, 1973. It had been discovered that Agnew had taken bribes when he was governor of Maryland. Also, Agnew hadn't paid income tax on some of his money. Once these things came out, Agnew could not remain in office.

Nixon chose Gerald Ford as his new vice-president. Then Nixon's scandal came to light, and Nixon resigned. Ford became president. He chose Nelson Rockefeller as his vice-president. For the first time in history, the United States was led by two men whom the nation had not elected.

## Learn More About It: Economic Inflation

In 1973 and 1974, inflation soared to the highest levels since 1947. "Inflation" means that the price of products goes way up. President Nixon and President Ford both blamed the inflation on heavy government spending.

Senior citizens are especially hard hit by inflation. Most are living on social security or retirement funds. Their incomes do not increase to meet rising prices.

## History Practice

Answer these questions on a separate sheet of paper

1. What role did the "silent majority" play in the presidential election of 1972?

2. What was the purpose of the Watergate break-in?

3. How did Gerald Ford become president?

## President Carter

Carter worried about the waste of resources in America. He called the United States "the most wasteful nation on earth." Carter got Congress to set up a new Department of Energy.

In 1976, Democrat Jimmy Carter won the presidential election over Gerald Ford. He was an unusual choice for president. Carter, from the state of Georgia, was the first president from the deep South since before the Civil War. He was a newcomer to Washington politics. He had been governor of Georgia. Before that he had been a peanut farmer. Most Americans had never heard of Jimmy Carter before he became a candidate for president. Carter would face new problems during his term as president. Some people criticized his lack of experience.

## Crisis in Iran

The country of Iran is in the Middle East. It was once called Persia. Iran is a small country. But it is rich in oil.

In 1953, an agency of the United States government had helped overthrow the government of Iran. The Shah of Iran, Mohammed Reza Pahlavi, took control of the country. While the Shah was in power, the United States continued to send military equipment and supplies to Iran.

The Shah tried to make Iran a more modern, western-style country. But many Iranians did not like the Shah's new ideas. They wanted to follow the old ways. The Shah was very hard on anyone who opposed him. Military police arrested those who were against the Shah. People were tortured and murdered.

The number of people who were opposed to the Shah grew. Finally a revolution broke out. The Shah was forced to flee the country. He was ill and asked to go to the United States for medical treatment. President Carter agreed to let him come into the country.

Iranians were now following a religious leader, the Ayatollah Khomeini. He had been forced into exile by the Shah fifteen years earlier. Iranians were angry at President Carter. They wanted the Shah returned to Iran to stand trial. The Ayatollah and his followers tried to force Carter to return the Shah to Iran. On November 4, 1979, the American **embassy** in Iran was attacked. Fifty-two Americans were taken as **hostages**.

**The Ayatollah Khomeini**

The American people expected President Carter to get the hostages back. Carter warned Iran that America would boycott Iranian exports. He encouraged other nations to boycott Iranian goods, too.

Carter organized a military rescue of the hostages. The rescue attempt ended in disaster. A helicopter and transport plane crashed. Eight of the rescuers were killed.

The Iranians held the Americans hostage for 444 days. They were finally set free on January 20, 1981.

## President Reagan

A new president welcomed the hostages home from Iran. Republican Ronald Reagan had won the 1980 election easily. Reagan was the former governor of California and a former film star. At 69, he was the oldest man to be elected president.

Reagan built up the nation's armed forces. He displayed military strength to the Soviets. Some people accused him of being a "hawk." They criticized his heavy military spending. Others felt he was doing what he had promised and was allowing America to "walk tall" again.

While spending large amounts on a military build-up, Reagan still cut taxes. To try to balance the budget, he cut social programs.

In 1982, a **recession** hit. Many people were without jobs. But other parts of the economy improved. Most Americans gave credit to President Reagan.

The cold war continued. President Reagan sent American troops to the Caribbean island of Grenada. Money and weapons were sent to El Salvador and Nicaragua in Central America.

President Reagan had another **landslide** victory when he ran for reelection in 1984. Even though the voting was not close, it was an interesting election.

For the first time a black person was considered as a candidate for the presidency. Many people supported Reverend Jesse Jackson, a civil rights leader, for the Democratic nomination.

The Democrats finally chose Walter Mondale. Mondale had served as vice-president in the Carter administration.

And there was another first in this election. Mondale picked Geraldine Ferraro as his running mate. Never before had a woman been chosen to run for the office of vice president.

A great many Americans were pleased with Reagan's second term. There was still poverty at home and unrest around the world. But the economy seemed stronger and more people had jobs. The Republicans won again in 1988. Reagan's vice-president, George Bush, was easily elected over his Democratic opponent, Governor Michael Dukakis of Massachusetts.

## History Practice

Answer these questions on a separate sheet of paper.

1. Why did Iranians take hostages from the American Embassy in 1979?

2. Explain President Reagan's policies concerning military readiness.

3. Name two "firsts" that occurred during the 1984 national elections.

## The United States and the Middle East

The Middle East is an area at the eastern end of the Mediterranean Sea. The map on the next page shows you which countries make up the area we call the Middle East. Most of the people of the Middle East are Arabs. Most Arabs follow the Islamic religion. Islam was founded by the prophet Muhammed in the 7th century. The followers of Islam are called Muslims. The Middle Eastern country of Israel is not Arab. Israel is a Jewish state.

There is more oil in the Middle East than in any other part of the world. About 25 percent of the world's oil supply comes from the Middle East. The United States cannot produce enough oil to meet its own needs. It depends on oil from the Middle East. What happens in the Middle East is very important to the United States.

## The State of Israel

The United States has supported the Jewish State of Israel. Israel was created in 1948 on land that had been part of Palestine. What had been Palestine was divided into Israel and Jordan. Many of the Palestinian Arabs living in Israel fled. They became refugees, people without a home. Arabs in the countries bordering Israel were not happy. They felt Palestine should be one Arab country. Since its creation, Israel has fought with surrounding Middle Eastern Arabic countries.

# The Middle East

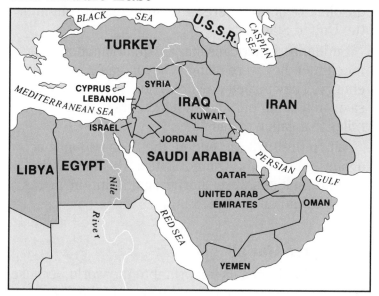

## Map Study

Study the map. Then answer the questions on a separate sheet of paper.

1. Which countries border Israel?
2. The Suez Canal is in Egypt. Which two seas are joined by the Suez Canal?
3. You read about Iran earlier in this chapter. Find Iran on the map.

## The Power of Oil

The United States sent military supplies to Israel. This made the neighboring Arab nations angry. These Middle Eastern Arabic nations had one thing everybody wanted—oil. In 1973, during a war in the Middle East, the Arabs refused to sell their oil to the United States. Although America has other sources of oil, the Arab oil embargo hurt. The price of oil and gasoline went up. There were shortages throughout the United States.

Suddenly, Americans started thinking about how much fuel they were using. They began conserving energy. They turned down the heat in their houses to save on heating oil. They bought cars that got more miles to a gallon of gasoline.

When the 1973 war ended, the Arab nations once again sent oil to the United States. The lines at the gasoline stations were shorter again. But the prices of gasoline and oil remained high.

## The Suez Canal

The Middle East is important to the world because of its oil. It is also important because of the Suez Canal. The canal links the Mediterranean Sea and the Red Sea. Without it, ships would have to travel all the way around Africa.

Wars have been fought over control of the canal. Egypt has tried to keep Israeli ships out of the canal. When the two nations went to war in 1973, the Soviet Union sent aid to the Arabs. And the United States supported Israel.

## Plans for Peace

In 1977, the leader of Egypt, Anwar El-Sadat, visited Israel. He met with Israeli Prime Minister Menachem Begin. At last Arabs and Israelis spoke of peace.

President Carter encouraged the talks. He invited Sadat and Begin to meet with him. In 1978, the three leaders met at Camp David in Maryland. In 1979, they signed the Camp David Accords, a peace treaty. The treaty ended 30 years of hostility between Egypt and Israel. Other Arab nations continued to battle with Israel, but Egypt and Israel had reached an **accord**.

At other times, the United States has also sent military supplies to Arabic countries.

## Violence and Terror

Palestinians wanted a Palestinian state for themselves. They wanted that state to be on land that Israel held. In December of 1987, an uprising by Palestinians began in territories occupied by Israel.

Some of the Palestinians used very violent means to make their demands known to the world. A group called the Palestine Liberation Organization (PLO) trained its members to use violence. Not only Israel felt the violence of the PLO. The organization claimed responsibility for acts of terror in other places of the world as well.

In the 1980s terrorism by different groups was on the rise. One of the most dramatic terrorist acts of the decade was the **hijacking** of a U.S. airplane on June 14, 1985. A group of rebel Muslims took control of TWA Flight 847 after it took off from Athens, Greece. The hijackers demanded that Israel release 766 prisoners. In October of that same year, terrorists struck again. PLO gunmen threatened to blow up a cruise ship unless Israel agreed to release 50 PLO prisoners. The terrorists killed a Jewish American tourist who was traveling aboard the ship. On December 21, 1988 a terrorist bomb exploded aboard Pan American Flight 103 as it was flying over Lockerbie, Scotland. All 259 people aboard were killed, including 38 American students.

Terrorist violence spread a blanket of fear, anger, and confusion around the world. Nations have expressed their outrage, but no one has found a way to end terrorism.

## U.S. Troops in Lebanon

During the 1970s, civil war raged in the Middle Eastern country of Lebanon. The city of Beirut was torn apart as the Muslim majority fought against Christians for congrol of the government. By the 1980s neighboring Middle Eastern nations had been drawn into the fight. To add to the violent climate, thousands of Palestinians who had fled Israel in 1984 were living in Lebanon. The PLO waged guerrilla war against Israel using Lebanon as its base. In 1982, Israel invaded Lebanon to try to wipe out the PLO.

United Nations peacekeeping forces entered Lebanon to try to end the violence. In 1982, U.S. President Reagan agreed to send American Marines to joint he peacekeepers. The peacekeeping forces came under attack. Terrorists bombed the American embassy in Beirut and U.S. Marine barracks. More than 200 Americans were killed in the attack. Muslim forces kidnapped American and European civilians and held them hostage. Americans at home protested the American involvement in Lebanon until President Reagan ordered the American troops home.

## Conflict in the Persian Gulf

During the 1980s the United States became involved in violence in the Persian Gulf. For years the nations of Iran and Iraq had been in conflict over control of a waterway dividing their nations. The fighting began when Iraq's leader, Saddam Hussein, launched an attack on Iran. Both nations soon were firing missiles. Tens of thousands of soldiers and civilians were killed.

Attacks began on oil tankers in the Persian Gulf. The United States sent navy ships to protect the flow of oil. In 1987 the *USS Stark* was hit by a missile from an Iraqi warplane. Thirty-seven Americans aboard the *Stark* were killed. Iraq called the attack a mistake.

Tension in the Gulf led to more errors and tragedies. On July 3, 1988 the U.S. cruiser *Vincennes* fired on an Iranian jet believing it was a hostile enemy aircraft. It was a passenger plane, and all 290 people aboard were killed.

Finally, in 1988, the United Nations arranged a cease-fire between Iran and Iraq. The eight-year war changed little politically in the Middle East, but it claimed more than a million lives. Iran and Iraq were left torn apart, and the United States had been drawn into a bitter conflict thousands of miles from its shores.

## The Gulf War and Operation Desert Storm

On August 2, 1990, Iraqi leader Saddam Hussein sent 100,000 troops into the small neighboring country of Kuwait. Hussein wanted to make Kuwait and its rich oil fields a part of Iraq. After the war between Iraq and Iran, Hussein had continued to build his military. Iraq bought missiles and developed chemical, biological, and nuclear weapons. The costs were heavy. Hussein needed Kuwait's oil profits to pay his military debts.

Kuwait fell only hours after the Iraqi attack. The take-over gave Saddam Hussein control of nearly 25% of the world's oil resources. It put him in a position of great power. Just days later, Hussein's troops were marching toward Kuwait's border with Saudi Arabia. The Iraqi leader appeared ready to go to war with Saudi Arabia if it protested the invasion of Kuwait.

When Hussein captured Kuwait, he did not count on the reaction of the United States and the rest of the world. U.S. President Bush and his advisers acted quickly. They cut off economic relations with Iraq. The U.S. launched Operation Desert Shield, sending military troops and equipment into Saudia Arabia's desert. Forces from Saudi Arabia, Britain, France, Egypt, Syria, and more than 20 other nations joined the American troops. Germany and Japan promised financial support. The United Nations demanded that Iraq leave Kuwait. On November 29, 1990, Hussein received a warning. The United Nations would "use all necessary means" if Iraq did not withdraw from Kuwait by January 15, 1991.

Meanwhile, President Bush doubled U.S. strength in the Gulf. January came, and Hussein still controlled Kuwait. On January 14, the U.S. Congress approved the use of force in the Gulf. By the evening of January 16, U.S. bombs and missiles rained down on Iraq. Operation Desert Shield had become Operation Desert Storm.

The United States led air attacks that pounded Iraq and shattered its air forces. In response, Iraq fired Scud missiles at Israel and Saudi Arabia. Hussein hoped to win support of other Arab nations by drawing Israel into the fight. The Scud missiles did no major damage, and Israel did not fight back. The United Nations used defense missiles to protect both Israel and Saudi Arabia.

A ground war began on February 23. Iraq was dealt a shattering defeat both on land and in the air. By February 28, Kuwait was free and a cease-fire had begun. Iraq left Kuwait with 600 oil wells on fire. The U.S. government estimated that 100,000 Iraqi soldiers died in combat during the 43 days of battle. Allied forces fighting against Hussein claimed that 200 of their troops had been killed.

**American women took up arms during the Gulf War. About 28,000 U.S. servicewomen were posted in combat zones.**

The Gulf War ended when Kuwait was freed. The war destroyed Iraq's military might. However, the defeat did not destroy Saddam Hussein's control over Iraq. During the war, President Bush spoke of a "new world order." The Gulf War did not create this new order. It did not end the tensions in the Middle East.

## History Practice

Answer these questions on a separate sheet of paper.

1. What was one result of the 1973 oil embargo?

2. Why is the Suez Canal important?

3. What do Palestinians want from Israel?

4. What was the goal of Operation Desert Storm?

## Summary

| CHRONOLOGY OF MAJOR EVENTS | |
| --- | --- |
| 1972 | Watergate break-in |
| 1973 | War in Middle East; oil embargo |
| 1974 | Nixon resigns; Gerald Ford becomes president |
| 1976 | Jimmy Carter elected 39th president |
| 1979 | Iran takes American hostages |
| 1979 | Camp David Accords |
| 1980 | Ronald Reagan elected 40th president |
| 1981 | Iran releases hostages |
| 1983 | U.S. Marines invade Grenada |
| 1984 | President Reagan reelected |
| 1988 | George Bush elected 41st president |
| 1991 | United States becomes involved in Persian Gulf War. |

- After the Watergate scandal, President Nixon resigned and Gerald Ford took over as president.

- President Carter faced problems when Iranians took American embassy workers as hostages for 444 days.

- President Reagan focused on military build-up and a stronger economy.

- Israel and the Arab nations surrounding it have been at war. The Arab nations feel Israel has no right to the land it occupies.

- There has also been much fighting within the Arabic world.

- Oil and control of the Suez Canal make the Middle East especially important.


## Chapter Quiz

Answer these questions on a separate sheet of paper.

1. Why did Richard Nixon leave office?

2. What happens to the cost of goods during times of inflation?

3. Which country was ruled by both Mohammed Reza Pahlavi and the Ayatolla Khomeini?

4. What was one way Ronald Reagan tried to balance the budget?

5. In 1948, Palestine was divided into two countries. What were they?

6. What important international event took place at Camp David, Maryland?


## Thinking and Writing

1. Do you think Gerald Ford should have pardoned Richard Nixon? Explain your answer.

2. Do you think a woman could become president of the United States? Do you think her presidency would be different from a man's? Explain your answer.

3. Have you read about any acts of terrorism during recent years? Describe the terrorist act and tell how it makes you feel. What do you think could be done to protect innocent people against terrorism?

# Chapter 28

# Today and Tomorrow at Home

**1969**
Neil Armstrong walks on the moon

Into the future...

In 1969 the United States became the first nation to land a manned spacecraft on the moon.

## Chapter Learning Objectives

- Name two major accomplishments of the U.S. space program since 1969.
- Describe changes in the roles of American women during modern times.
- Explain how the technology of the 1980s has improved American lives.
- Tell some of the problems and challenges that face Americans as they move into the 21st century.

# Words to Know

**environment**   everything that surrounds us, like air, earth, and water

**smog**   a mixture of fog and smoke

It often seems that we live in very troubled times. Conflict fills the news. Yet this is not the whole story. History is more than a record of failures. Is the world headed toward more peaceful relations? Are nations that were once enemies becoming friends? It does appear that there are more chances now for better understanding among the peoples of the world. The next two chapters are about the problems and challenges of today and tomorrow.

## The Continuing Struggle for Women's Rights

One struggle that gained strength in the 1970s was that of a minority group that was really a majority. More than half the people in the United States are women. They had gotten the vote in 1920. But they were still fighting laws and practices that kept them from what should have been theirs. They outnumbered men. But few women held powerful places in government or business.

The number of women who held jobs had grown from one in four in 1940 to one in two in 1970. But they made less money than men did, even when doing the same jobs. In 1945, a woman earned an average of 65% of what a man earned. By 1957, it had dropped to 57%. Even in 1987, a woman still earned an average of only 65% of what a man earned for the same work.

Joining together in groups like the National Organization for Women (NOW), women were able to change some laws. And they stopped some companies from discriminating against them in the work place. Also, they presented an amendment to the Constitution which would outlaw sex discrimination. In 1972, Congress passed the Equal Rights Amendment (ERA). Thirty-three states quickly approved it. But 38 of the 50 states had to vote for it before it could become law. Supporters of the ERA were unable to get the last three states they needed. In 1982, the amendment died. This happened even though 60% of all Americans were in favor of it.

The daily lives of American women have changed. Many women are waiting until an older age to marry. They are waiting still longer to have children. And they are having fewer children.

As more mothers enter the work force, businesses address new problems. Should women be given leave to take care of sick children? Will their jobs be kept open for them if they take time off to have children? Should businesses provide child care? Some companies are beginning to do this.

As the lives of women change, families change. Men appear to be assuming more responsibility for the daily care of their children and for household chores.

There is an old saying that "It's a man's world." It really did describe the United States of the past. It was once a place where women could not vote. They could not own property. They could not get most jobs. And when they did get jobs, they were paid less than men for their work. Women are still working for an America of equal opportunity.

Great Names in History: Betty Friedan

Betty Friedan was a magazine editor in New York City. In 1963, her book *The Feminine Mystique* was published. Friedan encouraged women to think of themselves as more than wives and mothers. She asked them if they were happy with themselves. She asked if they felt they were contributing to American society. The book started many American women thinking.

Not all women saw things as Friedan did. Some said they were happy with things as they were. But Friedan's book led others to question their lives. Many began to realize that they were, indeed, subject to discrimination.

Friedan and others organized. They marched. They carried banners. They worked for the passage of the Equal Rights Amendment. They made their voices heard.

## Resources and Energy Problems

During the 1970s it became plain that America's growth was causing some serious problems.

The pollution of the air by factories, cars, and power plants had been increasing for many years. It was becoming harmful and even deadly. Some cities posted **smog** warnings. On bad days, children were kept home from school. People were asked to stay indoors if they could.

Many rivers and lakes had been poisoned by industrial wastes. In Lake Erie and other places, all the fish and plants died. At Love Canal, New York, wastes buried 30 years before were poisoning people's water, food, and bodies. In 1969, so much waste built up in Cleveland, Ohio's Cuyahoga River that it actually caught fire.

In 1989, one of the largest oil spills in U.S. history occurred in Valdez, Alaska. The spill damaged wildlife and the state's fishing waters.

## Words from the Past: A Warning

In 1962, scientist and author Rachel Carson had published a book called *Silent Spring*. In it she warned America what would happen if we did not take care of our natural resources. She said that we were killing our wildlife and perhaps ourselves with the careless use of pesticides. "The mistakes made now," Carson wrote, "are being made for all time."

In 1971, the United States set up the **Environmental** Protection Agency (EPA). The EPA made rules to control pollution. They regulated factories' waste systems. They made automobiles meet certain standards in order to control air pollution. They outlawed the use of certain dangerous chemicals.

With only 7% of the world's population, the United States was using 33% of the world's energy. To meet this demand, the United States bought one third of its oil from other countries. Even so, there were sometimes small gas shortages. After the 1973 oil embargo, we looked closer at other energy sources. These included the sun, moving water, and atomic power. New sources of oil were found in this country. In 1977, the Trans-Alaska Pipeline was built. It sent oil from fields in Alaska.

Nuclear power provided another new source of energy. The splitting of atoms provided a clean, cheap source of power. But nuclear power plants posed certain risks. In 1979 the nation's most serious nuclear accident occurred at the Three Mile Island power plant near Harrisburg, Pennsylvania. The escape of deadly radiation was narrowly avoided and the American public became more concerned about the safety of producing nuclear power.

**A nuclear power plant**

Americans have begun to realize that our sources of energy are limited. People are taking steps to use less energy. Home owners are adding insulation to their dwellings and turning down the heat in the winter. Scientists and energy companies are looking for cleaner, safer sources of power.

## The Space Adventure Continues

John Kennedy had promised in 1960 that America would put someone on the moon within ten years. Although he didn't live to see it, his promise was kept. In 1969, the *Eagle*, a tiny landing craft, left its mother ship and circled the moon. While trying to touch down, the *Eagle* almost ran out of fuel. But it wasn't long before the earth received a message saying, "the *Eagle* has landed." A few hours later, Neil Armstrong became the first human being to set foot on the moon.

## Words from the Past:
## A Statement from the Moon

When Neil Armstrong stepped onto the moon, much of the world was watching him on television. They heard Armstrong say, "That was one small step for a man, one giant leap for mankind."

What do you think Armstrong meant?

In the 1970s, astronauts became more than space travelers. They became space workers. In 1973 and 1974, three different crews worked in *Skylab*. This was the first space station.

In the 1980s space shuttles like the *Columbia*, the *Challenger*, and the *Discovery* were launched. Earlier ships had made only one trip each. The space shuttles carry large loads into space again and again. Also to come are space stations on which people will probably be able to live and work for years at a time.

Tragedy struck the shuttle program on January 28, 1986. The space shuttle *Challenger* exploded right after take-off. All those aboard—six astronauts and a New Hampshire school teacher—were killed. The teacher, Krista McAuliffe, was to be the first civilian sent into space. The explosion was blamed on problems in the shuttle's engineering. The tragedy reminded America of the bravery of its space pioneers.

## Great Names in History: Sally Ride

Sally Ride had studied English and science in school. In 1977, she and 8,000 other people answered an ad for astronauts. She was one of the 35 chosen to be trained. Five-and-a-half years later, on June 18, 1983, Sally Ride was aboard a *Challenger* space shuttle when it lifted off. She became the first American woman in space.

## New Technology

The late 1970s and early 1980s saw the rise of the computer. Remember that early computers were very large and expensive. Today, there are home computers that cost a few hundred dollars. Most home computers are about the size of a TV set, or

The earliest computers were little more than high-speed adding machines.

smaller. They are faster and more powerful than any of the early models. As they have become smaller and cheaper, computers have become more a part of our lives. They're seen in supermarkets, banks, stores, factories, offices, and schools.

Many good things have come from computers. In factories, they control machines and work where humans can't. They find information in seconds and allow banks and businesses to work more quickly and cheaply. They keep round-the-clock watch on sick people in hospitals. Every day we are finding new ways to use them.

Of course, while computers can solve problems, they can also help bring them about. Some of the work they do was once done by people who have had to search for new jobs. Businesses that depend on computers come to a halt when the machines break down or the electricity goes out. And computers make spying on private citizens easier.

Computers invite us to gather, use, and share great amounts of information.

Today business and industry use robots as well as computers. Robot arms are used to assemble automobile engines in Detroit factories. They do jobs that were once done by human beings. What advantages can you see to using robots in industries? What disadvantages?

## Advances in Medicine

New technology has helped the medical community identify and treat disease. In the 1970s, CAT-scanners were developed to take computerized x-rays of soft body parts. In the 1980s, magnetic resonance imaging, or MRI, was used to take pictures of soft body tissues. The MRI uses magnets and sound energy to take pictures while avoiding harmful x-rays. Unlike x-rays, MRI can pass through

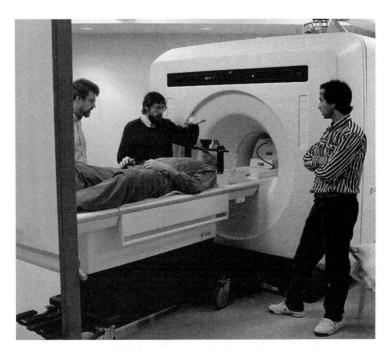

**Patient undergoing an MRI exam**

bone tissue. Doctors most often use MRI to look through the skull and take pictures of the brain. The development of the laser light beam has also enabled doctors to provide better medical care for seriously ill patients. It is used to seal wounds, clear blockages, and remove tumors.

Advances in medicine provide new devices to help the handicapped and new medicines to treat diseases that were once incurable. People today are living longer, healthier lives. In 1930 the average life expectancy for an American was about 60 years old. By 1990 it had increased to 75.

The laser could make light stronger, narrower, and hotter. Lasers are also used in photocopiers, compact disc players, and nuclear reactors.

## Home Entertainment Revolution

Advances in technology have produced a revolution in home entertainment. Video Tape Recorders (VCRs) allow families to tape televised programs to play back over their television at a later time. Or they can rent or buy tapes of movies to play in their own homes. Compact discs are replacing records and cassette tapes as a favorite way to play music at home.

## Learn More About It: Communities Change

A section of the United States known as the Sunbelt has grown rapidly throughout the seventies and eighties. This area includes California, Texas, Florida, and Arizona. It is an area of warm weather and sunny skies. Many older Americans are moving to the Sunbelt to spend their retirement years. Younger people have found jobs there in the space, oil, and computer fields.

### History Practice

Answer these questions on a separate sheet of paper.

1. What was the ERA? What happened to it?

2. Who was the first person to set foot on the moon?

3. What are three sources of energy besides oil?

## New Problems, Old Problems

During the 1980s the problem of homelessness in the United States became worse than at any time since the Great Depression of the 1930s. In 1985, the number of homeless people was estimated to range from 350,000 to 3 million. Government shelters have not been able to meet the needs of all the homeless.

The Department of Housing and Urban Development (HUD) has provided some money to build dwellings where the government pays part of the cost of rent. But the number of homeless Americans continues to grow. These people of the streets are a reminder that although America is a rich nation, there are many who do not share in the wealth.

During the 1980s, a new disease swept across the world. The United States was just one of the 140 countries where it hit. Scientists identified the disease in 1981, and they named it Acquired Immune Deficiency Syndrome (AIDS). They discovered it was caused by a virus they labeled HIV. The AIDS virus can be passed in only two ways: through blood-to-blood contact or through an exchange of bodily fluids. People could get AIDS from sexual contact with an infected person or from using a contaminated needle. In some cases the baby of an AIDS-infected mother could be born with the virus. AIDS attacks the body's immune system and usually leads to death. By 1990 more than 1 million cases of AIDS had been reported in the United States and Canada. It quickly became clear that education would be the key to halting the spread of AIDS. Many Americans called on their government to invest heavily in AIDS research.

Drugs and crime continued to be serious problems in the United States. During the 1980s drug users began turning to new, powerful, more addictive drugs. To get money for the drugs they needed, users often turned to crime. First President Reagan and later President Bush declared a war on drugs. The Reagan administration worked to stop the flow of drugs into the United States from Latin America. In 1988, Congress created a new post—the director of the national drug control policy. In 1989, President Bush appointed former Secretary of Education William J. Bennett to the position. Bennett became known as the "Drug Czar." In 1990 Bush and Bennett declared that America was winning the war. However, statistics show that drug-related crime is still a major problem on the streets of many American cities.

Race relations continue to be a problem in the United States. The civil rights movement has led African Americans closer to equality. They have gained political and economic power. Major cities, such as Los Angeles, New York, and Baltimore, have elected African American mayors. Many African Americans hold positions in state legislatures and in Congress. In the late 1980s General Colin Powell became the chairman of the Joint Chiefs of Staff, the nation's top military post.

However, discrimination has not disappeared. Too many African Americans still live in poverty. Too many feel thay have been denied America's wealth and opportunities. Urban African American communities have seen scores of angry young blacks join street gangs. Gang wars produce gunfire and lead to deaths, often those of innocent bystanders.

In 1992 violence rocked the city of Los Angeles. Angry mobs protested the outcome of a highly publicized trial. A jury found four policemen not-guilty of police brutality in the 1991 beating of a black man named Rodney King. The protest turned into a riot of burning and looting that left much of South-Central Los Angeles in ashes. In June, 1992, Los Angeles Police Chief Darryl Gates stepped down. He was replaced by Willie Williams, the city's first African American police chief.

## The 1992 Presidential Campaign

The year 1992 was a presidential election year. President Bush was running for reelection. He faced the Democrat's candidate, Arkansas Governor Bill

Clinton. A third-party candidate, H. Ross Perot, also gathered strong support. Americans were concerned about unemployment and a weak economy. They worried about the high costs of health care and of health insurance. President Bush assured the voters that the economy was improving. He reminded them of America's show of strength during the Persian Gulf War and warned that they needed a president with international experience.

Ross Perot, a self-made billionaire from Texas, declared that the United States needed a practical plan to balance the budget, pay up the national debt, and put Americans back to work. He offered a no-nonsense, businessman's approach to politics. Governor Clinton pointed out that unemployment was the highest it had been in eight years. He promised America a change. He pointed out that 12 years of Reagan-Bush politics had left many Americans with a lower standard of living.

The United States was ready for change. In November, 1992, Americans elected Democrat Bill Clinton president.

**Ross Perot gained more than 19% of the popular vote. That was the highest total for a third party candidate for president in U.S. history.**

## History Practice

Answer these questions on a separate sheet of paper.

1. What problem did the United States face in the 1980s that was worse than at anytime since the Great Depression?

2. How did the United States attempt to deal with the continuing drug problem during the 1980s?

3. What caused the Los Angeles riots of 1992?

4. Name a major issue that concerned voters during the 1992 presidential campaign.

# Chapter Review

## Summary

| CHRONOLOGY OF MAJOR EVENTS |
| --- |
| 1969      Astronauts walk on moon |
| 1971      Environmental Protection Agency (EPA) established |
| 1979      Three Mile Island nuclear accident |
| 1981      AIDS virus identified |
| 1982      Equal Rights Amendment defeated |
| 1986      Space Shuttle *Challenger* explodes |
| 1992      Bill Clinton elected president |

- Congress passed an Equal Rights Amendment that banned discrimination against women. Not enough states approved the amendment, and it failed to become part of the U.S. Constitution.

- Americans began to explore alternatives to oil and to use less energy.

- Regulations were passed to protect land, water, and air.

- American astronauts landed on the moon. Reusable space shuttles made trips into outer space.

- Computers played a larger role in American life.

- New medical technology allowed better images of the inside of the human body.

- The population of the Sunbelt region grew rapidly.

- Homelessness becomes a major problem in American cities.

- Scientists identify deadly AIDS virus and search for a cure.

- Presidents Reagan and Bush declare a war on drugs.

- Urban gangs and racial violence plague cities.

- Arkansas Governor Bill Clinton defeats George Bush in race for presidency.

## Chapter Quiz

Answer these questions on a separate sheet of paper.

1. What did the *Columbia*, the *Challenger*, and the *Discovery* have in common?

2. Name three sources of air pollution.

3. Describe two ways modern computers differ from the earliest computers.

4. Name four states included in the Sunbelt.

5. How is the AIDS virus spread?

6. Name three problems America still faces at this point in its history.

## Thinking and Writing

1. Name some women you know of who hold important positions in business or government. Name some women you know of who hold jobs that were once considered only for men.

2. What would you say is the most important change that has taken place in the United States since 1900? Why?

3. What would you like to see happen in the United States by the year 2000?

**Chapter 29**

# Today and Tomorrow:
# The United States and the World

**1972**
Nixon visits Communist China

Into the future...

President Bill Clinton
and Russian leader
Boris Yeltsin held
their first summit
in April 1993.

## Chapter Learning Objectives

- Explain how relations between the United States and other superpowers have changed since 1970.
- Describe U.S. relations with Latin America in the 1980s and 1990s.
- Explore incidences of American presence in the politics of other nations.
- Explain how the United States functions as part of a global economy.

# Words to Know

**global**   involving the whole world
**exported**   sent goods out of the
   country for sale in another country

**imported**   brought goods into one
   country from another
**symbol**   an object that stands for an
   idea

---

There were swift and dramatic changes in the
world during the 1980s and 1990s. Some of the
**global** political and economic changes were good
news for the United States. Old enemies became new
friends and trading partners. But problems also arose
to threaten U.S. interests and international peace.

## U.S. Relations with China

In 1972, President Nixon became the first sitting
U.S. president to visit Communist China. The visit
paved the way for better relations between the
United States, its Western allies, and China. For
many years Westerners had not been allowed to
visit The People's Republic of China. China did not
do business with the West. After Nixon's visit, China
developed new trade relations with the United States
as well as other Western nations. China also opened
its doors and allowed visitors from Western
countries.

During the 1980s the people of China began to call
for democratic freedoms and basic human rights.
Workers, students, and artists asked for changes
within the strict Communist government. But the
Communist party kept a firm hand. In May, 1989,
3,000 students gathered in Tiananmen Square in
the city of Beijing. They staged a hunger strike for
democratic reforms. Hundreds of thousands of
people joined the protest. Then, in the middle of the

night on June 4, the army made a sweep through the square. Hundreds of students were killed. More were arrested. China's democracy movement was violently crushed. The United States government spoke out against the force used in Tiananmen Square. President Bush took some small steps to punish the Chinese government, but refused to cut off all relations with it. The events in Tiananmen Square outraged many Americans and was a step backwards in U.S.- Chinese relations.

## U.S.–Soviet Relations and an End to the Cold War

Richard Nixon also visited the Soviet Union in 1972. It was the first time a U.S. president had gone there during peace time. Nixon met with Soviet leader Leonid Brezhnev. The two leaders worked out a treaty for slowing down the nuclear arms race. It was called the Strategic Arms Limitation Treaty (SALT). SALT slowed down the arms buildup for a time. However, a second attempt later in the decade to put together an arms limitation treaty failed. The SALT II talks were canceled when the Soviets invaded Afghanistan in 1979.

The biggest change in U.S.–Soviet relations began to occur at the beginning of Ronald Reagan's second term as president. In 1985, Mikhail Gorbachev became the Soviet leader. Gorbachev wanted his nation to be more open to information and ideas from the West. His new policy for the Soviet Union was sometimes described by the Russian word *glasnost*. It means "openness."

President Reagan and Secretary General Gorbachev attempted to reach an agreement on arms limitation. In 1987 they signed an historic treaty. For the first time both countries would destroy some of their nuclear weapons. Gorbachev continued to push for improved relations with the West. In 1988, he began pulling Soviet tanks out of eastern Europe. The next year he withdrew Soviet troops from Afghanistan. The 40-year Cold War was beginning to thaw.

Friendly relations with the United States were important to Gorbachev's plans for the Soviet Union. Good relations, he hoped, would lead to trade agreements and economic improvements. The thaw in the Cold War continued into President Bush's term of office. Bush met with Gorbachev to work on the Strategic Arms Reduction Treaty (START). The agreement would make further cuts in the number of U.S. and Soviet nuclear weapons.

START offered the United States a chance to make big cuts in military spending. Many Americans believed the money saved could be used at home to shelter the homeless and feed the hungry. Others worried that the end of the cold war would hurt the economy. They said that cuts in defense spending would mean heavy layoffs in many industries and would put more Americans out of work.

As the 1990s began, the Soviet Union faced widespread economic problems. The country was coming apart. The three Baltic republics, Latvia, Lithuania, and Estonia, had declared their independence. Eleven of the twelve remaining republics agreed to form a new group. They called themselves the Commonwealth of Independent States. The Communist Party was ousted from power. In December, 1991, Mikhail Gorbachev was forced to step down. Boris Yeltsin, president of the republic of Russia, became the leader of the new commonwealth. The people of the former Soviet Union still faced economic woes. Food and medicine continued to be in short supply. How would Yeltsin and the leaders of the new Commonwealth deal with their challenges?

Gorbachev's leadership brought new personal freedoms and a more open economy. But by late 1989 the Soviet economy was in trouble. Goods were in short supply. One Soviet citizen explained, "There is more freedom now, but life is harder."

## America Cheers Freedom in Eastern Europe

As dramatic change took place inside the Soviet Union, events were changing elsewhere within the Communist world. A wave of freedom swept through eastern Europe in 1989. It began in Poland. A workers' movement called Solidarity forced Communist leaders there to hold free elections. In Hungary Communist leaders were overthrown and soldiers began tearing down barbed wire fences that closed its border with Austria.

The wave of freedom roared from Hungary to Germany. On November 9, 1989, the Berlin Wall separating East and West Berlin was opened. East Germans by the thousands crossed into West Berlin. The Wall had been a **symbol** of all that separated Communism from democracy, tyranny from freedom. Many Americans traveled to Germany to celebrate the fall of the Berlin Wall. They brought home broken pieces of concrete as souvenirs of a new age of freedom.

A wave of rebellion also occurred in Bulgaria, Czechoslovakia, and Romania. Gorbachev and the Soviet Union did nothing to stop it. Unlike past episodes, no Soviet troops tried to crush the rebels. By January, 1990, six Soviet satellite nations were free of Communist control. Americans watched, thrilled and amazed by the changes that had happened so quickly and wondering what kind of future these changes would bring.

## History Practice

Answer these questions on a separate sheet of paper.

1. What event put an end to the SALT II talks?

2. How have U.S.–Soviet relations changed since 1972?

3. What event in Germany in 1989 symbolized the fall of communism?

## The United States Enters Conflicts in Central America

When Ronald Reagan took office in 1981, he saw the threat of communism casting a shadow on Central America. For many years the United States had encouraged democracy in Central America. Many times, however, the United States government had supported harsh anti-communist dictators when such support served U.S. interests. Partly because of such dictators, rebel communist movements took hold in parts of Central America. President Reagan declared that the United States must defend against communism in Central America. "The national security of all the Americas is at stake in Central America," Reagan said.

During the 1980s President Reagan turned his attention to the tiny country of El Salvador. A military government had come to power there in 1979. Now communist rebels were attacking government forces. Reagan asked Congress to send military aid to El Salvador. He warned that the rebels had the backing of communist Cuba and of the Soviet Union. The United States sent weapons, aircraft, and advisors to El Salvador. Some people thought that President Reagan was wrong to send military aid to El Salvador. They said that poverty and a cruel government were the real causes of rebellion there.

In 1984 El Salvador held national elections. A non-military president was elected with support from the United States. However, rebel guerrilla attacks continued throughout the decade. A 12-year civil war finally ended in El Salvador in January, 1992, when a peace treaty was signed.

During the Reagan years, the United States also responded to conflict in Nicaragua. A civil war there had ended in 1979 with the victory of a communist rebel party. The rebels, called *Sandinistas,* received economic and military aid from the Soviet Union and Cuba.

A Nicaraguan group known as the Contras rebelled against the communist Sandinistas. President Reagan announced that the United States would give aid to the Contras. Americans were divided over this policy. Many people believed that the United States should not interfere with the politics of another nation. Others agreed with Reagan that the Sandinistas presented a communist threat to the Americas. There were angry debates in Congress over aid to the Contras. Finally, in 1988, all military aid was stopped. Democratic elections in Nicaragua were held in February, 1990. The Sandinistas were defeated and peacefully gave up power.

**There were debates in Congress over sending U.S. money to aid the Nicaraguan Contras in their fight against the Sandinistas. "Didn't we learn our lesson in Vietnam?" asked members of Congress who were opposed to Contra aid. What do you think they meant?**

## U.S. Invasion of Panama

The other Central American country in which the United States became involved during the 1980s was Panama. In February, 1989, the U.S. government charged Panama's General Manuel Noriega with drug smuggling. As commander of his country's defense forces, Noriega held more power than even the country's president. After the drug charges were filed, Panama's president tried to fire Noriega from his post. But Noriega's troops remained loyal to him, and they drove the president into hiding.

Noriega fought all attempts to remove him from power. Finally, in December, 1989, U.S. President George Bush ordered 24,000 U.S. troops into Panama to drive Noriega out. Noriega went into hiding, and it took U.S. troops several days to establish order in the nation's capital. When the troops searched Noriega's office and home they found more than $3 million in cash and a stash of illegal drugs. A month later Noriega surrendered to American forces and was brought back to the United States to stand trial. A new president who had won an open election earlier that year was sworn into office.

**Learn More About It:**
**The Iran-Contra Scandal**

Was it a cover-up or a bad mistake? In late 1986 the American people learned about a secret arms deal between the United States and the Middle Eastern country of Iran. It was discovered that the Reagan administration secretly sold missiles and missile parts to Iran. After the weapons sales, Iranians persuaded terrorists in Lebanon to release some U.S. hostages. Yet U.S. policy forbade trading arms for political hostages.

There was even more to the scandal. Profits from the arms sales had been illegally used to aid the Contras in Nicaragua.

Marine Lieutenant Colonel Oliver North was charged with running the Contra aid operation. North was a staff member of the U.S. National Security Council. He insisted that he had been following orders from those above him.

President Reagan denied any knowledge of the affair. However, the Iran-Contra scandal badly damaged Reagan's popularity in his second term.

## America's Interest in the Third World

There are many nations in the world that have only begun to develop their industry and economy. These newly developing nations are sometimes called Third World nations. The Third World nations in Asia, Africa, and Latin America offer markets for products and political support from the larger advanced countries.

As the Third World nations have developed, their supply of available food has not kept up with their population growth. America wants to befriend the needy nations for political reasons. But Americans also have always believed in helping others. The United States has sent aid—food, money, tools, and medical supplies—to these nations. Americans themselves have gone to the Third World countries as teachers, doctors, and nurses.

Some people say that the United States is taking on the role of "peacekeeper" of the world. Others say that because we are the strongest, most powerful nation, we must come to the aid of those in need. What do you think?

As 1992 came to a close, America was lending its help to the tiny African nation of Somalia. Drought and civil war had left more than one million Somalis starving to death in this dry, barren land. Since 1960 various Somali warlords had fought for control of parts of their country. Their armies were stopping attempts to get food and medicine to the dying people. On December 3, 1992, President Bush and the United Nations approved a plan called Operation Restore Hope. U.S. troops would lead a multi-national military ground force into Somalia. These troops would see that food and medicine were safely distributed to the Somali people.

## The United States in a Global Economy

The story of United States history begins with a new nation struggling to stand on its own. As we move toward the 21st century, that story is one of a country whose strength and well-being is intertwined with the workings of all the nations of the world.

Every year, the economy becomes more global. Americans use products from many other countries. Many American companies have been purchased by foreign corporations. Since the 1970s, America has **imported** more goods from other nations than it has **exported**. Hundreds of American factories have closed or laid off workers because products are being made abroad.

How can the government ensure a strong American economy in this global age? Some economists believe the answer is to build barriers to foreign trade by putting taxes and quotas on imported products. Others believe it is time to tear down barriers to trade. They say free trade agreements will create more opportunities for everyone.

Americans have survived two world wars, the Depression, Watergate, and much more. America not only lived through all these things, it moved forward. Even though as 1993 began the national debt was more than two trillion dollars, America still had the largest economy in the world. For many people in other lands, coming to live and work in America is still a dream. Now Americans must, with care and courage, face the challenges of the future.

In 1989, the Honda Accord became the best-selling car in the United States. This was the first time a foreign car was the top U.S. seller.

## History Practice

Answer these questions on a separate sheet of paper.

1. Why did President Reagan feel the United States should give military aid to El Salvador and Nicaragua?

2. Why did some people feel it was wrong to give military aid to El Salvador and Nicaragua?

3. What phrase is sometimes used to describe newly developing nations?

# Chapter Review

## Summary

| CHRONOLOGY OF MAJOR EVENTS | |
|---|---|
| 1972 | Nixon visits China and the Soviet Union |
| 1972 | Strategic Arms Limitation Treaty (SALT) signed |
| 1979 | SALT II talks canceled |
| 1985 | Mikhail Gorbachev becomes leader of the Soviet Union |
| 1986 | Iran-Contra Scandal uncovered |
| 1987 | United States and Soviet Union sign treaty to destroy some of their nuclear weapons |
| 1989 | U.S. troops invade Panama to force Manuel Noriega from power |
| 1992 | President Bush sends U.S. troops to Somalia to lead Operation Restore Hope |

- U.S. relations with Communist China improved after President Nixon visited the People's Republic in 1972.

- Agreements were reached to limit nuclear arms buildup.

- Soviet leader Mikhail Gorbachev's policy of *glasnost* led to improved U.S.–Soviet relations.

- President Reagan sent military aid to El Salvador and Nicaragua to defeat communists in Central America.

- America watched democratic reforms sweep Russia and Eastern Europe.

- President Bush halted arms sales to China when Chinese leaders violently crushed democratic protests in Tiananmen Square.

- American consumers become increasingly dependent on foreign goods.

## Chapter Quiz

Answer these questions on a separate sheet of paper.

1. Wich president became the first sitting president to visit Communist China?

2. With which Soviet leader is the word *glasnost* linked?

3. Name three Eastern European countries where democratic movements took hold during the 1980s.

4. Which president sent military aid to stop communism in Central America?

5. How did President Bush respond to the starvation in Somalia?

6. What has happened to the balance between America's imports and exports?

## Thinking and Writing

1. What did democracy movements in the Soviet Union and Eastern Europe mean to the people of the United States?

2. Do you think the United States should aid foreign countries that face tyranny, hunger, and civil strife? Explain the reasons for your answer and tell what kind of aid you think the United States should provide.

3. Make a list of products you buy and use that are made in foreign countries. Why do you think Americans are buying so many foreign-made goods?

4. What would you like to see happen in the United States by the year 2000? Around the world?

# Unit Eight Review

Use the information in chapters 24 through 29 to answer the questions on this page. Write your answers on a separate sheet of paper.

**A. Who was there? Choose the U.S. president who was in office during each of the following events.**

Dwight Eisenhower

John Kennedy

Lyndon Johnson

Richard Nixon

Gerald Ford

Jimmy Carter

Ronald Reagan

George Bush

1. Cuban Missile Crisis
2. American hostages in Iran
3. Watergate scandal
4. SALT talks
5. Camp David Peace Talks
6. Integration of schools in Little Rock, Arkansas
7. Bay of Pigs invasion
8. Gulf of Tonkin Resolution
9. START talks with Gorbachev
10. Historic visit to communist China

**B. Think about what you have learned, then answer these questions.**

1. How has life changed for black Americans since World War II?
2. Give reasons for the search for non-oil energy sources.

# Appendix

# Glossary

**abolitionists**  people who worked to end slavery

**accord**  agreement

**accusations**  charges that someone has done something wrong

**act**  a law

**alien**  person from a foreign country who is not yet a citizen

**alliance**  a joining together for some purpose; an agreement by treaty

**ambush**  a surprise attack

**amendment**  a change or addition to a document

**annex**  to obtain; to include

**anthem**  the official song of a country

**antibiotics**  chemicals produced to kill or stop the growth of germs

**aqueducts**  large pipes that bring water from one place to another

**assemble**  to build

**astronaut**  a person trained to travel in outer space

**atmosphere**  all the air around the Earth

**bail**  money left with the court as a guarantee that an arrested person will show up for trial

**bill**  an idea for a law

**blockade**  to keep supplies from getting in or out of a place

**bodyguard**  a person who provides physical protection for another

**boycott**  to join together in refusing to buy goods or services

**bribes**  money given to get someone to do something against the law

**bugs**  tiny microphones

**building codes**  sets of laws and requirements that buildings must meet

**cabinet**  a group of people chosen by the president to give advice

**canal**  a waterway dug across a stretch of land

**candidate**  a person running for political office

**Carpetbaggers**  northerners who came south after the Civil War. They took power and used southern problems for their own gain.

**cease-fire**  a halt to fighting for an agreed upon time period

**charity**  kindness; good will

**charter**  an official government paper granting people certain rights

**chief justice**   the judge in charge of a court made up of several judges

**civil rights**   the rights of a citizen

**civilians**   people not belonging to the armed forces

**civilization**   the way of life of a people who have developed their own government, arts, and sciences

**climate**   the typical weather of a place over a period of years

**colonies**   lands settled and ruled by people from other countries

**committee**   a group of people chosen to do certain work

**communication**   the passing along of information, the exchange of messages

**concentration camp**   a prison camp for people feared by a government

**Confederacy**   the southern side in the Civil War

**conquistador**   Spanish conqueror

**conservation**   the protection of natural resources

**constitution**   the law and plan of a country's government

**consumers**   those who buy goods

**cooperate**   to work together toward a common goal

**corps**   a group of people working together

**correspond**   to write letters to someone and receive letters back

**corrupt**   dishonest

**cosmonaut**   a Soviet space explorer (like American "astronaut")

**crisis**   a time of great danger or trouble

**debt**   money that is owed

**decade**   ten years

**decay**   rot or decline

**decency**   proper behavior; goodness; kindness

**declaration**   a public statement

**delegate**   chosen spokesperson

**destined**   bound to happen

**dictator**   a ruler with complete power

**dictatorship**   a government in which power is held by a few people or by one person

**divine**   godlike

**doctrine**   a set of beliefs or principles

**drought**   a long period of dry weather

**duty**   a tax on goods brought in from a foreign country

**economy**   the way goods, wealth, and services are produced and used; the total amount of these and how they are divided among people

**Electoral College** group of people elected by voters to choose the president and vice-president

**embargo** an enforced halting of trade

**embassy** a building where representatives from foreign nations work

**empire** a group of countries or territories ruled by the same government

**environment** everything that surrounds us, like air, earth, and water

**epidemic** the rapid spread of a disease to a large part of a population

**equality** fairness; sameness

**escalate** to raise the level of conflict

**executive** the branch of government having power to carry out laws

**expand** to become larger

**expansion** growth outward

**expedition** a long journey of discovery

**exported** sent goods out of the country for sale in another country

**facilities** places, such as buildings or rooms, for certain activities; a school is a facility for learning

**fascism** a system of government under which each citizen's purpose is to serve the state

**figurehead** a person who holds a high position but has no real power

**foreign policy** the way a country deals with other countries

**freedom of association** the freedom to spend time with those one chooses

**frontier** the edge of settled country that lies next to wild, unsettled land

**galleon** a Spanish ship

**generation** the people born at about the same time

**ghettos** poor neighborhoods where people from one or more ethnic backgrounds live apart from others

**global** involving the whole world

**heir** a person who receives property or position when the person holding it dies

**hijacking** taking an airplane or vehicle over by force and directing it to a destination not originally intended

**Holocaust** the killing of millions of Jews by Nazi Germany; the word *holocaust* means great destruction of life by fire

**hostage** a person who is kidnapped and held until certain demands are met

**hostile** hateful, angry

**houses** groups of people who make laws

**immigrants** people who come into a country foreign to them to make a new home

**immunity** protection against disease

**impeach** to accuse a public official of doing wrong and to send that official to trial

**imperialism** the practice of setting up an empire by forming colonies in other lands or controlling the wealth or politics of weaker nations

**imported** brought goods into one country from another

**inauguration** the swearing in of a president

**income tax** tax on the money people earn

**indentured servants** people bound to work without pay for a certain number of years. After that time, the person is set free.

**independent** not controlled by others

**industry** the making of goods on a large scale

**inspire** to encourage

**integrate** to bring together

**interfere** to get in the way of

**internment** the keeping of people in a place, such as a prison, usually during wartime

**intolerance** an unwillingness to accept people of different races or backgrounds or with different ideas

**investigation** a search for facts

**isolation** separation

**judicial** the branch of government that settles arguments about the meaning of laws and that punishes law-breakers

**jury** a group of people who decide if a person on trial is guilty or not guilty

**landslide** the winning of an election by a huge number of votes

**Latin America** the Western Hemisphere south of the United States

**legislative** the branch of government that makes laws

**legislature** a group that makes laws

**loyal** faithful to someone or something

**Loyalists** Americans who supported the British in the Revolutionary War

**lynchings** killing by mobs, usually by hanging, without trial

**majority** more than half

**malice** ill will; anger; hatred

**mass production** the manufacturing of goods in large numbers at low cost

**migrant**   a worker who moves from one place to another as seasons change and crops ripen

**migrate**   to move from one place to another

**militia**   a group of citizens who are not regular soldiers but who get some military training

**missile**   an object shot or thrown through the air at a target

**nationalism**   love of country; patriotism

**natives**   people who live in the place where they were born

**natural resources**   things we need that are produced by nature; they include forests, minerals, water, and soil

**neutral**   not taking sides in a quarrel or war

**Neutralists**   colonists who did not care which side won the Revolutionary War

**nomads**   people who wander about from one area to another

**nominated**   named to run for office

**nuclear**   having to do with the nucleus, or center, of the atom

**opportunity**   chance; a "land of opportunity" is a place where people have a chance to improve their lives

**overcome**   to triumph over; to rise above

**overthrow**   to violently replace one government with another

**pacifist**   a person who believes problems between nations should be settled peacefully, never by war

**pamphlet**   a thin booklet with a paper cover

**panic**   a sudden great fear

**parallel**   one of the imaginary lines around the Earth that runs in the same direction as the equator

**pardon**   to forgive; to free from punishment

**patent**   the right given to someone by the government to be the only one to make or sell a new invention

**patriotic**   showing love and loyalty toward one's country

**Patriots**   Americans who wanted independence from Britain

**persecute**   to treat badly; to harm

**phonograph**   a record player

**pioneers**   people who go first, who open the way for others to follow

**plains**   large stretches of almost flat, nearly treeless land

**plantation**   a large farm that usually produces one main product. The workers live on the grounds.

**plot**   secret plan

**politics**   the art of running a government

**poll**   a place where people vote

**pollute**   to make dirty

**prairie**   large area of flat or rolling grassland

**prejudice**   hatred of a group of people, usually because of their race or religion

**primary**   an election in which people choose a political party's candidates

**proclamation**   a public statement

**prosperity**   wealth; well-being

**protest**   to speak out or act against

**pursuit**   the act of going after something, of seeking it

**quota system**   an immigration plan passed by Congress in the 1920s; it let in only a certain number of people from each country

**racism**   the belief that differences make one race better than another

**radicals**   people who favor big changes

**ratify**   to approve or accept

**ration**   to limit the amount of something given out

**recession**   a period when business is bad; less serious than a depression

**Reconstruction**   the time after the Civil War; the rebuilding of the South and the bringing of the southern states back into the Union

**recovery**   a return to health

**refinery**   a factory where something like oil or sugar is broken down into a purer form

**refuge**   a place a person can go for safety

**refugees**   people who have fled to a new country

**relocate**   to move to a new place

**repeal**   to cancel, put an end to

**repeal**   to take back or do away with

**reservation**   an area of land set aside for American Indians

**resign**   to leave a job or position

**resist**   to withstand; to oppose

**retire**   to stop working, usually because of age

**retreat**   to move back from; to escape

**rumors**   stories spread from person to person that may or may not be true

**satellite**   an object that circles the earth, another planet, or a moon

**Scalawags**   southerners who helped northern Republicans and southern blacks gain public office

**scandal**   something shameful that shocks people

**Scandinavia**   a part of northern Europe; it includes Denmark, Norway, Sweden, and Finland

**scourge** something that causes great pain and suffering

**secede** to separate from the rest of a country

**sectionalism** an interest in only one section or region of a country

**sedition** acts that stir up rebellion against the government

**segregated** separated by race

**sharecropping** farming someone else's land while paying a share of the crop as rent

**skyscraper** a very tall building

**slogan** a saying

**slums** crowded, run-down parts of town where poor people live

**smallpox** a deadly disease that Europeans brought to the New World. It spreads rapidly.

**smog** a mixture of fog and smoke

**spies** people sent by a government to learn military secrets

**stalemate** the halting of a struggle when neither side will give in

**statesman** a person who is good at handling government business

**steerage** the part of a ship where passengers paying the lowest fares stay

**submarines** boats that travel underwater

**suburbs** areas where people live near large cities

**suffrage** the right to vote

**Supreme Court** the United States court that has final say on law disputes

**surrender** to give up

**symbol** an object that stands for an idea

**tariff** a tax on goods brought in from another country

**tax** money people must pay to support a government

**technology** science put to practical use

**tenement** an apartment building, often in poor condition

**territory** the land ruled by a nation. A *territory* does not have the full rights of a state.

**tolerate** to let others have their own beliefs; to accept ways that may not be to one's liking

**traitor** a person who helps his country's enemies

**transcontinental** going across a continent

**transportation** the moving of goods and people from one place to another

**treaty** a written agreement

**truce**   an agreement to stop fighting

**typical**   usual

**unconstitutional**   not allowed by the Constitution

**underdeveloped**   having little or no industry

**unified**   joined together as one

**Union**   the northern side in the Civil War

**united**   joined together

**urban**   relating to a city

**veterans**   those who have served in the armed forces

**veto**   to reject

**wagon train**   a line of wagons that carried settlers westward

**war bonds**   certificates sold by the government as a way to raise money to support a war

**wilderness**   a wild place that people have not changed and that has no settlers

**zones**   sections marked off and divided

**zoning laws**   rules that control building in certain parts of a city

# Appendix A

# The Declaration of Independence

In Congress July 4, 1776

## The Unanimous Declaration of the Thirteen United States of America

When in the course of human events, it becomes necessary for one people to dissolve the political bands which have connected them with another, and to assume among the powers of the earth, the separate and equal station to which the laws of nature and of nature's God entitle them, a decent respect to the opinions of mankind requires that they should declare the causes which impel them to the separation.

## Political Theory of the Declaration

We hold these truths to be self-evident, that all men are created equal, that they are endowed by their Creator with certain unalienable rights, that among these are life, liberty, and the pursuit of happiness. That to secure these rights, governments are instituted among men, deriving their just powers from the consent of the governed. That whenever any form of government becomes destructive of these ends, it is the right of the people to alter or to abolish it, and to institute new government, laying its foundation on such principles and organizing its powers in such form, as to them shall seem most likely to effect their safety and happiness. Prudence, indeed, will dictate that governments long established should not be changed for light and transient causes; and accordingly all experience hath shown, that mankind are more disposed to suffer, while evils are sufferable, than to right themselves by abolishing the forms to which they are accustomed. But when a long train of abuses and usurpations, pursuing invariably the same object evinces a design to reduce them under absolute despotism, it is their right, it is their duty, to throw off such government, and to provide new guards for their future security.

## Grievances Against the King

Such has been the patient sufferance of these colonies; and such is now the necessity which constrains them to alter their former systems of government. The history of the present King of Great Britain is a history of repeated injuries and usurpations, all having in direct object the establishment of an absolute tyranny over these states. To prove this, let facts be submitted to a candid world.

He has refused his assent to laws, the most wholesome and necessary for the public good.

He has forbidden his governors to pass laws of immediate and pressing importance, unless suspended in their operation till his assent should be obtained; and when so suspended, he has utterly neglected to attend to them.

He has refused to pass other laws for the accommodation of large districts of people, unless those people would relinquish the right of representation in the legislature, a right inestimable to them and formidable to tyrants only.

He has called together legislative bodies at places unusual, uncomfortable, and distant from the depository of their public records, for the sole purpose of fatiguing them into compliance with his measures.

He has dissolved representative houses repeatedly, for opposing with manly firmness his invasions on the rights of the people.

He has refused for a long time, after such dissolutions, to cause others to be elected; whereby the legislative powers, incapable of annihilation, have returned to the people at large for their exercise; the state remaining in the meantime exposed to all the dangers of invasion from without, and convulsions within.

He has endeavored to prevent the population of these states; for that purpose obstructing the laws for naturalization of foreigners, refusing to pass others to encourage their migrations hither, and raising the conditions of new appropriations of lands.

He has obstructed the administration of justice, by refusing his assent to laws for establishing judiciary powers.

He has made judges dependent on his will alone, for the tenure of their offices, and the amount and payment of their salaries.

He has erected a multitude of new offices, and sent hither swarms of officers to harass our people, and eat out their substance.

He has kept among us, in times of peace, standing armies without the consent of our legislatures.

He has affected to render the military independent of and superior to the civil power.

He has combined with others to subject us to a jurisdiction foreign to our constitution, and unacknowledged by our laws; giving his assent to their acts of pretended legislation:

For quartering large bodies of armed troops among us;

For protecting them, by a mock trial, from punishment for any murders which they should commit on the inhabitants of these states;

For cutting off our trade with all parts of the world;

For imposing taxes on us without our consent;

For depriving us, in many cases, of the benefits of trial by jury;

For transporting us beyond seas to be tried for pretended offenses;

For abolishing the free system of English laws in a neighboring province, establishing therein an arbitrary government, and enlarging its boundaries so as to render it at once an example and fit instrument for introducing the same absolute rule into these colonies;

For taking away our charters, abolishing our most valuable laws, and altering fundamentally the forms of our governments;

For suspending our own legislatures; and declaring themselves invested with power to legislate for us in all cases whatsoever.

He has abdicated government here, by declaring us out of his protection and waging war against us.

He has plundered our seas, ravaged our coasts, burned our towns, and destroyed the lives of our people.

He is at this time transporting large armies of foreign mercenaries to complete the works of death, desolation, and tyranny, already begun with circumstances of cruelty and perfidy scarcely paralleled in the most barbarous ages, and totally unworthy the head of a civilized nation.

He has constrained our fellow citizens taken captive on the high seas to bear arms against their country, to become the executioners of their friends and brethren, or to fall themselves by their hands.

He has excited domestic insurrections amongst us, and has endeavored to bring on the inhabitants of our frontiers, the merciless Indian savages, whose known rule of warfare, is an undistinguished destruction of all ages, sexes, and conditions.

In every stage of these oppressions we have petitioned for redress in the most humble terms. Our repeated petitions have been answered only by repeated injury. A prince whose character is thus marked by every act which may define a tyrant is unfit to be the ruler of a free people.

Nor have we been wanting in attentions to our British brethren. We have warned them from time to time of attempts by their legislature to extend an unwarrantable jurisdiction over us. We have reminded them of the circumstances of our emigration and settlement here. We have appealed to their native justice and magnanimity, and we have conjured them by the ties of our common kindred to disavow these usurpations, which would inevitably interrupt our connections and correspondence. They too have been deaf to the voice of justice and of consanguinity. We must, therefore, acquiesce in the necessity, which denounces our separation, and hold them, as we hold the rest of mankind, enemies in war, in peace friends.

## A Proclamation of Independence

We, therefore, the representatives of the United States of America, in General Congress, assembled, appealing to the Supreme Judge of the world for the rectitude of our intentions, do, in the name, and by the authority of the good people of these colonies, solemnly publish and declare, that these united colonies are, and of right ought to be free and independent states; that they are absolved from all allegiance to the British Crown, and that all political connection between them and the state of Great Britain, is and ought to be totally dissolved; and that as free and independent states, they have full power to levy war, conclude peace, contract alliances, establish commerce, and to do all other acts and things which independent states may of right do. And for the support of this declaration, with a firm reliance on the protection of Divine Providence, we mutually pledge to each other our lives, our fortunes, and our sacred honor.

Signed by John Hancock of Massachusetts, President of the Congress, and by the fifty-five other Representatives of the thirteen United States of America.

# The Constitution of the United States of America

## Preamble

We the People of the United States, in order to form a more perfect Union, establish justice, insure domestic tranquility, provide for the common defense, promote the general welfare, and secure the blessings of liberty to ourselves and our posterity, do ordain and establish this Constitution for the United States of America.

## Article I

### The Legislative Branch

*Section 1.* All legislative powers herein granted shall be vested in a Congress of the United States, which shall consist of a Senate and House of Representatives.

### House of Representatives

*Section 2.* (1) The House of Representatives shall be composed of members chosen every second year by the people of the several states, and the electors in each state shall have the qualifications requisite for electors of the most numerous branch of the state legislature.

(2) No person shall be a representative who shall not have attained to the age of twenty-five years, and been seven years a citizen of the United States, and who shall not, when elected, be an inhabitant of that state in which he shall be chosen.

(3) Representatives *[and direct taxes] shall be apportioned among the several states which may be included within this Union, according to their respective numbers, [which shall be determined by adding to the whole number of free persons, including those bound to service for a term of years, and excluding Indians not taxed, three-fifths of all other persons]. The actual enumeration shall be made within three years after the first meeting of the Congress of the United States, and within every subsequent term of ten years, in such manner as they shall by law direct. The number of representatives shall not exceed one for every thirty thousand, but each state shall have at least one representative; and until such enumeration shall be made, the state of New Hampshire shall be entitled to choose 3, Massachusetts 8, Rhode Island and Providence Plantations 1, Connecticut 5, New York 6, New Jersey 4, Pennsylvania 8, Delaware 1, Maryland 6, Virginia 10, North Carolina 5, South Carolina 5, and Georgia 3.

(4) When vacancies happen in the representation from any state, the executive authority thereof shall issue writs of election to fill such vacancies.

(5) The House of Representatives shall choose their speaker and other officers; and shall have the sole power of impeachment.

## Senate

*Section 3.* (1) The Senate of the United States shall be composed of two senators from each state, [chosen by the legislature thereof,] for six years; and each senator shall have one vote.

*The blue lines indicate portions of the Constitution changed by amendments to the document.

(2) Immediately after they shall be assembled in consequence of the first election, they shall be divided as equally as may be into three classes. The seats of the senators of the first class shall be vacated at the expiration of the second year, of the second class at the expiration of the fourth year, and of the third class at the expiration of the sixth year, so that one-third may be chosen every second year; [and if vacancies happen by resignation, or otherwise, during the recess of the legislature of any state, the executive thereof may make temporary appointments until the next meeting of the legislature, which shall then fill such vacancies].

(3) No person shall be a senator who shall not have attained to the age of thirty years, and been nine years a citizen of the United States, and who shall not, when elected, be an inhabitant of that state for which he shall be chosen.

(4) The Vice-President of the United States shall be president of the Senate, but shall have no vote, unless they be equally divided.

(5) The Senate shall choose their other officers, and also a president *pro tempore,* in the absence of the Vice-President, or when he shall exercise the office of President of the United States.

(6) The Senate shall have the sole power to try all impeachments. When sitting for that purpose, they shall be on oath or affirmation. When the President of the United States is tried, the Chief Justice shall preside: and no person shall be convicted without the concurrence of two-thirds of the members present.

(7) Judgment in cases of impeachment shall not extend further than to removal from office, and disqualification to hold and enjoy any office of honor, trust, or profit under the United States: but the party

convicted shall nevertheless be liable and subject to indictment, trial, judgment, and punishment, according to law.

## Organization of Congress

*Section 4.* (1) The times, places, and manner of holding elections for senators and representatives, shall be prescribed in each state by the legislature thereof; but the Congress may at any time by law make or alter such regulations, except as to the places of choosing senators.

(2) The Congress shall assemble at least once in every year, [and such meeting shall be on the first Monday in December, unless they shall by law appoint a different day].

*Section 5.* (1) Each house shall be the judge of the elections, returns, and qualifications of its own members, and a majority of each shall constitute a quorum to do business; but a smaller number may adjourn from day to day, and may be authorized to compel the attendance of absent members, in such manner, and under such penalties as each house may provide.

(2) Each house may determine the rules of its proceedings, punish its members for disorderly behavior, and, with the concurrence of two-thirds, expel a member.

(3) Each house shall keep a journal of its proceedings, and from time to time publish the same, excepting such parts as may in their judgment require secrecy; and the yeas and nays of the members of either house on any question shall, at the desire of one-fifth of those present, be entered on the journal.

(4) Neither house, during the session of Congress, shall, without the consent of the other, adjourn for more than three days, nor to any other place than that in which the two houses shall be sitting.

*Section 6.* (1) The senators and representatives shall receive a compensation for their services, to be ascertained by law, and paid out of the treasury of the United States. They shall in all cases, except treason, felony, and breach of the peace, be privileged from arrest during their attendance at the session of their respective houses, and in going to and returning from the same; and for any speech or debate in either house, they shall not be questioned in any other place.

(2) No senator or representative shall, during the time for which he was elected, be appointed to any civil office under the authority of the United States, which shall have been created, or the emoluments whereof shall have been increased during such time; and no person holding any office under the United States, shall be a member of either house during his continuance in office.

*Section 7.* (1) All bills for raising revenue shall originate in the House of Representatives; but the Senate may propose or concur with amendments as on other bills.

(2) Every bill which shall have passed the House of Representatives and the Senate, shall, before it becomes a law, be presented to the President of the United States; if he approves he shall sign it, but if not he shall return it, with his objections to that house in which it shall have originated, who shall enter the objections at large on their journal, and proceed to reconsider it. If after such reconsideration two-thirds of that house shall agree

to pass the bill, it shall be sent, together with the objections, to the other house, by which it shall likewise be reconsidered, and if approved by two-thirds of that house, it shall become a law.  But in all such cases the votes of both houses shall be determined by yeas and nays, and the names of the persons voting for and against the bill shall be entered on the journal of each house respectively.  If any bill shall not be returned by the President within ten days (Sundays excepted) after it shall have been presented to him, the same shall be a law, in like manner as if he had signed it, unless the Congress by their adjournment prevent its return, in which case it shall not be a law.

(3) Every order, resolution, or vote to which the concurrence of the Senate and House of Representatives may be necessary (except on a question of adjournment) shall be presented to the President of the United States; and before the same shall take effect, shall be approved by him, or being disapproved by him, shall be repassed by two-thirds of the Senate and House of Representatives, according to the rules and limitations prescribed in the case of a bill.

## Powers of Congress

*Section 8.*  The Congress shall have power:

(1) To lay and collect taxes, duties, imposts, and excises, to pay the debts and provide for the common defense and general welfare of the United States; but all duties, imposts, and excises shall be uniform throughout the United States;

(2) To borrow money on the credit of the United States;

(3) To regulate commerce with foreign nations, and among the several states, and with the Indian tribes;

(4) To establish a uniform rule of naturalization, and uniform laws on the subject of bankruptcies throughout the United States;

(5) To coin money, regulate the value thereof, and of foreign coin, and fix the standard of weights and measures;

(6) To provide for the punishment of counterfeiting the securities and current coin of the United States;

(7) To establish post offices and post roads;

(8) To promote the progress of science and useful arts, by securing for limited times to authors and inventors the exclusive right to their respective writings and discoveries;

(9) To constitute tribunals inferior to the Supreme Court;

(10) To define and punish piracies and felonies committed on the high seas, and offenses against the law of nations;

(11) To declare war, grant letters of marque and reprisal, and make rules concerning captures on land and water;

(12) To raise and support armies, but no appropriation of money to that use shall be for a longer term than two years;

(13) To provide and maintain a navy;

(14) To make rules for the government and regulation of the land and naval forces;

(15) To provide for calling forth the militia to execute the laws of the Union, suppress insurrections and repel invasions;

(16) To provide for organizing, arming, and disciplining the militia, and for governing such part of them as may be employed in the service of the United States, reserving to the states respectively, the appointment of the officers, and the authority of

training the militia according to the discipline prescribed by Congress;

(17) To exercise exclusive legislation in all cases whatsoever, over such district (not exceeding ten miles square) as may, by cession of particular states, and the acceptance of Congress, become the seat of the government of the United States, and to exercise like authority over all places purchased by the consent of the legislature of the state in which the same shall be for the erection of forts, magazines, arsenals, dockyards, and other needful buildings;— And

(18) To make all laws which shall be necessary and proper for carrying into execution the foregoing powers, and all other powers vested by this Constitution in the government of the United States, or in any department or officer thereof.

## Powers Denied to Congress

*Section 9.* (1) The migration or importation of such persons as any of the states now existing shall think proper to admit, shall not be prohibited by the Congress prior to the year one thousand eight hundred and eight, but a tax or duty may be imposed on such importation, not exceeding ten dollars for each person.

(2) The privilege of the writ of *habeas corpus* shall not be suspended, unless when in cases of rebellion or invasion the public safety may require it.

(3) No bill of attainder or *ex post facto* law shall be passed.

(4) No capitation, [or other direct,] tax shall be laid, unless in proportion to the census or enumeration herein before directed to be taken.

(5) No tax or duty shall be laid on articles exported from any state.

(6) No preference shall be given by any regulation of commerce or revenue to the ports of one state over those of another: nor shall vessels bound to, or from, one state, be obliged to enter, clear, or pay duties in another.

(7) No money shall be drawn from the treasury, but in consequence of appropriations made by law; and a regular statement and account of the receipts and expenditures of all public money shall be published from time to time.

(8) No title of nobility shall be granted by the United States; and no person holding any office of profit or trust under them, shall, without the consent of the Congress, accept of any present, emolument, office, or title, of any kind whatever, from any king, prince, or foreign state.

### Powers Denied to the States

*Section 10.* (1) No state shall enter into any treaty, alliance, or confederation; grant letters of marque and reprisal; coin money; emit bills of credit; make anything but gold and silver coin a tender in payment of debts; pass any bill of attainder, *ex post facto* law, or law impairing the obligation of contracts, or grant any title of nobility.

(2) No state shall, without the consent of the Congress, lay any imposts or duties on imports or exports, except what may be absolutely necessary for executing its inspection laws; and the net produce of all duties and imposts, laid by any state on imports or exports, shall be for the use of the treasury of the United States; and all such laws shall be subject to the revision and control of the Congress.

(3) No state shall, without the consent of Congress, lay any duty of tonnage, keep troops, or ships of war in time of peace, enter into any

agreement or compact with another state, or with a foreign power, or engage in war, unless actually invaded, or in such imminent danger as will not admit of delay.

# Article II

## The Executive Branch

*Section 1.* (1) The executive power shall be vested in a President of the United States of America. He shall hold his office during the term of four years, and, together with the Vice-President, chosen for the same term, be elected, as follows:

(2) Each state shall appoint, in such manner as the legislature thereof may direct, a number of electors, equal to the whole number of senators and representatives to which the state may be entitled in the Congress; but no senator or representative, or person holding an office of trust or profit under the United States, shall be appointed an elector.

(3) [The electors shall meet in their respective states, and vote by ballot for two persons, of whom one at least shall not be an inhabitant of the same state with themselves. And they shall make a list of all the persons voted for, and of the number of votes for each; which list they shall sign and certify, and transmit sealed to the seat of the government of the United States, directed to the president of the Senate. The president of the Senate shall, in the presence of the Senate and House of Representatives, open all the certificates, and the votes shall then be counted. The person having the greatest number of votes shall be the President, if such number be a majority of the whole number of electors appointed; and there be more than one who have such majority, and have an equal number of votes, then the House of

Representatives shall immediately choose by ballot one of them for President; and if no person have a majority, then from the five highest on the list the said House shall in like manner choose the President. But in choosing the President, the votes shall be taken by states, the representation from each state having one vote; a quorum for this purpose shall consist of a member or members from two-thirds of the states, and a majority of all the states shall be necessary to a choice. In every case, after the choice of the President, the person having the greatest number of votes of the electors shall be the Vice-President. But if there should remain two or more who have equal votes, the Senate shall choose from them by ballot the Vice-President.]

(4) The Congress may determine the time of choosing the electors, and the day on which they shall give their votes; which day shall be the same throughout the United States.

(5) No person except a natural-born citizen, or a citizen of the United States at the time of the adoption of this Constitution, shall be eligible to the office of President; neither shall any person be eligible to that office who shall not have attained to the age of thirty-five years, and been fourteen years a resident within the United States.

(6) [In case of the removal of the President from office, or of his death, resignation, or inability to discharge the powers and duties of the said office, the same shall devolve on the Vice-President,] and the Congress may by law provide for the case of removal, death, or resignation or inability, both of the President and Vice-President, declaring what officer shall then act as President, and such officer shall act accordingly, until the disability be removed, or a President shall be elected.

(7) The President shall, at stated times, receive for his services, a compensation, which shall neither be

increased or diminished during the period for which he shall have been elected, and he shall not receive within that period any other emolument from the United States, or any of them.

(8) Before he enter on the execution of his office, he shall take the following oath or affirmation: —"I do solemnly swear (or affirm) that I will faithfully execute the Office of President of the United States, and will to the best of my Ability, preserve, protect, and defend the Constitution of the United States."

*Section 2.* (1) The President shall be commander in chief of the Army and Navy of the United States, and of the militia of the several states, when called into the actual service of the United States; he may require the opinion, in writing, of the principal officer in each of the executive departments, upon any subject relating to the duties of their respective offices, and he shall have power to grant reprieves and pardons for offenses against the United States, except in cases of impeachment.

(2) He shall have power, by and with the advice and consent of the Senate, to make treaties, provided two-thirds of the senators present concur; and he shall nominate, and by and with the advice and consent of the Senate, shall appoint ambassadors, other public ministers and consuls, judges of the Supreme Court, and all other officers of the United States, whose appointments are not herein otherwise provided for, and which shall be established by law; but the Congress may by law vest the appointment of such inferior officers, as they think proper, in the President alone, in the courts of law, or in the heads of the departments.

(3) The President shall have power to fill up all vacancies that may happen during the recess of the Senate, by granting commissions which shall expire at the end of their next session.

*Section 3.* He shall from time to time give to the Congress information of the state of the Union, and recommend to their consideration such measures as he shall judge necessary and expedient; he may, on extraordinary occasions, convene both houses, or either of them, and in case of disagreement between them, with respect to the time of adjournment, he may adjourn them to such time as he shall think proper; he shall receive ambassadors and other public ministers; he shall take care that the laws be faithfully executed, and shall commission all the officers of the United States.

*Section 4.* The President, Vice-President, and all civil officers on the United States, shall be removed from office on impeachment for, and conviction of, treason, bribery, or other high crimes and misdemeanors.

# Article III

## The Judicial Branch

*Section 1.* The judicial power of the United States shall be vested in one Supreme Court, and in such inferior courts as the Congress may from time to time ordain and establish. The judges, both of the Supreme and inferior courts, shall hold their offices during good behavior, and shall, at stated times, receive for their services, a compensation, which shall not be diminished during their continuance in office.

*Section 2.* (1) The judicial power shall extend to all cases, in law and equity, arising under this Constitution, the laws of the United States, and treaties made, or which shall be made, under their authority;—to all cases affecting ambassadors, other public ministers and consuls;—to all cases of admiralty and maritime jurisdiction;—to controversies to which the United States shall be a party;—to controversies between two or more states; [between a state and citizens of another state;] between citizens of different states;—between citizens of the same state claiming lands under grants of different states, [and between a state, or the citizens thereof, and foreign states, citizens or subjects].

(2) In all cases affecting ambassadors, other public ministers and consuls, and those in which a state shall be party, the Supreme Court shall have original jurisdiction. In all other cases before mentioned, the Supreme Court shall have appellate jurisdiction, both as to law and fact, with such exceptions, and under such regulations as the Congress shall make.

(3) The trial of all crimes, except in cases if impeachment, shall be by jury; and such trial shall be held in the state where the said crimes shall have been committed; but when not committed within any state, the trial shall be at such place or places as the Congress may by law have directed.

*Section 3.* (1) Treason against the United States, shall consist only in levying war against them, or in adhering to their enemies, giving them aid and comfort. No person shall be convicted of treason unless on the testimony of two witnesses to the same overt act, or on confession in open court.

(2) The Congress shall have power to declare the punishment of treason, but no attainder of treason shall work corruption of blood, or forfeiture except during the life of the person attained.

# Article IV

## Relations Among States

*Section 1.* Full faith and credit shall be given in each state to the public acts, records, and judicial proceedings of every other state. And the Congress may by general laws prescribe the manner in which such acts, records, and proceedings shall be proved, and the effect thereof.

*Section 2.* (1) The citizens of each state shall be entitled to all privileges and immunities of citizens in the several states.

(2) A person charged in any state with treason, felony, or other crime, who shall flee from justice, and be found in another state, shall on demand of the executive authority of the state from which he fled, be delivered up, to be removed to the state having jurisdiction of the crime.

[(3) No person held to service or labor in one state, under the laws thereof, escaping into another, shall, in consequence of any law or regulation therein, be discharged from such service or labor, but shall be delivered up on claim of the party to whom such service or labor may be due.]

## Federal-State Relations

*Section 3.* (1) New states may be admitted by the Congress into this Union; but no new state shall be formed or erected within the jurisdiction of any other state; nor any state be formed by the junction of two or more states, or parts of states, without the consent of the legislatures of the states concerned as well as of the Congress.

(2) The Congress shall have power to dispose of and make all needful rules and regulations respecting the territory or other property belonging to the United States; and nothing in this Constitution shall be so construed as to prejudice any claims of the United States, or any particular state.

*Section 4.* The United States shall guarantee to every state in this Union a republican form of government, and shall protect each of them against invasion; and on application of the legislature, or of the executive (when the legislature cannot be convened) against domestic violence.

# Article V

## Provisions for Amendments

The Congress, whenever two-thirds of both houses shall deem it necessary, shall propose amendments to this Constitution, or, on the application of the legislatures of two-thirds of the several states, shall call a convention for proposing amendments, which, in either case, shall be valid to all intents and purposes, as part of this Constitution, when ratified by the legislatures of two-thirds of the several states, or by conventions in three-fourths thereof, as the one or the other mode of ratification may be proposed by the Congress; provided ~~[that no amendment which may be made prior to the year one thousand eight hundred and eight shall in any manner affect the first and fourth clauses in the ninth section of the first article; and]~~ that no state, without its consent, shall be deprived of its equal suffrage in the Senate.

# Article VI

### National Debts

(1) All debts contracted and engagements entered into, before the adoption of this Constitution, shall be as valid against the United States under this Constitution, as under the Confederation.

### Supremacy of National Law

(2) This Constitution, and the laws of the United States which shall be made in pursuance thereof, and all treaties made, or which shall be made, under the authority of the United States, shall be the supreme law of the land; and the judges in every state shall be bound thereby, anything in the constitution or laws of any state to the contrary notwithstanding.

(3) The senators and representatives before mentioned, and the members of the several state legislatures, and all executive and judicial officers, both of the United States and of the several states, shall be bound by oath or affirmation, to support this Constitution; but no religious test shall ever be required as a qualification to any office or public trust under the United States.

# Article VII

### Ratification of Constitution

The ratification of the conventions of nine states, shall be sufficient for the establishment of this Constitution between the states so ratifying the same.

Done in convention by the unanimous consent of the states present the seventeenth day of September in the year of our Lord one thousand seven hundred and eighty-seven and of the independence of the United State of America the twelfth. In witness whereof we have hereunto subscribed our names,

George Washington—President and deputy from Virginia

Attest: William Jackson—Secretary

## Delaware

George Read
Gunning Bedord, Jr.
John Dickinson
Richard Bassett
Jacob Broom

## Maryland

James McHenry
Dan of St. Thomas Jennifer
Daniel Carroll

## Virginia

John Blair
James Madison, Jr.

## North Carolina

William Blount
Richard Dobbs Spaight
Hugh Williamson

## South Carolina

John Rutledge
Charles Cotesworth Pinckney
Charles Pinckney
Pierce Butler

## Georgia

William Few
Abraham Baldwin

## New Hampshire

John Langdon
Nicholas Gilman

## Massachusetts

Nathaniel Gorman
Rufus King

## Connecticut

William Samuel Johnson
Roger Sherman

## New York

Alexander Hamilton

## New Jersey

William Livingston
David Brearley
William Paterson
Jonathan Dayton

## Pennsylvania

Benjamin Franklin
Thomas Mifflin
Robert Morris
George Clymer
Thomas Fitzsimons
Jared Ingersoll
James Wilson
Gouverneur Morris

# Amendments to the Constitution

(The first ten amendments are the Bill of Rights.)

**Amendment 1.** *Freedom of Religion, Speech, and the Press; Rights of Assembly and Petition*

Congress shall make no law respecting an establishment of religion, or prohibiting the free exercise thereof; or abridging the freedom of speech, or of the press; or the right of the people peaceably to assemble, and to petition the government for a redress of grievances.

**Amendment 2.** *Right to Bear Arms*

A well-regulated militia, being necessary to the security of a free state, the right of the people to keep and bear arms shall not be infringed.

**Amendment 3.** *Housing of Soldiers*

No soldier shall, in time of peace, be quartered in any house, without the consent of the owner; nor in time of war, but in a manner to be prescribed by law.

**Amendment 4.** *Search and Arrest Warrants*

The right of the people to be secure in their persons, houses, papers, and effects, against unreasonable searches and seizures, shall not be violated; and no warrants shall issue, but upon probable cause, supported by oath or affirmation, and particularly describing the place to be searched, and the persons or things to be seized.

**Amendment 5.** *Rights in Criminal Cases*

No person shall be held to answer for a capital, or otherwise infamous crime, unless on a presentment or indictment of a grand jury, except in cases arising in the land or naval forces, or in the militia, when in actual service in time of war or public danger; nor shall any person be subject for the same offense to be twice put in jeopardy of life or limb; nor shall be compelled in any criminal case to be a witness against himself; nor be deprived of life, liberty, or property, without due process of law; nor shall private property be taken for public use, without just compensation.

### Amendment 6. *Rights to a Fair Trial*

In all criminal prosecutions, the accused shall enjoy the right to a speedy and public trial, by an impartial jury of the state and district wherein the crime shall have been committed, which district shall have been previously ascertained by law, and to be informed of the nature and cause of the accusation; to be confronted with the witnesses against him; to have compulsory process for obtaining witnesses in his favor, and to have the assistance of counsel for his defense.

### Amendment 7. *Rights in Civil Cases*

In suits at common law, where the value in controversy shall exceed twenty dollars, the right of trial by jury shall be preserved; and no fact tried by a jury, shall be otherwise re-examined in any court of the United States, than according to the rules of the common law.

### Amendment 8. *Bails, Fines, and Punishments*

Excessive bail shall not be required, nor excessive fines imposed, nor cruel and unusual punishment inflicted.

**Amendment 9.** *Rights Retained by the People*

The enumeration in the Constitution of certain rights shall not be construed to deny or disparage others retained by the people.

**Amendment 10.** *Powers Reserved to the States and the People*

The powers not delegated to the United States by the Constitution, nor prohibited by it to the states, are reserved to the states respectively, or to the people.

**Amendment 11.** *Lawsuits Against States*

The judicial power of United States shall not be construed to extend to any suit in law or equity, commenced or prosecuted against one of the United States by citizens of another state, or by citizens or subjects of any foreign state.

**Amendment 12.** *Election of the President and Vice-President*

The electors shall meet in their respective states and vote by ballot for President and Vice-President, one of whom, at least, shall not be an inhabitant of the same state with themselves; they shall name in their ballots the person voted for as President, and in distinct ballots the person voted for as Vice-President, and they shall make distinct lists of all persons voted for as President, and of all persons voted for as Vice-President; and of the number of votes for each, which lists they shall sign and certify, and transmit sealed to the seat of the government of the United States, directed to the president of the Senate;—the president of the Senate shall, in the presence of the Senate and House of

Representatives, open all the certificates and the votes shall then be counted;—the person having the greatest number of votes for President, shall be the President, if such number be a majority of the whole number of electors appointed; and if no person have such majority, then from the persons having the highest numbers not exceeding three on the list of those voted for as President, the House of Representatives shall choose immediately, by ballot, the President. But in choosing the President, the votes shall be taken by states, the representation from each state having one vote; a quorum for this purpose shall consist of a member or members from two-thirds of the states, and a majority of all the states shall be necessary to a choice. And if the House of Representatives shall not choose a President whenever the right of choice shall devolve upon them, [before the fourth day of March next following,] then the Vice-President shall act as President, as in the case of the death or other constitutional disability of the President. The Person having the greatest number of votes as Vice-President, shall be the Vice-President, if such number be a majority of the whole number of electors appointed, and if no person have a majority, then from the two highest numbers on the list, the Senate shall choose the Vice-President; a quorum for the purpose shall consist of two-thirds of the whole number of senators, and a majority of the whole number shall be necessary to a choice. But no person constitutionally ineligible to the office of President shall be eligible to that of Vice-President of the United States.

**Amendment 13.** *Abolition of Slavery*

*Section 1.* Neither slavery nor involuntary servitude, except as a punishment for crime whereof the party shall have been duly convicted, shall exist within the United States, or any place subject to their jurisdiction.

*Section 2.* Congress shall have power to enforce this article by appropriate legislation.

**Amendment 14.** *Rights of Citizens*

*Section 1.* All persons born or naturalized in the United States, and subject to the jurisdiction thereof, are citizens of the United States and of the state wherein they reside. No state shall make or enforce any law which shall abridge the privileges or immunities of citizens of the United States; nor shall any state deprive any person of life, liberty, or property, without due process of law; nor deny to any person within its jurisdiction the equal protection of the laws.

*Section 2.* Representatives shall be apportioned among the several states according to their respective numbers, counting the whole number of persons in each state, [excluding Indians not taxed]. But when the right to vote at any election for the choice of electors for President and Vice-President of the United States, representatives in Congress, the executive and judicial officers of a state, or the members of the legislature thereof, is denied to any of the male inhabitants of such state, being twenty-one years of age, and citizens of the United States, or in any way abridged, except for participation in rebellion, or other crime, the basis of representation therein shall be reduced in the proportion which the number of such male citizens shall bear to the whole number of male citizens twenty-one years of age in such state.

*Section 3.* No person shall be a senator or representative in Congress, or elector of President and Vice-President, or hold any office, civil or military, under the United States, or under any state, who, having previously taken an oath, as a member of Congress, or as an officer of the United States, or as a member of any state legislature, or as an executive or judicial officer of any state, to support the Constitution of the United States, shall have engaged in insurrection or rebellion against the same, or given aid or comfort to the enemies thereof. But Congress may by a vote of two-thirds of each House, remove such disability.

*Section 4.* The validity of the public debt of the United States, authorized by law, including debts incurred for payment of pensions and bounties for services in suppressing insurrection or rebellion, shall not be questioned. But neither the United States nor any state shall assume or pay any debt or obligation incurred in aid of insurrection or rebellion against the United States, or any claim for the loss or emancipation of any slave, but all such debts, obligations, and claims shall be held illegal and void.

*Section 5.* The Congress shall have power to enforce, by appropriate legislation, the provisions of this article.

**Amendment 15.** *Negro Suffrage*

*Section 1.* The right of citizens of the United States to vote shall not be denied or abridged by the United States or by any state on account of race, color, or previous condition of servitude.

*Section 2.* The Congress shall have power to enforce this article by appropriate legislation.

**Amendment 16.** *Income Taxes*

The Congress shall have power to lay and collect taxes on incomes, from whatever source derived, without apportionment among the several states, and without regard to any census or enumeration.

**Amendment 17.** *Popular Election of Senators*

(1) The Senate of the United States shall be composed of two senators from each state, elected by the people thereof for six years; and each senator shall have one vote. The electors in each state shall have the qualifications requisite for electors of the most numerous branch of the state legislatures.

(2) When vacancies happen in the representation of any state in the Senate, the executive authority of such state shall issue writs of election to fill such vacancies: *Provided,* That the legislature of any state may empower the executive thereof to make temporary appointments until the people fill the vacancies by election as the legislature may direct.

(3) This amendment shall not be so construed as to affect the election or term of any senator chosen before it becomes valid as part of the Constitution.

**Amendment 18.** *Prohibition of Liquor*

~~Section 1.~~ ~~[After one year from the ratification of~~ ~~this article the manufacture, sale, or transportation of~~ ~~intoxicating liquors within, the importation thereof~~ ~~into, or the exportation thereof from the United~~ ~~States and all territory subject to the jurisdiction~~ ~~thereof for beverage purposes is hereby prohibited.~~

~~Section 2.~~ ~~The Congress and the several states~~ ~~shall have concurrent power to enforce this article by~~ ~~appropriate legislation.~~

~~Section 3.~~ ~~This article shall be inoperative unless it~~ ~~shall have been ratified as an amendment to the~~ ~~Constitution by the legislatures of the several states,~~ ~~as provided in the Constitution, within seven years~~ ~~from the date of the submission hereof to the states~~ ~~by Congress.]~~

**Amendment 19.** *Women's Suffrage*

*Section 1.* The right of citizens of the United States to vote shall not be denied or abridged by the United States or by any state on account of sex.

*Section 2.* Congress shall have power to enforce this article by appropriate legislation.

**Amendment 20.** *Terms of the President and Congress*

*Section 1.* The terms of the President and Vice-President shall end at noon on the 20th day of January, and the terms of senators and representatives at noon on the third day of January, of the year in which such terms would have ended if this article had not been ratified; and the terms of their successors shall then begin.

*Section 2.* The Congress shall assemble at least once in every year, and such meeting shall begin at noon on the third day of January, unless they shall by law appoint a different day.

*Section 3.* If, at the time fixed for the beginning of the term of the President, the President elect shall have died, the Vice-President elect shall become President. If a President shall not have been chosen before the time fixed for the beginning of his term, or if the President elect shall have failed to qualify, then the Vice-President elect shall act as President until a President shall have qualified; and the Congress may by law provide for the case wherein neither a President elect nor a Vice-President elect shall have qualified, declaring who shall then act as President, or the manner in which one who is to act shall be selected, and such person shall act accordingly until a President or Vice-President shall have qualified.

*Section 4.* The Congress may by law provide for the case of the death of any of the persons from whom the House of Representatives may choose a President whenever the right of choice shall have devolved upon them, and for the case of the death of any of the persons from whom the Senate may choose a Vice-President whenever the right of choice shall have devolved upon them.

*Section 5.* Sections 1 and 2 shall take effect on the 15th day of October following the ratification of this article.

*Section 6.* This article shall be inoperative unless it shall have been ratified as an amendment to the Constitution by the legislatures of three-fourths of the several states within seven years from the date of its submission.

**Amendment 21.** *Repeal of 18th Amendment*

*Section 1.* The eighteenth article of amendment to the Constitution of the United States is hereby repealed.

*Section 2.* The transportation or importation into any state, territory, or possession of the United States for delivery or use therein of intoxicating liquors, in violation of the laws thereof, is hereby prohibited.

*Section 3.* This article shall be inoperative unless it shall have been ratified as an amendment to the Constitution by conventions in the several states, as provided in the Constitution, within seven years from the date of the submission hereof to the states by the Congress.

**Amendment 22.** *Limitation of Presidential Terms*

*Section 1.* No person shall be elected to the office of the President more than twice, and no person who has held the office of President, or acted as President, for more than two years of a term to which some other person was elected President shall be elected to the office of the President more than once. But this article shall not apply to any person holding the office of President when this article was proposed by the Congress, and shall not prevent any person who may be holding the office of President, or acting as President, during the term within which this article becomes operative from holding the office of President or acting as President during the remainder of such term.

*Section 2.* This article shall be inoperative unless it shall have been ratified as an amendment to the Constitution by the legislatures of three-fourths of the several states within seven years from the day of its submission to the states by the Congress.

**Amendment 23.** *Presidential Electors in the District of Columbia*

*Section 1.* The district constituting the seat of government of the United States shall appoint in such manner as the Congress may direct: A number of electors of President and Vice-President equal to the whole number of senators and representatives in Congress to which the district would be entitled if it were a state, but in no event more than the least populous state; they shall be in addition to those appointed by the states, but they shall be considered, for the purposes of the election of President and Vice-President, to be electors appointed by a state; and they shall meet in the district and perform such duties as provided by the twelfth article of amendment.

*Section 2.* The Congress shall have power to enforce this article by appropriate legislation.

**Amendment 24.** *Poll Taxes*

*Section 1.* The right of citizens of the United States to vote in any primary or other election for President or Vice-President for electors for President or Vice-President, or for senator or representative in Congress, shall not be denied or abridged by the United States or any state by reason of failure to pay any poll tax or other tax.

*Section 2.* The Congress shall have power to enforce this article by appropriate legislation.

**Amendment 25.** *Presidential Disability and Succession*

*Section 1.* In case of the removal of the President from office or of his death or resignation, the Vice-President shall become President.

*Section 2.* Whenever there is a vacancy in the office of the Vice-President, the President shall nominate a Vice-President who shall take office upon confirmation by a majority vote of both houses of Congress.

*Section 3.* Whenever the President transmits to the president pro tempore of the Senate and the speaker of the House of Representatives his written declaration that he is unable to discharge the powers and duties of his office, and until he transmits to them a written declaration to the contrary, such powers and duties shall be discharged by the Vice-President as acting President.

*Section 4.*  Whenever the Vice-President and a majority of either the principal officers of the executive departments or of such other body as Congress may by law provide, transmit to the president pro tempore of the Senate and the speaker of the House of Representatives their written declaration that the President is unable to discharge the powers and duties of his office, the Vice-President shall immediately assume the powers and duties of the office as acting President.

Thereafter, when the President transmits to the president pro tempore of the Senate and the speaker of the House of Representatives his written declaration that no inability exists, he shall resume the powers and duties of his office unless the Vice-President and a majority of either the principal officers of the executive department or of such other body as Congress may by law provide, transmit within four days to the president pro tempore of the Senate and the speaker of the House of Representatives their written declaration that the President is unable to discharge the powers and duties of his office.  Thereupon Congress shall decide the issue, assembling within forty-eight hours for that purpose if not in session.  If the Congress, within twenty-one days after receipt of the latter written declaration, or, if Congress is not in session within twenty-one days after Congress is required to assemble, determines by two-thirds vote of both houses that the President is unable to discharge the powers and duties of his office, the Vice-President shall continue to discharge the same as acting President; otherwise, the President shall resume the powers and duties of his office.

**Amendment 26.** *Suffrage for 18-Year-Olds*

*Section 1.* The right of citizens of the United States, who are eighteen years of age or older, to vote shall not be denied or abridged by the United States or by any state on account of age.

*Section 2.* The Congress shall have power to enforce this article by appropriate legislation.

# Presidents of the United States

1. George Washington
   birth: February 22, 1732
   term of office: 1789–1797
   death: December 14, 1799

2. John Adams
   birth: October 30, 1735
   term of office: 1797–1801
   death: July 4, 1826

3. Thomas Jefferson
   birth: April 13, 1743
   term of office: 1801–1809
   death: July 4, 1826

4. James Madison
   birth: March 16, 1751
   term of office: 1809–1817
   death: June 28, 1836

5. James Monroe
   birth: April 28, 1758
   term of office: 1817–1825
   death: July 4, 1831

6. John Quincy Adams
   birth:  July 11, 1767
   term of office: 1825–1829
   death: February 23, 1848

7. Andrew Jackson
   birth: March 15, 1767
   term of office: 1829–1837
   death: June 8, 1845

8. Martin Van Buren
   birth: December 5, 1782
   term of office: 1837–1841
   death: July 24, 1862

9. William H. Harrison
   birth: February 9, 1773
   term of office: 1841
   death: April 4, 1841

10. John Tyler
    birth: March 29, 1790
    term of office: 1841–1845
    death: January 18, 1862

11. James K. Polk
    birth: November 2, 1795
    term of office: 1845–1849
    death: June 15, 1849

12. Zachary Taylor
    birth: November 24, 1784
    term of office: 1849–1850
    death: July 9, 1850

13. Millard Fillmore
    birth: January 7, 1800
    term of office: 1850–1853
    death: March 8, 1874

14. Franklin Pierce
    birth: November 23, 1804
    term of office: 1853–1857
    death: October 8, 1869

15. James Buchanan
    birth: April 23, 1791
    term of office: 1857–1861
    death: June 1, 1868

16. Abraham Lincoln
    birth: February 12, 1809
    term of office: 1861–1865
    death: April 15, 1865

17. Andrew Johnson
    birth: December 29, 1808
    term of office: 1865–1869
    death: July 31, 1875

18. Ulysses S. Grant
    birth: April 27, 1822
    term of office: 1869–1877
    death: July 23, 1885

19. Rutherford B. Hayes
    birth: October 4, 1822
    term of office: 1877–1881
    death: January 17, 1893

20. James A. Garfield
    birth: November 19, 1831
    term of office: 1881
    death: September 19, 1881

21. Chester A. Arthur
    birth: October 5, 1829
    term of office: 1881–1885
    death: November 18, 1886

22. Grover Cleveland
    birth: March 18, 1837
    term of office: 1885–1889
    death: June 24, 1908

23. Benjamin Harrison
    birth: August 20, 1833
    term of office: 1889–1893
    death: March 13, 1901

24. Grover Cleveland
    birth: March 18, 1837
    second term of office:
    1893–1897
    death: June 24, 1908

25. William McKinley
    birth: January 29, 1843
    term of office: 1897–1901
    death: September 14, 1901

26. Theodore Roosevelt
    birth: October 27, 1858
    term of office: 1901–1909
    death: January 6, 1919

27. William H. Taft
    birth: September 15, 1857
    term of office: 1909–1913
    death: March 8, 1930

28. Woodrow Wilson
    birth: December 28, 1856
    term of office: 1913–1921
    death: February 3, 1924

29. Warren G. Harding
    birth: November 2, 1865
    term of office: 1921–1923
    death: August 2, 1923

30. Calvin Coolidge
    birth: July 4, 1872
    term of office: 1923–1929
    death: January 5, 1933

31. Herbert C. Hoover
    birth: August 10, 1874
    term of office: 1929–1933
    death: October 20, 1964

32. Franklin D. Roosevelt
    birth: January 30, 1882
    term of office: 1933–1945
    death: April 12, 1945

33. Harry S Truman
    birth: May 8, 1884
    term of office: 1945–1953
    death: December 26, 1972

34. Dwight D. Eisenhower
    birth: October 14, 1890
    term of office: 1953–1961
    death: March 28, 1969

35. John F. Kennedy
    birth: May 29, 1917
    term of office: 1961–1963
    death: November 22, 1963

36. Lyndon B. Johnson
    birth: August 27, 1908
    term of office: 1963–1969
    death: January 22, 1973

37. Richard M. Nixon
    birth: January 9, 1913
    term of office: 1969–1974

38. Gerald R. Ford
    birth: July 14, 1913
    term of office: 1974–1977

39. James E. Carter, Jr.
    birth: October 1, 1924
    term of office: 1977–1981

40. Ronald Reagan
    birth: February 6, 1911
    term of office: 1981–1988

41. George Bush
    birth: June 12, 1924
    term of office: 1989–1992

42. William J. Clinton
    birth: August 19, 1946
    term of office: 1993–

# Almanac of the States

## Alabama

Statehood: December 14, 1819
Population: 4,040,587
Total Area: 51,705 square miles
Capital: Montgomery
Nickname: The Heart of Dixie
Motto: We Dare Maintain Our Rights

## Alaska

Statehood: January 3, 1959
Population: 550,043
Total Area: 586,412 square miles
Capital: Juneau
Nickname: The Last Frontier
Motto: North to the Future

## Arizona

Statehood: February 14, 1912
Population: 3,665,228
Total Area: 114,000 square miles
Capital: Phoenix
Nickname: The Grand Canyon State
Motto: God Enriches

## Arkansas

Statehood: June 15, 1836
Population: 2,350,725
Total Area: 53,187 square miles
Capital: Little Rock
Nickname: Land of Opportunity
Motto: The People Rule

## California

Statehood: September 9, 1850
Population: 29,760,021
Total Area: 158,706 square miles
Capital: Sacramento
Nickname: The Golden State
Motto: Eureka, I Have Found It

## Colorado

Statehood: August 1, 1876
Population: 3,294,394
Total Area: 104,091 square miles
Capital: Denver
Nickname: The Centennial State
Motto: Nothing Without Providence

## Connecticut

Statehood: January 9, 1788
Population: 3,287,116
Total Area: 5,018 square miles
Capital: Hartford
Nickname: The Constitution State
Motto: He Who Transplanted Still Survives

## Delaware

Statehood: December 7, 1787
Population: 666,168
Total Area: 2,044 square miles
Capital: Dover
Nickname: The First State
Motto: Liberty and Independence

## Florida

Statehood: March 3, 1845
Population: 12,937,926
Total Area: 58,664 square miles
Capital: Tallahassee
Nickname: The Sunshine State
Motto: In God We Trust

## Georgia

Statehood: January 2, 1788
Population: 6,478,216
Total Area: 58,910 square miles
Capital: Atlanta
Nickname: The Peach State
Motto: Agriculture and Commerce

## Hawaii

Statehood: August 21, 1959
Population: 1,108,229
Total Area: 6,471 square miles
Capital: Honolulu
Nickname: The Aloha State
Motto: The Life of the Land is
    Perpetuated in Righteousness

## Idaho

Statehood: July 3, 1890
Population: 1,006,749
Total Area: 83,564 square miles
Capital: Boise
Nickname: The Gem State
Motto: It Is Forever

## Illinois

Statehood: December 3, 1818
Population: 11,430,602
Total Area: 55,645 square miles
Capital: Springfield
Nickname: The Prairie State
Motto: State Sovereignty, National
    Union

## Indiana

Statehood: December 11, 1816
Population: 5,544,159
Total Area: 35,932 square miles
Capital: Indianapolis
Nickname: The Hoosier State
Motto: The Crossroads of America

## Iowa

Statehood: December 28, 1846
Population: 2,776,755
Total Area: 56,275 square miles
Capital: Des Moines
Nickname: The Hawkeye State
Motto: Our Liberties We Prize, and
    Our Rights We Will Maintain

## Kansas

Statehood: January 29, 1861
Population: 2,477,574
Total Area: 82,277 square miles
Capital: Topeka
Nickname: The Sunflower State
Motto: To the Stars Through
    Difficulty

## Kentucky

Statehood: June 1, 1792
Population: 3,685,296
Total Area: 40,409 square miles
Capital: Frankfort
Nickname: The Bluegrass State
Motto: United We Stand, Divided
  We Fall

## Louisiana

Statehood: April 30, 1812
Population: 4,219,973
Total Area: 47,752 square miles
Capital: Baton Rouge
Nickname: The Pelican State
Motto: Union, Justice, and Confidence

## Maine

Statehood: March 15, 1820
Population: 1,227,928
Total Area: 33,265 square miles
Capital: Augusta
Nickname: The Pine Tree State
Motto: I Direct

## Maryland

Statehood: April 28, 1788
Population: 4,781,468
Total Area: 10,460 square miles
Capital: Annapolis
Nickname: The Old Line State
Motto: Manly Deeds, Womanly
  Words

## Massachusetts

Statehood: February 6, 1788
Population: 6,016,425
Total Area: 8,284 square miles
Capital: Boston
Nickname: The Bay State
Motto: By the Sword We Seek Peace,
  but Peace Only Under Liberty

## Michigan

Statehood: January 26, 1837
Population: 9,295,297
Total Area: 59,954 square miles
Capital: Lansing
Nickname: The Wolverine State
Motto: If You Seek a Pleasant
  Peninsula, Look About You

## Minnesota

Statehood: May 11, 1858
Population: 4,375,099
Total Area: 84,402 square miles
Capital: St. Paul
Nickname: The Gopher State
Motto: Star of the North

## Mississippi

Statehood: December 10, 1817
Population: 2,573,216
Total Area: 47,689 square miles
Capital: Jackson
Nickname: The Magnolia State
Motto: By Valor and Arms

## Missouri

Statehood: August 10, 1821
Population: 5,117,073
Total Area: 69,697 square miles
Capital: Jefferson City
Nickname: The Show Me State
Motto: The Welfare of the People
    Shall Be the Supreme Law

## Montana

Statehood: November 8, 1899
Population: 799,065
Total Area: 147,046 square miles
Capital: Helena
Nickname: The Treasure State
Motto: Gold and Silver

## Nebraska

Statehood: March 1, 1867
Population: 1,578,385
Total Area: 77,355 square miles
Capital: Lincoln
Nickname: The Cornhusker State
Motto: Equality Before the Law

## Nevada

Statehood: October 31, 1864
Population: 1,201,833
Total Area: 110,561 square miles
Capital: Carson City
Nickname: The Silver State
Motto: All for Our Country

## New Hampshire

Statehood: June 21, 1788
Population: 1,109,252
Total Area: 9,297 square miles
Capital: Concord
Nickname: The Granite State
Motto: Live Free or Die

## New Jersey

Statehood: December 18, 1787
Population: 7,730,188
Total Area: 7,787 square miles
Capital: Trenton
Nickname: The Garden State
Motto: Liberty and Prosperity

## New Mexico

Statehood: January 6, 1912
Population: 1,515,069
Total Area: 121,593 square miles
Capital: Santa Fe
Nickname: The Land of Enchantment
Motto: It Grows as It Goes

## New York

Statehood: July 26, 1788
Population: 17,990,455
Total Area: 49,108 square miles
Capital: Albany
Nickname: The Empire State
Motto: Higher

## North Carolina

Statehood: November 21, 1789
Population: 6,628,637
Total Area: 52,669 square miles
Capital: Raleigh
Nickname: The Tar Heel State
Motto: To Be Rather Than To Seem

## North Dakota

Statehood: November 2, 1889
Population: 638,800
Total Area: 70,702 square miles
Capital: Bismarck
Nickname: The Flickertail State
Motto: Liberty and Union Now and
Forever, One and Inseparable

## Ohio

Statehood: March 1, 1803
Population: 10,847,115
Total Area: 41,004 square miles
Capital: Columbus
Nickname: The Buckeye State
Motto: With God, All Things Are
Possible

## Oklahoma

Statehood: November 16, 1907
Population: 3,145,585
Total Area: 69,956 square miles
Capital: Oklahoma City
Nickname: The Sooner State
Motto: Labor Conquers All Things

## Oregon

Statehood: February 14, 1859
Population: 2,842,321
Total Area: 97,073 square miles
Capital: Salem
Nickname: The Beaver State
Motto: The Union

## Pennsylvania

Statehood: December 12, 1787
Population: 11,881,643
Total Area: 45,308 square miles
Capital: Harrisburg
Nickname: The Keystone State
Motto: Virtue, Liberty, and
Independence

## Rhode Island

Statehood: May 29, 1790
Population: 1,003,464
Total Area: 1,212 square miles
Capital: Providence
Nickname: The Ocean State
Motto: Hope

## South Carolina

Statehood: May 23, 1788
Population: 3,486,703
Total Area: 31,113 square miles
Capital: Columbia
Nickname: The Palmetto State
Motto: Prepared in Mind and
Resources

## South Dakota

Statehood: November 2, 1889
Population: 696,004
Total Area: 77,116 square miles
Capital: Pierre
Nickname: The Coyote State
Motto: Under God the People Rule

## Tennessee

Statehood: June 1, 1796
Population: 4,877,185
Total Area: 42,114 square miles
Capital: Nashville
Nickname: The Volunteer State
Motto: Agriculture and Commerce

## Texas

Statehood: December 29, 1845
Population: 16,986,510
Total Area: 266,807 square miles
Capital: Austin
Nickname: The Lone Star State
Motto: Friendship

## Utah

Statehood: January 4, 1896
Population: 1,722,850
Total Area: 84,899 square miles
Capital: Salt Lake City
Nickname: The Beehive State
Motto: Industry

## Vermont

Statehood: March 4, 1791
Population: 562,758
Total Area: 9,614 square miles
Capital: Montpelier
Nickname: The Green Mountain State
Motto: Freedom and Unity

## Virginia

Statehood: June 25, 1788
Population: 6,187,358
Total Area: 40,767 square miles
Capital: Richmond
Nickname: Old Dominion
Motto: Thus Ever to Tyrants

## Washington

Statehood: November 11, 1889
Population: 4,866,692
Total Area: 68,139 square miles
Capital: Olympia
Nickname: The Evergreen State
Motto: Bye and Bye

## West Virginia

Statehood: June 20, 1863
Population: 1,793,477
Total Area: 24,231 square miles
Capital: Charleston
Nickname: The Mountain State
Motto: Mountaineers Are Always Free

**Wisconsin**

Statehood: May 29, 1848
Population: 4,891,769
Total Area: 55,426 square miles
Capital: Madison
Nickname: The Badger State
Motto: Forward

**Wyoming**

Statehood: July 10, 1890
Population: 453,588
Total Area: 97,809 square miles
Capital: Cheyenne
Nickname: The Equality State
Motto: Equal Rights

# Index

popularity of, 128

spoils system, 128–129

takes Indian lands, 134

Jackson, Jesse, 445

Jackson, Stonewall, 182

James I, King of England, 22

Jamestown colony, 22–23

Japan

aerial bombardment of, 354–356

attacks Pearl Harbor, 346

Axis Pact, 346

postwar recovery, 370

trade with, 292

U.S. relations with, 383

in World War II, 353–356

Japanese Americans

internment camps, 350

in World War II, 350

Jay, John, 92, 96

Jazz Age, 319

Jefferson, Thomas, 96, 98–99, 128

death, 106

elected President, 105

Louisiana Purchase and, 107–108

orders embargo, 112

political ideology, 106–107

writes Declaration of Independence, 69

Jim Crow laws, 210–211

Johnson, Andrew

elected President, 199

impeachment of, 206

Radical Republicans and, 200

Johnson, Henry, 306

Johnson, James Weldon, 319

Johnson, Lyndon B.

Great Society programs, 424–425

Vietnam policy, 428–429

Joliet, Louis, 20

*Jungle, The* (Sinclair), 265

## K

Kansas-Nebraska Act, 171

Kansas Pacific Railroad, 225

Kansas Territory, 171

Kennedy, John F., 16, 415

assassination of, 421–422, 432

Bay of Pigs invasion, 420

Berlin crisis, 419–420

changes immigration laws, 258

Cuban Missile Crisis, 420–421

space program, 461

Vietnam policy, 426

Kennedy, Robert, 432

Kent State University, 433

Key, Francis Scott, 113

Khomeini, Ayatollah, 443

Khrushchev, Nikita, 384, 419

Cuban Missile Crisis, 421

King, Martin Luther, Jr.

assassination of, 405, 424, 432

peaceful resistance strategy, 404–405

King, Rodney, 468

Knox, Henry, 96

Korean War, 378–380

Kosciusko, Thaddeus, 75

Ku Klux Klan, 212, 316–317

Kuwait, Iraqi invasion of, 451–452

## L

Labor unions, 240–241, 243

Depression years, 335

postwar, 362–363

strikes, 243, 244–245, 412

weakening of, 311

Lafayette, Marquis de, 75

La Salle, Jacques, 29

Laser technology, 465

Political parties
    nominating convention, 129
    one-party system, 116
    two-party system, 99
Polk, James K., 149
Poll tax, 211, 411
Pollution
    air and water, 459
    controlling, 460
    urban, 386
Polo, Marco, 8
Ponce de Leon, Juan, 17
Pony Express, 146 – 147
Powell, Colin, 468
Powers, Francis Gary, 385
Prescott, Samuel, 65
Presidents, 533 – 535
    election of, 105 – 106, 124, 125
    first, 96 – 97
    impeachment process, 206
    nomination of, 129
    televised campaigns, 398
Presley, Elvis, 398
Princip, Gavrilo, 298
Progressives, 269 – 270
Prohibition, 317 – 318
    repeal of, 330 – 331
Promontory Point, 221
Prosser, Gabriel, 162 – 163, 164
Public works projects, 329
Pueblo Indians, 6
    Coronado and, 16
Puerto Rico
    American control of, 284
    immigrants from, 412
Pulaski, Count Casimir, 75
Pure Food and Drug Act, 265
Puritans, 25, 27
    religious intolerance, 32

## R

Racism, 316 – 317
Radical Republicans, 198, 199
    Andrew Johnson and, 200
    reconstruction acts, 200, 201
Railroad
    buffalo and, 225
    business and, 245
    immigrant laborers, 221, 257
    Standard Oil Company and, 266
    steam locomotives, 143 – 145
    transcontinental, 220 – 221
Raleigh, Sir Walter, 22
Randolph, Edmund, 96
Rankin, Jeannette, 69
Ray, James Earl, 405
Reagan, Ronald
    aid to contras, 478
    Central American policy, 477
    Iran-Contra scandal, 479
    military buildup, 444
    Soviet policy, 474 – 475
    war on drugs, 467
Reconstruction
    congressional plans for, 200
    end of, 208 – 209
    Lincoln's plan for, 197 – 198
    Second, 410
    under Johnson, 199 – 200
Reconstruction Finance Corporation, 329
Red Scare, 312, 312 – 313, 377, 382
Reed, Walter, 285
Reform, Age of, 262 – 273
Refugees, 259
    Indochinese, 432
Regional differences, 158
    between colonies, 31 – 32, 38
    election of 1824 and, 123 – 124

War of 1812, 113–115
    results of, 115
War on drugs, 467–468
Washington, Booker T., 202
Washington, D.C., 97–98
Washington, George, 86, 128, 164
    at Constitutional Convention, 87, 88
    elected President, 96
    at First Continental Congress, 58
    leads American army, 68
Watergate, 438–440
Webster, Daniel, 127, 170
Welch, Joseph, 383
Westward expansion, 41–43, 152.
    *See also* Manifest Destiny
    land and climatic factors, 3–5
    transportation and, 141–145, 219–223
Whaling industry, 33
Wheatly, Phyllis, 59
Whigs, 127
White House, 113
Whitman, Narcissa, 220
Whitney, Eli, 161
Williams, Roger, 25
Williams, Willie, 468
Wilson, Woodrow, 299
    League of Nations, 306–307
Women
    in Civil War, 187
    Colonial Period, 54
    education, 133
    in Gulf War, 452
    in Jamestown colony, 23
    Prohibition activities, 318
    rights of, 69, 133, 271–272, 457–458
    in space, 463

suffrage, 209, 271, 318
    in the work force, 318–319, 457–458
    in World War I, 305
    in World War II, 349
Women's Christian Temperance Union, 318
World War I
    air warfare, 303
    alliances, 297–298
    events leading to, 298–299
    home effort, 305
    peace treaty, 306
    United States in, 299–305
World War II
    aerial bombing, 354–356
    alliances in, 343, 346
    D-Day, 352
    end of, 356
    European battles, 351–352
    events leading to, 341–342
    Fighting 442nd, 350
    home effort, 349
    North African front, 351
    opposition to U.S. involvement, 345–346
    Pacific battles, 353–356
    United States in, 348–356
    V-E Day, 352
Wright, Orville and Wilbur, 233

## Y

Yeltsin, Boris, 475
Yorktown, battle of, 75

## Z

Zimmerman, Arthur, 301